DETROIT
AFTER BANKRUPTCY

Are There Trends towards an Inclusive City?

Joe T. Darden

BRISTOL
UNIVERSITY
PRESS

First published in Great Britain in 2023 by

Bristol University Press
University of Bristol
1–9 Old Park Hill
Bristol
BS2 8BB
UK
t: +44 (0)117 374 6645
e: bup-info@bristol.ac.uk

Details of international sales and distribution partners are available at bristoluniversitypress.co.uk

© Bristol University Press 2023

British Library Cataloguing in Publication Data
A catalogue record for this book is available from the British Library

ISBN 978-1-5292-3566-1 hardcover
ISBN 978-1-5292-3567-8 paperback
ISBN 978-1-5292-3569-2 ePub
ISBN 978-1-5292-3568-5 ePdf

The right of Joe T. Darden to be identified as author of this work has been asserted by him in accordance with the Copyright, Designs and Patents Act 1988.

All rights reserved: no part of this publication may be reproduced, stored in a retrieval system, or transmitted in any form or by any means, electronic, mechanical, photocopying, recording, or otherwise without the prior permission of Bristol University Press.

Every reasonable effort has been made to obtain permission to reproduce copyrighted material. If, however, anyone knows of an oversight, please contact the publisher.

The statements and opinions contained within this publication are solely those of the author and not of the University of Bristol or Bristol University Press. The University of Bristol and Bristol University Press disclaim responsibility for any injury to persons or property resulting from any material published in this publication.

Bristol University Press work to counter discrimination on grounds of gender, race, disability, age and sexuality.

Cover design: Liam Roberts Design
Front cover image: alamy/Dennis Cox
Bristol University Press use environmentally responsible print partners.
Printed and bound in Great Britain by CPI Group (UK) Ltd, Croydon, CR0 4YY
Maps throughout this book were created using ArcGIS® software by Esri. ArcGIS® and ArcMap™ are the intellectual property of Esri and are used herein under license. Copyright © Esri. All rights reserved. For more information about Esri® software, please visit http://www.esri.com.

This book is dedicated to residents
of Detroit, especially those who live
in very low and low socioeconomic
characteristic neighborhoods

Contents

List of Figures and Tables

Figures

Tables

Acknowledgments

The assistance in completing this book on Detroit came primarily from graduate students at Michigan State University. I am most grateful for all their assistance. I am most thankful for the very helpful editorial contributions and proofreading provided by Andra Durham, who contributed to every chapter in the book. I also want to thank Cordelia Martin-Ikpe, who assisted with the gathering of data from such sources as the US Census, the Home Mortgage Disclosure database, and the Detroit Portal database. I would also like to thank Kyeesha Wilcox for using her geographic information system (GIS) skills to construct all of the maps used in the book. Thanks also to Jen Fry (now PhD) for gathering data on crimes by type and neighborhood. In the early stages of the book, I relied upon clerical assistance from Lisa Eldred and Hope Lewis. I want to thank them for their assistance. Finally, I would like to thank my spouse, Catherine Gibson, for her ongoing support and assistance. Because of the contributions of all of these individuals, I was able to complete the book and provide knowledge about postbankruptcy Detroit that I hope will be beneficial to the residents of the city and enable them to improve the quality of their lives.

Preface

Bankruptcy ended in Detroit on December 11, 2014. This book begins its assessment of the major questions that policy makers, city residents, and the private sector want answered: have there been *measurable changes* in the city in certain critical areas that impact the quality life of the city's residents? Is there *measurable evidence* that the residents are experiencing a higher quality of life? This book is my third investigation of these questions. The first book, *Detroit: Race and Uneven Development* (1987), with co authors Richard Hill (sociology), June Thomas (urban planning), and Richard Thomas (American history), included a detailed investigation that revealed that racial differences in the quality of life in Detroit presented a deep problem for many Blacks in the city that was getting worse over time. Moreover, the problems of the city could not be addressed without examining the Detroit Metropolitan region as a whole. After the investigation we concluded that "racial polarization between Detroit and its suburbs will increase along with the class gap between the poor in the central city and affluent in the suburbs. Detroit's financial problems are likely to worsen and the city's political influence in the region will continue to decline" (Darden et al, 1987: 254). We further concluded that "most who leave Detroit will continue to be white and affluent, but a sizable number of middle class Blacks will also migrate to the suburbs. The geographical line between Blacks and whites will still be rigidly drawn. Those remaining in the central city will be mostly Black and mostly poor" (Darden et al, 1987: 255). The book was published more than 25 years before Detroit's bankruptcy. We investigated the City of Detroit from different perspectives and came to a consensus that the rigid race and class divides were the driving forces that helped to explain the continued problems of Detroit following the Second World War. We argued that the problems of Metropolitan Detroit, such as economic decentralization, chronic racial and class residential segregation, and regional political fragmentation, were predicable trends that had gradually escalated throughout the post-Second World War period. We presented policy recommendations for Detroit's problems that focused on how to handle the rigid divide by race, class, and place of residence. We also warned Detroit's policy makers and residents that "if present trends continue, racial polarization between Detroit and its suburbs would increase along with a wider class gap between the poor in the central city and the affluent in the suburbs. Detroit's financial problems would worsen, and the city's political influence in the region would continue to decline" (Darden et al, 1987: 254).

Unfortunately, the policy makers did not take the necessary actions to address the problems of persistent housing discrimination, school segregation, and employment discrimination and city–suburban inequality in economic development. Blacks, on the other hand, continued to peacefully protest for change. Most whites continued to oppose change in the area of racial equality. White racism was a key reason for white inaction. The extent of that racism was documented in my second book, which was published with historian Richard Thomas in 2013. In that book, *Detroit: Race Riots, Racial Conflicts, and Efforts to Bridge the Racial Divide*, we examined the white reaction to Blacks who wanted more racial equality in housing, education, jobs, and neighborhoods. Black protests to improve their socioeconomic conditions in Detroit led to more racial conflict.

The book documents why, during the summer of 1967, Detroit experienced the worst racial conflict in the city's history and the most severe racial conflict in the entire nation. The book examined six basic questions:

(1) What happened?
(2) Where did it happen?
(3) Why did it happen?
(4) To what extent have the conditions that caused the racial conflict changed?
(5) What efforts have occurred since the racial conflict to build bridges across racial lines?
(6) What are the alternative futures for the Detroit residents? (Darden and Thomas, 2013: xv).

Like the 1987 book *Detroit: Race and Uneven Development*, our socioeconomic analysis of neighborhoods revealed inequality by race and class by neighborhood of residence. This inequality led to two key political questions: "How effective has the Black political leadership been in Detroit in reducing the racial divides? What did the results tell us about the effectiveness of Black political power and Black demographic dominance in driving socioeconomic change in Detroit?" (p 202). The book examined Black and white inequality and conflict in the public schools, employment and unemployment, and housing (residential segregation). The book also explored an alternative spatial mobility strategy within the context of a *geography of opportunity* for those residents who wanted to move to greater economic and social opportunities that lie beyond the City of Detroit.

In this third book, of which I am the sole author, I again examine the problems of Detroit within the city and the search for answers within the wider Detroit Metropolitan region. This book shows that the social and economic characteristics of neighborhoods in Detroit were influenced tremendously by the bankruptcy, which made conditions for a large segment of the Detroit population much more difficult. Many residents of Black and Hispanic neighborhoods were exposed to higher rates of unemployment and poverty. Some residents had more difficulty finding jobs in higher occupations at the management and professional levels. Other residents did not reside in the same neighborhoods as highly educated residents and they noticed income inequality by race. Other residents had difficulty becoming homeowners due to differential rates of mortgage loan denials by race. Some residents were negatively affected by the undervaluation of their homes. When such multiple problems and racial inequality persist in a place (municipality), it is quite common for residents to search for neighborhoods and places that will improve the quality of life, even if it means moving away from the city and neighborhood where they have lived most of their lives. Urban geographers call this search by residents for the *geography of opportunity*. This book will determine whether such movement made a difference in the class and racial inequality.

Antecedents to Bankruptcy

Introduction

On July 18, 2013, Kevyn Orr, the Emergency Manager appointed by Rick Snyder, the Republican Governor of Michigan, made the legal decision to declare the City of Detroit bankrupt. According to *Bloomberg News* (2013), Orr rushed the $18 billion bankruptcy petition into federal court on July 18 just minutes before a State judge could stop him. The decision by the Emergency Manager made the City of Detroit the largest city in the US to experience bankruptcy.

This chapter examines the historical, economic, social, demographic, racial, and non cooperative relationship between the State of Michigan and the City of Detroit that led to the bankruptcy decision. There is evidence to suggest that the seeds of Detroit's bankruptcy were planted over time by the actions of investors, who reduced their investments in the city and increased investment in the suburbs over a period of 60 years (Darden et al, 1987). These actions resulted in increased unemployment in the city, the outmigration of the white middle class, a decline in property values, an increase in housing abandonment, and a reduction in tax revenue for city services (Gillette, 2014). Instead of financial assistance from the State, Detroit, like other cities in Michigan, was faced with a reduction in revenue sharing (Lavelle, 2014; Sapotichne et al, 2015). Such disinvestment by the private sector and a reduction in revenue sharing by the State made the financial problems of the city very difficult to solve (McFarland and Pagano, 2014).

Instead of providing the financial support needed, the Governor used a new, stronger Republican-passed Emergency Manager Law in 2011 to remove the democratically elected African American mayor and city council from power (Pew Charitable Trusts, 2013). The Governor then appointed an Emergency Manager to govern Detroit. The Emergency Manager served on behalf of the Governor, who made the final political decision to declare bankruptcy.

What led to the City of Detroit's bankruptcy?

The cause of Detroit's bankruptcy can best be understood by tracing the city's decline in population and economic status after 1950. The auto industry, which was concentrated in the city, made Detroit a very wealthy city in 1950 (Darden et al, 1987). Detroit has been declining in terms of population and socioeconomic status since 1950 (Darden et al, 1987; Orr, 2013b). The key factors that led to this decline will be given subsequently. This chapter uses most of the scholarly published articles and court documents to explain the economic situation in Detroit that led up to the bankruptcy. The most recent scholarly articles are being used. The legal and court documents and scholarly articles are being used to develop the conclusion that the most important reasons why bankruptcy eventually occurred were related to the severe economic condition of the city, and the State of Michigan's unwillingness to provide economic support to a city that was predominantly Black and politically Democratic. The chapter also indicates a secondary factor which was related to the outmigration of both white and to some extent middle-class Blacks to suburbs such as Southfield, which was located on the border of Detroit.

White flight and economic disinvestment

Due to the decline of manufacturing and the relocation of the auto industry to plants in the suburbs, overall economic restructuring, and selective suburbanization by race, most investors changed their priority *place* of investment from the City of Detroit to the suburbs (Darden et al, 1987). Hackworth wrote about the manufacturing decline in Detroit (2019: 117–33). He argued that it was related to the fact that political power was under the control of conservative Republicans. He discussed the limits imposed on Detroit, which was and is an economically distressed city that is majority-Black, and how these limits accelerated the process of decline.

Whites, encouraged by public policy and subsidized by the federal government, moved to the suburbs, but Blacks were not allowed to move there because of racial discrimination in housing. This discrimination took the form of racially restrictive covenants and the outright refusal by white real estate brokers to sell and by white apartment managers to rent to Blacks seeking housing in the suburbs (Sugrue, 1996). These practices were very effective in preventing Blacks from moving or even attempting to move outside of the city limits of Detroit before the 1968 *Fair Housing Act* was passed, outlawing racial discrimination in housing.

There were many suburban whites who cooperated with the real estate brokers and apartment managers in discriminating against Blacks (Farley et al, 2000). A well-documented example is the discriminatory behavior of whites in the five suburbs of Grosse Pointe, which borders the City of Detroit. To exclude Blacks and other "undesirable groups," the white residents developed secret, private exclusionary agreements. The white property owners and associations worked with white real estate brokers to create and apply a point system for "scoring" families seeking residence in these suburbs. Blacks, Asians, and Mexicans were categorically excluded regardless of their score. In other words, those groups were excluded not based on ability to pay for housing or their socioeconomic status, but on their race or ethnicity (Sugrue, 1996).

As middle-class whites left Detroit for the suburbs, banks continued to invest in the suburbs. Job growth, high-quality public schools, neighborhoods, and public services likewise moved outward, leaving poor services in the city.

Redlining, a multifaceted concept involving the discriminatory behavior of mortgage lenders and the geographic location of property, became a common practice in Detroit (Farley et al, 2000). Banks in Detroit actually drew a red line on a map around the borders of certain neighborhoods to indicate to the staff that loans were not to be made to the neighborhoods in that area of the city (Vojnovic and Darden, 2013). Those areas were where Blacks or Mexican Americans resided.

Consequences of disinvestment and discrimination

As a result of *disinvestment*, *redlining*, and *continued racial discrimination*, barriers to Black movement to the suburbs of Detroit—where there were far more employment opportunities, along with high-achieving public schools—the city became increasingly Black and increasingly poor, while the suburbs became increasingly white and affluent (Darden and Thomas, 2013).

In addition, following the 1967 civil disorders—or, as Blacks referred to them, "Black rebellion" (that is, riots)—which were caused by institutionalized racism in education, housing, and employment, Detroit experienced accelerated white population loss as whites continued to move to the Detroit suburban region (Darden and Thomas, 2013).

The Black rebellion of 1967 destroyed several businesses, especially white-owned ones, and many of the remaining businesses started to leave the neighborhoods in Detroit for the suburbs, taking jobs with them (Darden and Thomas, 2013). More properties (including commercial buildings) were abandoned. Racial discrimination and racial steering in housing continued to prevent Blacks from migrating to certain suburban municipalities (Darden and Thomas, 2013). Chapter 9 will provide greater details on Black movement to certain municipalities.

The myth of living cheaply in Detroit

Yet, many whites did not believe that discrimination was the major reason why Blacks did not move to the suburbs. Instead, many of them believed that Blacks simply could not afford to leave Detroit, which they erroneously thought was less costly than the suburbs. In fact, it is a myth that it is cheaper to live in Detroit than in the suburbs and this is why so many poor people have continued to live there. In reality, the data showed that on the eve of bankruptcy, it was *more* expensive to live in Detroit than in the suburbs because of high taxes and high insurance rates in the city.

Taxes had continued to increase in the city compared to the suburbs, while services continued to decline. Some residents and businesses left Detroit to escape these high taxes and insurance costs.

Detroit residents were paying the highest total property tax rates (inclusive of property taxes paid to all overlapping jurisdictions—for example, the City, the State, and Wayne County) of those paid by residents of Michigan cities with a population over 50,000 (Orr, 2013b). Detroit was also the only city in Michigan that levied an excise tax on utility users (at a rate of 5 percent). In addition, Detroit residents were paying the highest auto insurance rates (see Table 1.1).

Detroit was also experiencing declining property values and there was an increase in the number of abandoned structures as the population fell each decade after 1950. A shortage of businesses forced residents to shop outside of the city. This process, in economic terms, is called *negative circular causation* and *cumulative effects* (Fusfeld, 1981). This means that the more money the residents of Detroit spent outside of the city, the poorer their city became, and the more the suburban businesses and neighborhoods gained and prospered as a result. One of the more important factors that led to Detroit's bankruptcy was the continued population decline in the city, which was differential by race and class.

Table 1.1: Comparative average annual auto insurance rates (Detroit and selected suburbs)

Selected suburbs	Rate	Distance from Detroit (miles)
Detroit	$3,993	–
Southfield	$3,108	0
Dearborn	$2,908	0
Livonia	$2,052	3

Note: 0 = Detroit's geographic border.

Source: Orr, City of Detroit (2013b) *Report to Creditors.*

Most whites, some poor but mostly the middle class, continued to move to the suburbs and most Blacks and the poor continued to live in the city. This created a *demographic imbalance* in the Detroit Metropolitan Area. What is meant by *demographic imbalance* is that there was an uneven spatial distribution of the population, resulting in a sharp degree of residential segregation of whites from Blacks separating neighborhoods by socioeconomic characteristics (see Chapter 3 for an analysis of this) (Darden et al, 1987; Darden et al, 2010).

Geographic, social, and economic conditions in Detroit on the eve of bankruptcy

When the Emergency Manager, Kevyn Orr, who was appointed by Rick Snyder, the Republican Governor of Michigan, made the legal decision to declare the City of Detroit bankrupt in July 2013, the total population of Detroit had declined to 695,437. The white, non-Hispanic population was only 60,407 (or 8.7 percent) compared to a Black population of 561,034 (or 80.7 percent) (US Bureau of the Census, 2014). The racial divide, which had been increasing since 1950, became greater. The suburbs of Detroit were overwhelmingly white, at 82.1 percent, 74 percent, and 49.8 percent in Macomb, Oakland, and Wayne Counties respectively—that is, the counties that surround Detroit and constitute the Detroit Metropolitan Area for the purposes of this chapter. Blacks continued to reside in Detroit, with a small but growing number in the suburbs, a trend which became more prevalent following the *Fair Housing Act of 1968* (Darden and Thomas, 2013). All three suburban counties (Macomb, Oakland, and Wayne) had at least a 10 percent Black population, excluding the population of the City of Detroit, which is in Wayne County.

Suburban Wayne County had 146,095 Blacks, second only to Oakland County at 166,763. Throughout the three county areas, the Black population accounted for 80.7 percent in Detroit, 20.6 percent in the rest of Wayne County, 13.7 percent in Oakland County, and 9.8 percent in Macomb County (US Bureau of the Census, 2014). The spatial pattern of population distribution by race showed an increase in the socioeconomic status of the populations as they moved outward from the City of Detroit to suburban Wayne County, to Macomb County, and to Oakland County (see Table 1.2).

However, in order to fully reveal the *inequality* by class, neighborhood, and race in the three-county area, an analysis was done at the census tract level using the Darden-Kamel Composite Socioeconomic Index and the *index of dissimilarity* between Blacks and whites over neighborhoods by characteristics (Darden et al, 2010). Census tracts are used as surrogates for neighborhoods (see Chapter 3).

Table 1.2: The socioeconomic characteristics of the population in Detroit and its suburbs, 2010–14

Socioeconomic status (SES)	Detroit City	Wayne County	Macomb County	Oakland County	Ratio of greatest inequality: Detroit vs. Oakland County
BA degree or higher	13.2	21.7	23.1	43.7	3.3
Unemployment rate	27.1	16.8	10.9	9.1	2.9
Black unemployment rate	28.7	26.5	17.0	15.5	1.9
White non Hispanic unemployment rate	18.6	10.5	10.1	8.1	2.3
Median household income	$26,095	$41,421	$54,059	$66,436	2.5
Black median household income	$25,444	$27,124	$35,329	$46,809	1.8
White median household income	$29,781	$53,768	$56,646	$69,369	2.3
Homeownership	50.7	63.9	74.2	70.9	1.4 (Macomb County was highest)
Median year structure was built	1947	1955	1973	1973	Difference in median year structure (homes/ houses were built 26 years older)
Median gross rent	$756	$797	$852	$934	1.2
Poverty rate	34.8	19.6	10.0	7.7	4.5
Black poverty rate	39.5	37.3	27.9	18.8	2.1
White poverty rate, non Hispanic	38.9	14.4	10.4	8.3	4.7
No health insurance	19.0	13.9	10.5	9.3	2.0

Source: US Bureau of the Census, 2015.

The importance of neighborhood socioeconomic characteristics, racial residential segregation, school quality, and the academic achievement gap

On the eve of bankruptcy, despite the clear evidence that Black students in Detroit were attending grossly unequal schools compared to white students in the suburbs, the Emergency Manager representing the Governor focused less on the inequity and instead advocated more charter schools as the solution, combined with a limited amount of choice over schools. However, a large body of research has concluded that low-income Black students generally do not take advantage of school choice or open enrollment policies as policy makers had expected. Therefore, such policies have had a limited impact on reducing racial residential segregation and reducing the achievement gap (Orfield and Lee, 2005). Thus, most Black students compared to white students remained in low-achieving schools in Detroit, while most whites were attending higher-quality schools in the suburbs.

Although the success of charter schools in reducing the gap varies, most research suggests that charter schools are not the most effective solution to the problem of the persistent racial gap in academic achievement. For example, Frankenberg et al (2010) have concluded, based on research nationally, that charter schools have created the illusion of real choice for parents with children attending low-achieving schools. Such schools do not provide strong evidence of higher academic achievement for the students who attend them. Moreover, charter schools on average are more racially segregated than traditional public schools (Frankenberg et al, 2010). When it comes to the academic achievement *gap*, the structure of the school, whether charter or traditional, is less important than whether the school is *located* in a low socioeconomic characteristic neighborhood and is low achieving. In Metropolitan Detroit, whether the school is traditional or charter, the Black students on the eve of bankruptcy were disproportionately in low-achieving schools compared to their white counterparts (Darden and Thomas, 2013).

The fact that Black students were, at the time of bankruptcy, overwhelmingly attending school in the city where resources and overall quality were inferior compared to white students attending school in the suburbs was the real nature of the problem related to the academic achievement gap. Whether the State, in cooperation with the city and school board, adequately addressed the problem in the postbankruptcy period will be discussed in Chapter 7. The following discussion focuses on the extent of the racial gap problem by neighborhood characteristics.

The State of Michigan not only refused to provide the resources needed to bring the Detroit public schools up to a level of equality with schools in the suburbs, but the entire City of Detroit was also denied an equal share of the financial support needed for essential public services as the population continued to decline. The relationship between the City and the State has not been very cooperative, nor has it benefited the students of Detroit. The following section also shows that the relationship between the State and the City has also not benefited the population of Detroit as a whole.

The history and impact of declining state revenue sharing to Detroit compared to other municipalities

The evidence suggests that although Detroit has been experiencing severe economic decline since the 1950s, State of Michigan policies on the eve of bankruptcy were still less concerned about Detroit's economic decline. Instead, the State was concerned about the cost of assisting the city financially since from the State's perspective, the problem was due to the city's fiscal mismanagement. The State acted instead to reduce revenue sharing to Detroit, which made the city's financial condition worse. This created accelerated fiscal stress to manage the City of Detroit.

According to the Task Force on Local Government Services and Fiscal Stability (2006), a healthy fiscal balance between revenue and expenditure is necessary in the provision of local public services, without which economic development efforts will falter. Ignoring this report while insisting that the problem was due to mismanagement, the Governor appointed an emergency manager, Kevyn Orr, on March 14, 2013. In addition, the State of Michigan government cut the revenue sharing to the city that it had been giving the city over a 20-year period, that is, since 2002 (see Table 1.3).

This made the financial problem in Detroit even worse. Using the Emergency Manager Law *Public Act 72*, which broadened the Emergency Manager's powers beyond only handling matters of finances, the Emergency Manager investigated the City of Detroit and found that the entire city had been drained of resources and tax revenue. However, the State did not restore revenue sharing, which had a severe impact on Detroit. The impact of the Emergency Manager on Detroit will be discussed in more detail later on in this chapter.

State revenue sharing is a program to redistribute to cities tax dollars collected at the state level. This was implemented in part as recognition that Detroit and other cities hold limited control over the level of taxation. The structured limitations imposed on property tax collection were done when, in 1964, the State legislation prohibited local governments from levying any tax not authorized by State law (State of Michigan, 1963).

In 1978, Michigan voters approved a constitutional amendment commonly referred to as the *Headlee Amendment*. This amendment: (1) limited the growth of local government property tax revenues by providing millage

8

Table 1.3: The amount of revenue sharing lost to Detroit, 2003-13

Year	Reduction (in millions)
2003	$10,032.00
2004	$39,465.69
2005	$50,619.92
2006	$59,660.61
2007	$61,007.02
2008	$72,351.77
2009	$67,951.15
2010	$70,731.20
2011	$73,769.33
2012	$78,519.57
2013	$80,145.75
Total	$664,254 million

Source: State of Michigan, 2006.

rollbacks whenever revenue from existing property grew by more than the rate of inflation unless voters overrode the rollback; (2) required voter approval for any new local taxes or an increase in a tax rate not authorized at the time the amendment was adopted; and (3) required that the State provide reimbursement for any additional costs resulting from new requirements mandated by State law (State of Michigan, 1998).

The *Headlee Amendment* limited revenue to Detroit. Moreover, citizens continued to complain about rising tax assessments. As a result, *Proposal A* was adopted in 1994, which was a constitutional amendment. It further limited local property tax revenue growth by changing the system of tax assessment to cap individual property values and prohibited Detroit and other cities from increasing a millage to the rate of inflation if actual property value growth was lower than inflation (Sapotichne et al, 2015). It included a limitation on assessment increases for individual parcels of property, excluding new construction on the property to a lessor of 5 percent of the rate of inflation.

In 1996, the State consolidated income tax and single business tax shared revenues into an expanded percentage of sales tax. As a result of this action, past revenue reductions were made permanent through a lower sales tax percentage (Citizens Research Council, 2000). In 1998, although the State of Michigan had a constitutional requirement to return 15 percent of the 4 percent State sales tax, the State stopped returning State income taxes and single business taxes to Detroit and other local governments. Instead, it passed a statute that required sharing 21.3 percent of the 4 percent sales tax with local governments. However, after one year, the State broke its pledge to return state sales taxes to local governments and retained the funds for State purposes (Citizens Research Council, 2000). This was a serious blow to Detroit in 2000. From 2001 to 2005, the State continued to cut revenue sharing in order to balance its own budget. In every State budget since it changed its agreement on revenue sharing, the State did not fully return State sales taxes to cities as required by State statute between 2001 and 2005 (Task Force on Local Government Services and Fiscal Stability, 2006). The amount of reduced revenue sharing for Detroit amounted to millions from 2003 to 2013 and is shown in Table 1.3. Detroit lost a total of $664,254 million over the 11-year period.

The data contained in the Task Force on Local Government Services and Fiscal Stability Report (2006) and the Citizens Research Council on Michigan Report (2000) suggest that revenue sharing to Detroit has been declining for years. In Detroit, statutory revenue-sharing reductions had a very inequitable impact on the city. This is because revenue sharing is the only State resource that has traditionally been designed to reduce disparities between low and high tax base local units of government. When revenue sharing was reduced, the reductions impacted Detroit (a high-poverty municipality) to a much greater extent than low-poverty municipalities and exacerbated the inequities between high- and low-poverty municipalities. Statutory revenue-sharing reductions partly played a role in producing a growing gap between Detroit (a "have not" city) and the low-poverty ("have") suburbs (Task Force on Local Government Services and Fiscal Stability, 2006).

Local difficulties in Detroit and other units of government

It appears that the State's reduction in revenue sharing was not directly correlated to the position of the State's economy. For example, even during the economically robust 1990s, statutory revenue sharing was rarely shared to the agreed upon level with Detroit and other cities. Instead, the State continued to reduce revenue sharing, which caused Detroit and other cities to bear a greater burden in order to provide essential services to their residents. The only choice for Detroit was to cut or eliminate services.

Local governments perceived the State's actions as a broken promise that hamstrung Detroit and other units of local government, causing them to reduce police, fire, and other essential services that produce the quality of life necessary for the city to grow or sustain its economic status and attract new workers (Florida, 2002; Task Force on Local Government Services and Fiscal Stability, 2006). At the same time, the State's fiscal stress was translated into minimal increases from 2006 to 2007 or even more cuts to local government revenue sharing (Task Force on Local Government Services and Fiscal Stability, 2006).

However, the cost of providing essential services continued to rise at a rate greater than the Consumer Price Index. Since 2001, Detroit and other units of government have received less in revenue-sharing payments compared to the full amount outlined in the Michigan Constitution. Notwithstanding this fact, instead of providing the revenue sharing to assist Detroit, the State of Michigan passed a law to force the city to manage with fewer financial resources. That law was the *Emergency Finance Act, Public Act 72*, which was passed in 1990. The impact of the Emergency Manager Law will be addressed later on; for now, it is important to discuss the decisions by the State to address the financial stress in Michigan cities.

Michigan, by virtue of its superior constitutional status, has strong legal powers to regulate finance (Sapotichne et al, 2015). Michigan also has a superior role in local fiscal distress by controlling the two dominant sources of city revenue: State and local united taxes. Detroit, like the other cities in Michigan, was dependent on the sources of income the State was to provide, and the amount of taxes the State was to allow it to raise and retain (Berman, 1995; Berman, 2003).

According to Sapotichne et al (2015), Michigan is one of a few States that increased financial stress by cutting shared revenue to its largest city while limiting the city's capacity to raise its own critical revenue. Such legislation has resulted in the city becoming more dependent on the State, which has limited Detroit's ability to provide for essential services. Michigan law makers were accused of enhancing the fiscal distress faced by Detroit by placing limitations on its local revenue and providing a relatively low level of financial assistance (Sapotichne et al, 2015).

In summary, the history of the relationship between Detroit and the State of Michigan in addressing the city's fiscal stress has been one of blame instead of cooperation to address the problem. The next section explains how Michigan intervened after Detroit could not pay its creditors or make timely pension contributions. This intervention followed the passage of Michigan's Emergency Manager Law.

The premise of the Emergency Manager Law

The major premise of the Emergency Manager Law from the State of Michigan's perspective was that Detroit's fiscal distress was due to mismanagement and not a lack of financial support from the State. The State law makers who supported the law argued that Detroit should have cut pension obligations, cut personnel, and contracted out services traditionally provided by the City of Detroit. The law makers believed that the revenue side of the solution was adequate to provide for public safety and debt payment if only the city had competent management (Anderson, 2011).

Most research does not support this position (Honadle et al, 2004; Anderson, 2011; Sapotichne et al, 2015). Instead of assuming that there was mismanagement, some researchers have suggested that Michigan law makers should have paid more attention to monitoring the city early on—that is, before the crisis—and that they should have allowed the city to take the leading role in the path toward recovery (Spiotto et al, 2012).

Although cities in other states have had financial stress, Michigan's aggressive Emergency Manager Law is unlike any other. In fact, nationwide, 23 states have laws that allow them to intervene with municipalities and school districts, but none of these allow such dictatorial power to be given to an Emergency Manager as the law passed by Republicans and signed by Republican Governor Rick Snyder on December 26, 2012. Michigan law gave the power to the Emergency Manager to change union contracts, remove elected officials, and sell city assets (Detroit NAACP, 2013; Dawsey, 2014).

The history and provisions of the Emergency Manager Law in Michigan

The Emergency Manager Law was first passed in Michigan in 1988. It was called *Public Act 101*, or the *Local Government Fiscal Responsibility Act of 1988*. The State of Michigan would impose certain actions if a municipality had a deficit that it could not remove. The 1988 *Act* created the Emergency Financial Manager position for a specific financial emergency in Hamtramck, Michigan. The *Act* provided certain triggers for an initial review, which included: (1) failure to pay debts; (2) failure to pay employees' salaries; and (3) a request for an emergency manager by local residents or officials, a State legislature, or State treasurer. If the review concluded that a financial emergency existed, the local Emergency Assistance Board would make the appointment of an Emergency Financial Manager for the governmental unit (State of Michigan, 1988).

The *Local Government Fiscal Responsibility Act 101 of 1988* was repealed in 1990 and replaced with *Public Act 72*, which broadened the Emergency Financial Manager's powers to handle all matters of finances of a city and provided a statute to apply to public schools as well. The name was changed from Emergency Financial Manager to Emergency Manager. The individual was an official appointed by the Governor to take *control* of a local government under a financial emergency. In fact, the Emergency Manager's powers supplanted the powers of the mayor, the city council, and the school superintendent and the school board. The Emergency Manager could remove elected officials should they refuse to provide any information requested or assistance (Michigan Legislature, 2016).

Public Act 72 was repealed and replaced by Public Act 4 of 2011, called the Local Government and School District Fiscal Accountability Act. The Act was approved by Republican Governor Snyder on March 16, 2011. However, on February 29, 2012, a petition seeking a referendum on Public Act 4 of 2011 was filed with the Secretary of State. The supporters of the referendum quoted Article 2, Section 9 of the Michigan Constitution of 1963, which stated that "no law as to which the power of referendum properly has been invoked shall be effective thereafter unless approved by a majority of the electors voting thereon at the next general election" (State of Michigan, 1963).

A referendum was presented at the November 2012 general election as Proposal 12–1. According to the State of Michigan, the Proposal read as follows:

> PROPOSAL 12–1 A REFERENDUM ON PUBLIC ACT 4 OF 2011 – THE EMERGENCY MANAGER LAW Public Act 4 of 2011 would: (i) Establish criteria to assess the financial condition of local government units, including school districts; (ii) Authorize the Governor to appoint an emergency manager (EM) upon state finding of a financial emergency, and allow the EM to act in place of local government officials; (iii) Require the EM to develop financial and operating plans, which may include modification or termination of contracts, reorganization of government, and determination of expenditures, services, and use of assets until the emergency is resolved; and (iv) Alternatively, authorize state-appointed review team to enter into a local government approved consent decree.
>
> Should this law be approved? YES __ NO ___
> (Michigan Legislature, 2016)

Public Act 4 of 2011 was rejected by a majority of the voters at the November 2012 general election. The vote was certified by the State Board of Canvassers on November 25, 2012. Act 72 of 1990, which had been repealed by Act 4 of 2011, came back into effect while the referendum on Act 4 of 2011 was pending. Act 436 of 2012, approved by the Governor on December 26, 2012 and filed with the Secretary of State on December 27, 2012, provided a new act (MCL 141.1541 to 141.1575) known as the Local Financial Stability and Choice Act, effective as of March 28, 2013. Act 436 of 2012 repealed Act 72 of 1990, effective as of March 28, 2013 (State of Michigan, 2011). Act 436 of 2012 was called the Local Financial Stability and Choice Act and was virtually identical to Act 4 of 2011, which voters in the State had rejected via a referendum.

Public Act 436 of 2012 was created with the following parameters: to safeguard and assure the financial accountability of local units of government and school districts; to preserve the capacity of local units of government and school districts to provide or cause to be provided necessary services essential to the public health, safety, and welfare; to provide for review, management, planning, and control of the financial operation of local units of government and school districts; to provide criteria to be used in determining the financial condition of local units of government and school districts; to authorize a declaration of the existence of a financial emergency within a local unit of government or school district; to prescribe remedial measures to address a financial emergency within a local unit of government or school district; to provide for a review and appeal process; to provide for the appointment and to prescribe the powers and duties of an Emergency Manager for a local unit of government or school district; to provide for the modification or termination of a financial emergency within a local unit of government or school district; to provide a process by which a local unit of government or school district may file for bankruptcy; to prescribe the powers and duties of certain state agencies and officials and officials within local units of government and school districts; to provide for appropriations; and to repeal acts and parts of acts (State of Michigan, 2012).

This was the first Act that specifically listed bankruptcy as an option for the Emergency Manager to use to address a local unit of government's financial problems. Michigan has a substantial number of local governments, ranking 13th among the 50 states. It has 275 cities and 552 school districts (State of Michigan, 2009). Beginning in 1909, Detroit and other cities had been granted home rule by the *Home Rule City Act*, enacted by the Michigan Legislature as *Public Act 279*. This statute provided the authority that permitted cities to draft and adopt their own charters by vote of the people (State of Michigan, 2009). As an explanation as to why, among the 275 cities and 552 school districts, some were selected by the governors to receive an Emergency Manager (even though the officials did not request one), the answer appears to be related to: (1) the racial composition and class characteristics of the city and/or school district; and (2) the political affiliation of the Governor.

There were nine cities and three school districts governed and controlled by an Emergency Manager between 2000 and 2013. Five of the cities were majority-Black: Benton Harbor (87 percent); Detroit (81 percent); Flint (55 percent); Highland Park (90.8 percent); and Pontiac (51 percent). Among the four cities that were majority-white were the suburban municipalities of Allen Park, Ecorse, Lincoln Park, and the municipal enclave of Hamtramck. Allen Park invited the Governor to appoint an Emergency Manager in 2012 (see Table 1.4).

Table 1.4: Race and class characteristics of cities and school districts where Emergency Managers were appointed

Emergency Managers appointed under Democratic Governor		
City/school district	Percentage Black	Percentage in poverty
Highland Park City	90.8	35.6
Benton Harbor school district	89.2	47.4
Ecorse school district	46.4	28.5
Pontiac school district	52.1	37.8
Detroit school district	82.7	39.8
Ecorse suburb	42.5	27.1
Pontiac City	51.0	33.4
Emergency Managers appointed under Republican Governor		
Benton Harbor school district	89.2	47.4
Allen Park suburb★	2.4	4.7
Detroit City	81.0	34.8
Flint City	55.0	36.0
Hamtramck City	13.9	43.1
Highland Park school district	93.5	47.6
Lincoln Park school district	5.8	16.9
Muskegon Heights school district	78.3	44.5
Pontiac City	51.0	33.4
Benton Harbor City	87.0	43.3

Note: ★ Allen Park, a suburb of Detroit, was the only place to request an Emergency Manager. Among the Governors appointing Emergency Managers, John Engler and Rick Snyder are Republicans, and Jennifer Granholm is a Democrat.

Source: US Bureau of the Census, 2015.

The three school districts with Emergency Managers were Detroit, Highland Park, and Muskegon Heights. These districts were all majority-Black. More important, however, is the differential impact that such Emergency Managers had on the loss of decision making by the elected officials who were Black, which reduced the democratic freedom of the Black population. Unlike the white population of Michigan, which constituted 7.5 million, only 2.3 percent of the State's white population resided in municipalities and school districts with Emergency Managers. By contrast, of the Black population of 1.3 million, 48 percent resided in municipalities and school districts with Emergency Managers.

In addition to a majority-Black population, most of the municipalities and/ or school districts had a high poverty rate. The urban municipalities ranged from a poverty rate of 34.8 percent in the City of Detroit to 43.3 percent in Benton Harbor (see Table 1.4). The poverty rate for Michigan was 12.1 percent (US Bureau of the Census, 2014).

The Emergency Manager appointments also appeared to have had a partisan dimension. Governor Jennifer Granholm, a Democrat, appointed two Emergency Managers to govern cities and one to govern a suburb. She also appointed four Emergency Managers to govern school districts, including one to govern Detroit. Republican Governor Rick Snyder and former Republican Governor John Engler together appointed four Emergency Managers to govern cities, including Detroit, and two to govern suburbs. One suburb, Allen Park, actually requested an Emergency Manager. In addition, Republican governors appointed six Emergency Managers to govern school districts.

The majority-white residents of municipalities and school districts were opposed to the appointment of Emergency Managers to run their cities and school districts, since such appointments effectively removed their democratically elected officials from power. Since cities and school districts with Emergency Managers appointed were majority-Black and politically Democratic, many viewed the appointments as a way to nullify their elections by keeping the cities and school districts under the control of the Republican Party. After all, control in practice meant the power to dismiss elected officials, abrogate labor contracts, sell off public assets, and impose new taxes on residents (Abbey-Lambertz, 2013).

On May 13, 2013, the National Association for the Advancement of Colored People (NAACP) brought a legal complaint against Governor Snyder over the Emergency Manager Law. The case was brought under the Equal Protection and Substantive Due Processes Clauses of the *Fourteenth Amendment* (US Constitution, 1983). The action challenged Michigan's *Local Financial Stability and Choice Act*, that is, the *Public Acts of 2012*, especially *Public Act 436* (Detroit NAACP, 2013).

The major argument made by the NAACP was that the Emergency Manager statute has had a *disparate impact* on Michigan's voters of color. At the time that the complaint was filed, roughly a majority (50.4 percent) of Michigan's 1,413,320 African Americans were being ruled by an unelected Emergency Manager. The NAACP also argued that *Public Act 436* had been applied in a discriminatory manner because the law was imposed on cities with a majority-Black population even though there were majority-white cities with the same or worse "fiscal health scores." For example, in Oakland County, the State imposed an Emergency Manager on the suburb of Pontiac, which had a majority-Black population of 52.1 percent according to the NAACP, but did not impose an Emergency Manager on the suburb of Hazel Park, which had a 9.8 percent African American population and was also located in Oakland County. Yet Hazel Park had an identical fiscal health score

(Detroit NAACP, 2013; see also US Bureau of the Census, 2014; Michigan Department of Treasury, n.d.). Under the law at the time, the Michigan Department of Treasury was required to wait until local units of government showed signs of fiscal stress before being able to directly address the local government issues. Rather than take this reactive approach, the Department developed a process to review certain fiscal indicators that encouraged sound fiscal health for all of Michigan's 1,858 units of local government. The Department's process also provided guidance, upon request, for local units of government (Michigan Department of Treasury, n.d.).

Finally, the NAACP argued that Emergency Managers had exercised powers and duties exclusively reserved for local elected branches of Michigan government, thereby degrading the electorate's voting rights. *Public Act 436* resulted in the State placing the value of one person's vote over that of another, which violates the *Fourteenth Amendment*'s Equal Protection Clause (US Constitution, 1983). Further discussion of the Emergency Manager Law that is relevant to the court cases, and its legal implications and impact, will be given in later chapters.

Conclusion

Throughout Detroit's history, the State of Michigan has played an active role in influencing the city's social and economic decline, its financial problems, and its ultimate bankruptcy. It is important to note that it was not the elected officials of Detroit or the residents of the city who decided to place the city into bankruptcy; instead, it was Emergency Manager Kevyn Orr, under the direction of Republican Governor Richard Snyder, who made the decision (Orr, 2013b). The next chapter will examine the struggles of the city during the bankruptcy period.

2

Detroit Bankruptcy: The Characteristics of the Decision Makers and the Differential Benefits Afterwards

Introduction

On July 18, 2013, Detroit filed for the largest municipal bankruptcy in US history. The city emerged 17 months later with a *Plan of Adjustment*. This chapter examines: (1) the legal origin of the city's bankruptcy; (2) the summary of oral opinion and reasons why the decision was made for bankruptcy by Judge Steven Rhodes; (3) the characteristics of the decision makers; and (4) the characteristics of the creditors and of winners and losers resulting from the Plan of Adjustment. This chapter is based on a critical examination of the bankruptcy decision, and a Plan of Adjustment that was the resolution. It focuses on the decision makers after discussing that the State of Michigan did not provide full revenue sharing. The most important decision maker was Emergency Manager Kevyn Orr, who wrote the *Proposal to Creditors* in 2013. Kevyn Orr was born May 11, 1958, in Fort Lauderdale, Florida. He received his law degree from the University of Michigan in 1983 and worked as an Assistant General Counsel for complex litigation and bankruptcy. In 1995 he was the Deputy Director of the Executive Office for United States Trustees, a division of the US Department of Justice that monitors the nation's bankruptcy system (Davey, 2013). In 2001, he was hired by Jones Day International Law firm as a partner, where he advised Chrysler on its bankruptcy. He was also honored as a Fellow of the American College of Bankruptcy.

The Proposal to Creditors document was among the most important documents to use for the chapter. It was relied upon in detail for this chapter. After meeting with 150 invited representatives, Emergency Manager Kevyn

Orr wrote that Detroit be authorized to file for relief under Chapter IX of the Bankruptcy Code. The Plan of Adjustment process set forth in the Bankruptcy Code created a mechanism by which Detroit may bind all of its creditors even if all creditors did not assent to the city's restructuring plan (Orr, 2013a: 10).

The case was then turned over to Judge Steven Rhodes and the other key decision makers for their views. The third decision maker was US District Chief Judge Gerald Rosen, who supported a plan that: (1) dissolved more than $7 billion of the city's $18 billion of debt; (2) enhanced the city's credit rating; and (3) included a ten-year, $1.7 billion investment in city services. Rosen considered that his role in this case was to protect the pensions, the Detroit Institute's art collections, and, most importantly, to save the city. The remaining chapters of the book will examine whether the city has become more inclusive by race and class after bankruptcy.

The legal origin of and reasoning behind the bankruptcy

The legal origin of the bankruptcy can be traced back to 1937. This was when Congress enacted new municipal bankruptcy provisions to the 1934 *Bankruptcy Act,* which added a new Chapter IX to the *Act.* The provisions were necessary because the US Supreme Court ruled that the 1934 *Act* was unconstitutional because it was an improper enforcement on the sovereign powers of the states (see *Ashton V, Cameron County Water Improvement District No. 1* 298 US 513 [1936]). Based on that decision, Judge Steven Rhodes issued the following opinion on November 7, 2014: "'The Plan of Adjustment' filed by the City of Detroit meets all of the requirements of confirmations under the United States Bankruptcy Code" (City of Detroit, 2014a). Judge Steven Rhodes is a white male. He received his law degree from the University of Michigan in 1972. He was appointed as the US Bankruptcy Judge for the Eastern District of Michigan in Detroit in 1985 and was reappointed in 1999 and 2013. He retired in February 2015.

What was the Plan of Adjustment?

The Plan of Adjustment (hereinafter "the Plan") that the City of Detroit filed with the US Bankruptcy Court for the Eastern District of Michigan on February 21, 2014 represented a critical step toward the city's rehabilitation and recovery from a decades-long downward spiral. The Plan provided for the adjustment of up to as much as $18 billion in secured and unsecured debt, and offered the greatest possible recoveries for the city's creditors, while simultaneously allowing for meaningful and necessary investment in the city. Detroit promised to invest approximately $1.5 billion over ten years to achieve the following:

1. Improve and provide essential municipal services to the city's 700,000 residents, including the police, fire, and emergency medical services, garbage removal, and functioning streetlights.
2. Attract and retain residents and businesses to foster growth and redevelopment.
3. Improve the city's information technology systems, thereby increasing efficiency and decreasing costs.
4. Provide pension treatment that was intended to deliver pensions that the city could afford, and by which retirees could continue to meet their needs and maintain their current quality of life.
5. If police and fire retirees agreed to the Plan, they had the possibility of receiving in excess of 90 percent of their earned pensions after the elimination of cost-of-living allowances.
6. If general retirees agreed to the Plan, they would have had the possibility of receiving in excess of 70 percent of their pensions after the elimination of cost-of-living allowances.
7. Detroit's current active employees would continue to earn pensions in the future under traditional defined benefit formulas rather than defined contribution arrangements (City of Detroit, 2014a). The two pension funds—the Police & Fire Retirement System and the General Retirement System—would operate under more conservative investment return assumptions, and contributions to the two pension funds would come from three sources over the following ten years after the Plan was accepted.

The judge then wrote that those accepting the Plan were the following classes of creditors: (1) Police and Fire Retirement System (PFRS) pensioners; (2) General Retirement System (GRS) creditors; (3) Other Past-Employment Benefits (OPEB) creditors; (4) Unlimited Tax General Obligations (UTGO) bondholders; (5) Limited Tax General Obligations (LTGO) bondholders; and (6) Swaps, which were financial agreements to exchange cash for a set period of time.

Judge Rhodes also wrote that the Plan was not accepted by the classes of other, unsecured creditors. What follows is the in-depth rationale as to why, despite some objections, Judge Rhodes approved the Plan and concluded that it was in the best interests of the City of Detroit.

Judge Rhodes' rationale for approving the Plan

Despite the acceptance of the Plan by the pension classes, many pension claimants still strongly opposed the impairment of their pension rights in the bankruptcy. They believed that under the Michigan Constitution, their pension rights were not subject to impairment. They argued that they worked hard for the city, that they had done nothing wrong, and that these impairments would cause them real hardship. Some also argued that the pension impairments in the Plan were unnecessary because their pension plans were, in fact, fully funded. They further argued that if the pension plans were underfunded, the city should sell the art at the Detroit Institute of Arts or other city assets to cover the cost. Many of those objecting parties took the time to come to court to give a strong, sincere, and personal voice to their objections. However, the US Bankruptcy Court for the Eastern District of Michigan Court found that the pension settlement was reasonable and overruled those objections to confirmation and to the pension settlement. It argued that the Plan was only possible because of the pension settlement and the Grand Bargain. The pension reductions in the pension settlement were minor compared to any reasonably foreseeable outcome for these creditors without the pension settlement and the Grand Bargain.

The State contribution agreement

The Court also addressed the State contribution agreement in which the State of Michigan supported the city's Plan by agreeing to give $194.8 million to fulfill its goals.

The Detroit Institute of Arts settlement

The Detroit Institute of Arts (DIA) was a key factor in Detroit's bankruptcy settlement. In 2012, voters in Wayne, Oakland, and Macomb Counties—that is, Metropolitan Detroit—passed a millage to provide long-term regional support for the DIA. These tax dollars provided about $22 million of the museum's $32 million operating budget. The next year (2013), the DIA's decision that those funds should go to maintenance was on the bargaining table in Detroit's bankruptcy case (Wright, 2015). Even though hundreds of thousands of voters from Wayne, Oakland, and Macomb Counties had voted to support one of most impressive fine art museums, some individuals wanted the value of the DIA's art collection to be used to lessen the blow to pensioners. Thus, questions were asked regarding who owned the collection and how much it was worth. This discussion resulted in a deal called the "Grand Bargain." It was designed by southeast Michigan's chief, US District Judge Gerald Rosen, who served as chief mediator in the case. The agreement would tie together the plight of the pensioners and the ongoing financial debate related to the future of the DIA (Wright, 2015). The key points of this settlement were as follows:

- The DIA would secure and guarantee commitments for contributions of $100 million to the GRS for the City of Detroit and the PFRS over a 20-year period.
- Various local and national charitable foundations would contribute $366 million to the GRS and the PFRS over a 20-year period.
- The city would agree to transfer the art to the DIA Corporation, which would hold it in a perpetual charitable trust for the benefit of the people of the city and the State.

Two issues arose from this: whether the DIA settlement was a fair settlement and whether it was in line with the best interests of creditors.

Both the Michigan Republican Attorney General and the DIA took the position that the DIA art was subject to a trust that prohibited the city from selling it to pay debts and placed it beyond creditors' reach. The DIA board also asserted that the donors of many of the pieces of art had imposed specific transfer restrictions on them. The Court concluded that the DIA settlement was a most reasonable and favorable settlement for the city and its pension creditors, and readily approved it. Accordingly, it approved all aspects of the Grand Bargain (City of Detroit, 2014b: 12).

The Other Past-Employment Benefits settlement

The city was obligated at the time to its retirees for OPEB. The city claimed the OPEB liability was $3.8 billion. The retiree committee asserted that it was $5 billion. The parties settled. The key points of this settlement were as follows:

- The allowed amount of OPEB claims was $4.3 billion.
- Of that, $2.2 billion was for the PFRS and retirees and $2.1 billion was for the GRS for City of Detroit GRS retirees (City of Detroit, 2014b: 14).

The 36th District Court settlement

When the city was under bankruptcy, the 36th District Court was defending several employment-related claims. Because the city is legally required to fund the 36th District Court, it would ultimately be responsible for any judgments against the 36th District Court in those proceedings. The parties in the litigation settled with the city. The aggregate liquidated allowed amount of the claims was $6 million. The Court found that the settlement was reasonable and approved it.

Unlimited Tax General Obligation bonds settlement

The city defaulted on its obligation to make payments on UTGO bonds, resulting in the bond insurers paying claims on the defaulted payments. The city opposed the litigation, contending that the UTGO claims were unsecured claims, and the city and the bond insurers settled. The key points of this settlement were as follows:

- The allowed claim on the UTGO bonds would be $388 million.
- Just under $288 million of the UTGO bonds would be restructured and re allocated among the holders of the bonds.

The 36th District Court concluded that the UTGO settlement was within the range of possible reasonable settlements, albeit at the upper end of that range. It also concluded that the circumstances did warrant the premium that the settlement reflected and therefore approved it (City of Detroit, 2014b: 16).

The Limited Tax General Obligation bonds settlement

The city had almost $164 million in outstanding LTGO bonds and defaulted on its obligation to make interest payments. The LTGO claimants argued that their claims were entitled to secured treatment and that State law required the city to pay the LTGO bonds as a first budget obligation. The city asserted that the LTGO claims were unsecured claims, and the parties settled their disputes. The key point of this settlement was the city would either issue new LTGO bonds to the amount of $55 million or pay $55 million in cash using exit financing.

The city elected to make the $55 million cash payment from the exit financing. The Court approved the settlement (City of Detroit, 2014b: 15).

What has been presented are the major settlements concluding the Court's approval of the settlements in the city's Plan. Following these approvals, the Court then addressed some of the other confirmation requirements that the Plan had to meet, including good faith, the best interests of creditors, and the reasonableness of attorney fees.

Discussion related to classes 14 and 15 of creditors that rejected the Plan

The Court addressed the requirements that applied because two classes of creditors, classes 14 and 15, rejected the Plan. These rejections raised questions about whether the Plan was fair and equitable or unfairly discriminatory. The Court also briefly addressed the objections of certain creditors holding constitutional claims against the city.

The importance of good faith

Section 1129(a)(3) of the Bankruptcy Code required the city to establish that it proposed its Plan in good faith. When the Court decided that the city was eligible to be in bankruptcy, it also found that the city had acted in good faith in seeking the relief that the Court could provide.

In relation to both of these points, the Court argued that the record demonstrated the city had worked honestly, diligently, and tirelessly to accomplish precisely the remedy that the Bankruptcy Code establishes for municipalities, the necessary adjustment of the city's debt. It also argued that the record demonstrated that the city was committed to maintaining its debt at a level that it could manage in the long term (City of Detroit, 2014b). The testimony of several city representatives directly supported these findings. The representatives were a very racially diverse group of individuals: Emergency Manager Kevyn Orr (Black); Mayor Mike Duggan (white); City Council President Brenda Jones (Black); the city's Chief Financial Officer John Hill (Black); the city's Chief Information Officer Beth Niblock (white); Police Chief James Craig (Black); and Executive Fire Commissioner Edsel Jenkins (Black) (City of Detroit, 2014b: 21).

On the second point, the Court found that the city had treated its creditors in a fundamentally fair way, citing the high level of creditor support for the Plan as evidence of this. Section 943(b)(7) of the Bankruptcy Code required that the Plan be in the best interests of creditors, and the Court found that the city had proposed its Plan in good faith (City of Detroit, 2014b: 21). It held that the Plan would provide creditors all that they could reasonably expect under the circumstances and that it was in their best interests. It also found that the Plan did not unfairly discriminate against the two rejecting unsecured classes, 14 and 15. In fact, very few of the creditors in classes 14 and 15 filed objections to the Plan and although the classes did vote to reject the Plan, the margins for doing so were small—in class 14, the margin was 51 percent rejecting and 49 percent accepting, while in class 15, the margin was slightly more significant, with 58 percent rejecting and 42 percent accepting (City of Detroit, 2014b: 34). The Court decision on this matter was highly controversial. According to Hynes and Walt:

> The Bankruptcy Code incorporates a standard of unfair discrimination that it leaves unclear. The standard does not allow the *Plan* proponent the complete discretion to favor one class over other co-equal classes. Instead, case law requires *Plan* to treat classes equally unless the favorable treatment of a class falls within a limited number of judicially recognized categories. (Hynes and Walt, 2015: 69)

Hynes and Walt concluded that considerations of fairness, such as those based on need, did not support treating retirees and active workers better than other creditors in a municipality's bankruptcy. However, the Court argued that it was equitable to confirm this Plan over the dissent of a handful of unsecured creditors—most of whom had claims under $25,000—when thousands of creditors with claims in the billions of dollars supported the Plan (City of Detroit, 2014b: 32). The Court did accept the likelihood that the dividend to the creditors in classes 14 and 15 would cause those creditors real hardship, but it said that it must analyze and balance the hardship on the other side too (City of Detroit, 2014b: 35).

The hardship was that a large number of people in Detroit were experiencing a lack of basic municipal services such as police, fire, and emergency medical services to protect their health and safety. The Court argued that this hardship was inhumane and intolerable, and must be fixed. As the city's Plan was committed to addressing these issues, the Court argued that the few creditors who had rejected the Plan must share in the sacrifice that the other creditors had agreed to endure. It concluded that there were no viable alternatives to the Plan that would solve the city's problems and at the same time pay more to classes 14 and 15 to get their support (City of Detroit, 2014b: 35). Accordingly, the Court concluded that it should exercise its power under the Bankruptcy Code to impose the Plan on classes 14 and 15 despite their dissenting votes. It found that the Plan was fair and equitable in relation to classes 14 and 15 (City of Detroit, 2014b: 35).

The constitutional claims against the city

The Court stated its objections to the creditor's constitutional claims against the city. It first concluded that the Fourteenth Amendment does not provide a constitutional right to damages for a constitutional violation (City of Detroit, 2014b: 36). After all the arguments had been made about the Plan, Judge Rhodes ruled that:

> The City filed the Plan in good faith
> The Plan was in the best interests of creditors
> The Plan did not unfairly discriminate
> The Plan was fair and equitable
> The Plan was feasible. (City of Detroit, 2014a: 1)

Judge Rhodes also concluded that all of the city's settlements with its creditors were "reasonable" and then wrote that he approved them (City of Detroit, 2014a). His approval included the Annuity Savings Fund recoupment settlement to which several retirees had objected. He also approved the city's existing financing with Barclays. As a result, Detroit's Plan resulted in the city shedding $7 billion in debts.

The decision makers supporting the Plan

Detroit at the time of bankruptcy was—and continues to be—a majority-Black city. The city also leans heavily toward the Democrats, politically speaking. As many residents feared that race would matter in the bankruptcy Plan (Farley, 2015), it is important to detail the demographic characteristics of the major decision makers in support of the Plan who influenced Judge Rhodes' final decision. Of those decision makers, Emergency Manager Kevyn Orr, a Black lawyer, was the most influential.

When Republican Governor Rick Snyder was searching for an Emergency Manager to address the financial situation in Detroit—a Democratic city—Orr was on his shortlist (Pinho, 2013). On March 14, 2013, Snyder appointed Orr (Williams, 2013). He asked Orr to first study whether Detroit should declare bankruptcy, making him a major decision maker in the process. The position gave Orr control over all of Detroit's finances and the ability to make a recommendation to Snyder and to the State Treasurer about whether the city should enter Chapter IX bankruptcy (Pinho, 2013). Before Orr made a recommendation, he conducted a study and issued a report entitled "Proposal to Creditors."

The Proposal to Creditors

The report focused on an assessment of Detroit's assets. The proposal focused on: (1) the economic headwinds that the city faced; (2) the key objective for the financial restructuring and rehabilitation of the city; (3) the current financial status of the city and the action it had taken to address its financial challenges; (4) the restructuring and reinvestment in city government; (5) the revenue adjustments and tax reform; and (6) the realization of the value of assets held by the city. After this investigation, Orr then made ten-year projections: a restructuring proposal for the City after the Emergency Manager's tenure had ended.

Among the economic headwinds faced by Detroit was a declining population—the city had gone from 1.8 million people in 1950 to 684,000 by 2012. In addition, the city suffered from an increasing unemployment rate—from 7.5 percent in June 2000 to 18.6 percent in June 2012 (Orr, 2013a).

Detroit was also facing declining property tax revenues, which had decreased by 18.7 percent over a five-year period from 2008 to 2012. Moreover, income tax revenues had decreased by $91 million between 2002 and 2012. The primary cause of the decreases, according to Orr, was high unemployment, which resulted in lower taxable income of city residents and nonresidents who worked in the City. Orr also noted that revenues from the city's utility users' tax declined from approximately $55.3 million in fiscal year (FY) 2003 to approximately $39.8 million in FY 2012 or by 28 percent (Orr, 2013a).

Orr then turned to State revenue sharing and found that the city's share had decreased by $161 million between FY 2002 and FY 2012, or by 48 percent. The decline in revenue was due to the declining population and significant reductions in statutory revenue sharing by the State of Michigan (see Chapter 1). Revenue sharing is based on populations and revenue-sharing amounts decrease further if the city's population continues to decline.

The outmigration of residents and businesses

Orr then noted the increasing tax burden placed on the city due to the outmigration of residents and businesses. He found that the per capita tax burden on city residents was the highest in Michigan. The burden was especially severe, he noted, because it was imposed on a population that had low levels of per capita income. Moreover, the income tax burden on Detroit residents was greater than the tax burden for residents in suburban Dearborn—$1,207 in Detroit compared to $668 in Dearborn, $590 in Livonia, and $930 in Southfield (Orr, 2013a). The city's income tax of 2.4 percent for residents, 1.2 percent for nonresidents, and 2.0 percent for businesses was the highest in Michigan. Contrary to what some residents in the suburbs believed—that those residents in Detroit pay for less in property taxes than residents in the suburbs—Orr stated that Detroit residents paid higher total property tax rates than residents in the suburbs, as well as in other cities with a population of 50,000 or more (Orr, 2013a). Finally, he noted that Detroit residents were paying more for auto insurance than residents in the surrounding suburbs—in Detroit the cost was $3,993, compared to $2,908 in Dearborn, $2,052 in Livonia, and $3,108 in Southfield.

Given such loss of revenue and population decline, what was Detroit's debt? Orr noted that the city's accumulated general fund deficit had increased over the years so that by the end of FY 2012, the city's accumulated general fund deficit was $326.6 million, with the city's operations budget deficit estimated at $47 million (Orr, 2013a). He wrote that without interventions and/or restructuring, the city was projected to have negative cashflows of $198.5 million in FY 2014 (Orr, 2013a). He also noted that at the end of May 2013, one month before he made his recommendations about Detroit's bankruptcy, the city had $68 million of cashflow before property tax distributions, but had outstanding deferrals and amounts (due to other funds and entities) of approximately $216 million. These were effectively borrowed and had to be repaid.

Detroit was not paying its debts

Orr then turned to Detroit's unpaid debts. For example, the city had deferred payment of its year-end PFRS contributions. It also deferred approximately $50 million on June 30, 2013 for that year of PFRS pension contributions. Thus, by the end of FY 2013, the city would have deferred over $100 million in pension contributions. Moreover, Orr wrote that Detroit would not make the scheduled $39.7 million in payments due on its pension-related certificates of participation (COPS) due on June 14, 2013 (Orr, 2013a).

Given such debts and the lack of ability to pay them, the city's credit ratings by Moody's had continued to decline from Baa1 on June 30, 2003 to B3 on June 30, 2012. The credit rating by Standard & Poor's dropped from A- to B, and the ratings by Fitch dropped from A to CCC over the same time period (Orr, 2013a). It is important to note that no comparable major city had lower credit ratings. The negative credit ratings supported Orr's report, confirming his excellent characterization of Detroit's financial conditions. Orr's findings were also validated by other researchers (Sands and Skidmore, 2014).

Sands and Skidmore (2014) examined the City of Detroit 2012–13 executive budget departments and the agencies/budget departments 2011–12 executive budget. They found that the high rate of unemployment, declining populations, poverty, and lack of revenue from taxes had a significant effect on Detroit's finances and its ability to provide services, resulting in a double-digit cumulative deficit over $800 million. They also validated Orr's conclusions that Detroit residents and businesses were paying some of the highest tax rates in Michigan. Detroit is one of 22 Michigan cities that levy income taxes; at a rate of 2.5 percent for residents, Detroit's income tax was the highest in Michigan (Sands and Skidmore, 2014: 684).

Although the average property tax rate in Michigan is slightly below the median rate among States that offer property tax relief as an economic development incentive, the tax burden on industrial property in Detroit is almost double the Statewide average, according to Sands and Skidmore (2014) (see also Fisher and Peters, 1998). Sands and Skidmore (2014) also concluded, based on their analysis of Detroit's comprehensive annual financial reports, that compared to other municipalities, the local and city tax rates were among the highest of any municipality in Michigan (see also Michigan Department of Treasury, 2012).

Additionally, Detroit did not receive the revenue it could have due to the large number of properties that are owned by the city from property tax foreclosures. Such foreclosures have increased substantially in recent years due to the collapse of the housing market. With a property tax delinquency rate of 54 percent at the end of 2014 and 62,000 tax foreclosures being expected in 2015 alone, improving the administration of the property tax was critical (Sands and Skidmore, 2015). Such properties were transferred from the private homeowner to either the city's Land Bank Authority or Wayne County (Sands and Skidmore, 2014). Sands and Skidmore note that with fewer properties contributing revenue, the burden on those homeowners who continued to pay taxes increased (Sands and Skidmore, 2014). As a result of tax procedures, the city acquired the title to almost 46,500 properties. The authors state that while the city gains ownership of an asset, it is an asset that is in great need of repair and maintenance before generating any revenue (Sands and Skidmore, 2014).

Sands and Skidmore's analysis found that the problems Detroit faced included unfairly distributed tax burdens, inflated assessments, high rates of tax delinquency, and thousands of foreclosures that reduce the tax base and depress property values. The erosion of Detroit's property tax base was a symptom of changing social, economic, and cultural forces—challenges that have accumulated over more than six decades. This report suggested that property tax reform was not only necessary but could also help in Detroit's recovery (Sands and Skidmore, 2015). The authors' analysis reinforced the analysis by Orr that Detroit continued to struggle to balance its budget, and additional city revenue cuts, layoffs, and deferred pensions would be a solution to its problem.

Lack of resources for public safety

Orr then examined the city's resources to provide adequate services to its residents. Specifically, he examined the resources to address crime. He noted that in 2012, Detroit had the highest rate of violent crime of any city with a population of over 200,000, based on the FBI's Uniform Crime Report Database (Orr, 2013a). Detroit's violent crime rate at that time was five times the national average. He also stated that some residents and business owners in some neighborhoods had hired private security forces to ensure their safety.

Lack of resources to address the deterioration of the city

The next examination by Orr was the condition of the physical infrastructure of the city. He noted that there were 28,000 abandoned and blighted structures in the city and nearly 50 percent were considered dangerous. There were also 66,000 blighted and vacant lots in the city. Moreover, the number of city parks was dwindling and many more were in poor or fair condition as a result of neglect due to the lack of funding (Orr, 2013a).

The key objective for a financial restructuring and rehabilitation according to Orr

Given its financial position, Orr then wrote the financial and restructuring objectives for Detroit:

- Provide incentives and eliminate disincentives for businesses and residents to locate and remain in Detroit. This would require improvements in city services, particularly in the areas of public safety and tax reform, to reduce the high cost of living in Detroit. The aim was to make the cost of living in the city equal to the cost of living in nearby areas.
- Maximize recoveries for creditors.
- Provide affordable pension and health insurance benefits, and restructure governance of pension arrangement.
- Eliminate blight to assist in stabilizing and revitalizing neighborhoods in the city.
- Reform city government operations to improve efficiency and reduce costs.
- Maximize the collections of taxes and fees that are levied or imposed.
- Generate value from city assets where appropriate. (Orr, 2013a)

To achieve these objectives would not be easy. Orr noted that revenues had declined more quickly while legacy expenditures had increased between 2008 and 2013. Furthermore, excluding proceeds from debt issuances, the city's expenditures had exceeded revenues from FY 2008 to FY 2012 by an average of $100 million annually (Orr, 2013). Property tax revenues had been decreasing primarily due to declining taxable property valuations by −12 percent since FY 2008.

Limited options for further revenue generating

Given Detroit's financial situation and increasing debt, Orr concluded that the city had limited options for generating additional revenue. This was because, according to him, the city's legacy obligations were continuing to increase. Compounding this, it had limited or no access to capital markets. There were diminishing returns from further tax increases and there was municipal potential for further payroll-related reductions (Orr, 2013a). He then predicted that, without structural changes, the city's accumulated deficit would grow three to four times its current level of $326.6 million to over $1.35 billion by FY 2017.

What assets the city owned at the time of the assessments

The City of Detroit owned the US portion of the Detroit–Windsor Tunnel and the City of Windsor owned the portion located in Canada. Operating revenue for the Detroit side of the tunnel was less than $5 million per year.

Belle Isle Park

The City of Detroit also owned Belle Isle Park, a 982-acre park on an island in the Detroit River. The park has a museum, a conservatory, a golf course, and other attractions. The Detroit Recreation Department managed Belle Isle Park at a cost of $6 million per year in maintenance and operations costs (Orr, 2013a). In January 2013, Governor Rick Snyder proposed that the city lease Belle Isle Park to the State of Michigan, turning it into a State park and charging an admission fee to cover the cost of maintenance. This proposal was later adopted (Orr, 2013a).

The Detroit Institute of Arts

The City owned the DIA.

City-owned land

An estimated 22 square miles of land within the city limits of Detroit was government-owned, including parcels owned by the city, Wayne County, and the State of Michigan.

Parking garages/lots

The city owned some parking facilities among the 58,688 parking spaces in the city.

Conclusion

After an extensive investigation of Detroit's financial conditions and its lack of funds to pay its debts, Orr made a ten-year projection. He concluded that the city would continue to experience an even larger deficit. Orr then wrote to the Honorable Richard Snyder, Governor, and the Honorable Andrew Dillion, State Treasurer: "I hereby recommend that the city be authorized immediately to file a case and proceed to adjust its debts, under Chapter IX by title 11 of the United States Bankruptcy Code" (Orr, 2013b).

Orr also wrote that:

> Based on the current facts and circumstances, I have concluded that
> no reasonable alternative to rectifying the city's financial emergency
> exists other than the confirmation of a *Plan of Adjustment* for the city's
> debts pursuant to Chapter IX of the Bankruptcy Code because the
> city cannot adopt a feasible financial plan that can satisfactorily rectify
> the financial emergency outside of a Chapter IX process in a timely
> manner. (2013b: 2)

To support his recommendations, Orr provided information about
Detroit's inadequate city services and infrastructure, which were negatively
impacting the quality of life of its residents. He wrote that "after decades
of fiscal mismanagement; plummeting population, employment and
revenues; decaying city infrastructure, deteriorating city sewers, Detroit
today (2013) is a shell of the thriving metropolis that it once was"
(Orr, 2013b).

Orr continued: "Basic infrastructure is in failing such as the city's
streetlights, many of which do not work. Crime is endemic. The city is
plagued by blight and diminishing quality of life." He also noted that:

> For an extended period of time, the city has simply failed to make
> the investments required to provide its residents with an adequate
> quality of life, as limited resources have been diverted elsewhere. The
> failure of the city to address the large and growing legacy liabilities
> will prevent the city from devoting sufficient resources to providing
> basic and essential services to its residents. (2013b: 2)

Moreover, he wrote that "the city must devote a larger share of its revenues
to A) providing basic services B) attracting new residents and businesses
to foster growth and redevelopment and C) ultimately begin what will
be a long process of rehabilitation and revitalization of the city," and "the
city's debt and legacy liabilities must be reduced to permit the retirement"
(2013b: 2).

Orr then stated the details of Detroit's debts:

> The city had over $18 million in accrued obligations including A)
> $3.5 billion in underfunding pension liabilities; B) $5.7 billion in
> other past employment benefit liabilities; C) $1.13 billion in general
> obligation liabilities; D) $1.43 billion in liabilities under pension
> related certificates of participation; $343.6 million in swap liabilities
> related to the certificates of participation and $30.0 million in other
> liabilities. (2013b: 3)

In sum, Orr concluded that the city's substantial long-term obligations and legacy liabilities impeded its ability to operate within its budget. According to him, the level of debt "was simply unsustainable" (2013b: 3).

Orr then discussed the growing budget deficits. He wrote that, for many years, "the city's expenditures have exceeded its revenues, and the city has deferred paying certain obligations just to make ends meet" (2013b: 3). He also stated that "the city has funded its continuing deficits in a variety of unorthodox and financially imprudent ways including the deferral of pension contributions in later periods" (2013b: 3). He then discussed the city's negative cashflows: "the city had negative cash flows of $115.5 million in fiscal year 2012 absent interventions and restructuring, the city was projected to have a negative cash flow of $11.6 million as early as December 2013" (2013b: 4).

Orr noted that the city had taken certain measures to address the perceived challenges, such as: (1) entering into a financial stability agreement with the State of Michigan; and (2) reducing the number of city employees by more than 22 percent since FY 2010. Orr wrote that the city could not increase revenues by raising taxes since the current rate was already at the statutory maximum (2013b: 5).

Meetings to discuss his Proposal to Creditors

Orr wrote that on June 14, 2013, he had held a two-hour meeting to present the Executive Summary of the June 14 creditor proposal to approximately 150 invited representatives of the city's creditors, including all of the city's union employees, certain retiree associations, and bondholders. He also held individual follow-up meetings on June 20 and 25, and July 9, 10, and 11, 2013. After the meetings, he concluded that there was no realistic prospect for reaching agreements with all of the affected constituencies in a timely manner. Yet he noted that "the City did try and achieve in good faith an out of court resolution with creditors" (2013b: 9). Thus, he made his recommendations to seek relief under Chapter IX:

> I am unable to negotiate an out-of-court resolution that simultaneously addresses the city's dire financial situation while laying the foundation for a strong and prosperous city going forward and having exhausted all other available options, I hereby recommend in accordance with section 18(1) of PA 436 that the city be authorized to file for relief under Chapter IX of the Bankruptcy Code. ... The *Plan of Adjustment* process set forth in the Bankruptcy Code creates a mechanism by which the City may bind all of its creditors even if all creditors do not assent to the city's restructuring plan. (2013b: 10)

In sum, Orr concluded that, despite aggressive cost-cutting measures already implemented by the city, and despite good faith negotiations, no reasonable alternatives for restructuring the city's operations and obligations existed other than Chapter IX. Without Chapter IX relief, there was no clear path for rectifying the city's financial emergency and its deteriorating financial cycle would not only continue but also accelerate (Davey and Walsh, 2014a; Davey and Walsh, 2014b).

Judge Steven Rhodes and the other decision makers

The case was then turned over to Judge Steven Rhodes and the other key decision makers for their views. Rhodes, as mentioned earlier, is a white male and was the US Bankruptcy Judge for the Eastern District of Michigan. He made the final decision about Detroit's bankruptcy case. The *Detroit Mews* called him the top "Engineer of Detroit's Bankruptcy" (Gulick, 2015).

Rhodes had worked in his role as decision maker for 28 years prior to taking on the bankruptcy case. The case, which took 18 months, delayed his retirement plans. US District Judge Gerald Rosen believed that "democracy had to be taken from Detroiters to get the city's finances figured out" (Gulick, 2015). What was the nature of the plan that Judge Rhodes supported? He supported a plan that: (1) dissolved more than $7 billion of the city's $18 billion of debt; (2) enhanced the city's credit rating; and (3) included a ten-year, $1.7 billion investment in city services (Gulick, 2015).

The third decision maker was US District Chief Judge Gerald Rosen.

Judge Gerald Rosen

Judge Rosen was appointed by Rhodes to serve as chief mediator in the Detroit bankruptcy case. Rosen, a white male, was born in 1951 in Chandler, Arizona, and received his law degree from George Washington University Law School. He was a legislative assistant to US Senator Robert Griffin of Michigan. He was appointed judge of the United States District Court for the Eastern District of Michigan in 1990 by then President George W. Bush. It was Rosen who created the original structure of the Grand Bargain. In other words, he negotiated the $816 million Grand Bargain, which produced funds to help with city pensions and protect the DIA from the sale of many of its prized possessions. Rhodes said it was the smartest thing he did during the bankruptcy case (Gulick, 2015). Rosen had served on the bench for 25 years and has been called the "Judge who helped save Detroit" (Baldas, 2017). He stated: "My role in the Detroit bankruptcy was to protect the pensions, the art collections and most importantly saving the city" (Baldas, 2017). The City of Detroit was saved. The remaining chapters will examine whether the city has become more inclusive in terms of race and class after bankruptcy.

3

The Postbankruptcy Social and Spatial Structure of Metropolitan Detroit: Anatomy of Class and Racial Residential Segregation

Introduction

This chapter is based on my analysis of the social and spatial structure of the Detroit Metropolitan Area (DMA) postbankruptcy. It also examines racial residential segregation through socioeconomic neighborhood characteristics. For the purposes of this chapter, the study area consists of Wayne, Oakland, and Macomb Counties.

Such analysis allows for the measurement of racial residential segregation combined with inequality in neighborhood socioeconomic characteristics related to the racial composition of neighborhoods. To analyze these three counties for the purposes of determining the extent of inequality, I use census tracts from the American Community Survey Five-Year Estimates as spatial units, as they are surrogates for neighborhoods. Most of the analyses are based on data from the 2011–15 and 2016–20 Five-Year Estimates databases. I use the Darden-Kamel Composite Socioeconomic Index (CSI) to analyze Metropolitan Detroit (DMA) by neighborhoods in order to determine the extent of class inequality, and the *index of dissimilarity* to determine the extent of racial residential segregation and socioeconomic neighborhood inequality by race (Darden et al, 2010). The analysis of the data shows that the *inequality gap* between neighborhoods increased between the 2011–15 and 2016–20 censuses. This inequality has negatively impacted Black and Hispanic residents more than white residents as Black and Hispanic residents disproportionately reside in neighborhoods with very low and low socioeconomic characteristics. Most whites, on the other hand, reside in neighborhoods with high and very high socioeconomic characteristics. The data and analyses in this chapter answer questions

35

about inequality after bankruptcy. Detroit is not moving toward a more inclusive city racially and socially. Both race and class inequality remain, and more actions need to be taken with policies to reduce the inequality. The implications of the data and analyses are that racial discrimination continues after bankruptcy.

Explaining the Darden–Kamel Composite Socioeconomic Index

The Darden–Kamel CSI incorporates nine variables:

1. Percentage of households below poverty
2. Unemployment rate
3. Median household income
4. Occupational status
5. Educational attainment
6. Median value of dwelling
7. Median rent of dwelling
8. Percentage of households that own homes
9. Percentage of households with a vehicle available

Definitions of the variables

1. Percentage below poverty: the percentage of all families whose income in the past 12 months is below the US poverty level. The poverty thresholds vary depending on the size of family, the number of related children, and, for one- and two-person families, the age of the householder as defined by the US Census Bureau.
2. Unemployment rate: the percentage of civilians aged 16 and over who were neither at work nor held a job during the reference week and who were actively seeking work during the previous four weeks and available to start a job.
3. Median household income: the median income of all households among family members aged 16 and over, including those without an income.
4. Occupation (defined as the percentage of residents with management, business, science, and arts occupations): the percentage of workers aged 16 and over based on the US Bureau of the Census.
5. Educational attainment (defined as the percentage of residents with bachelor's degrees or higher): the percentage of the total population aged 25 years and over who hold at least a bachelor's degree (for example, four or more years of schooling in addition to a high school education).

6. Median value of dwelling (in dollars): the median value of owner-occupied housing, which is the respondent's estimate of how much the property would sell for if it were for sale.
7. Median gross rent of dwelling (in dollars): the contract rent value plus the estimated average monthly cost of utilities.
8. Percent homeownership: the percentage of owner-occupied housing units regardless of mortgage status.
9. Percentage of households with a vehicle available.

Calculating and standardizing these composite socioeconomic variables

To standardize the contribution of each census variable included in the CSI, a Z-score was created for each of the nine census tract variables by subtracting the mean from the grand mean for each of the variables used in the study and dividing it by the standard deviation of the respective variable for the DMA as a whole. To ensure that each variable contributed appropriately when calculating this index, the Z-scores for two depreciating variables—unemployment rate and percentage of the population below poverty—were multiplied by -1 before they were added to the remainder variables (see Darden et al, 2010). The formula for the CSI index is as follows:

$$CSI_i = \sum_{j=i}^{k} \frac{V_{ij} - V_{jDMA}}{S(V_{jDMA})}$$

The parts of this equation are defined as follows:

- CSI_i = the composite socioeconomic Z-score index for census tract i and the sum of Z-scores for the socioeconomic status variables j, relative to the DMA's socioeconomic status.
- DMA = the specific Metropolitan Area.
- k = the number of variables in the index.
- V_{ij} = the jth socioeconomic position variable (Z-score) for a given census tract i.
- V_{jDMA} = the mean of the jth variable in the DMA.
- $S(V_{jDMA})$ = the standard deviation of the jth variable in the DMA.

The socioeconomic results for the DMA (defined here as Wayne, Oakland, and Macomb Counties) resulted in it being divided into five separate and unequal clusters of neighborhoods. The clusters range in socioeconomic status (SES) with boundaries at the 20th, 40th, 60th, and 80th percentiles (quintiles) of the CSI frequency distribution.

This categorization allows for a division of the DMA census tracts of residence into five approximately equal proportions of the population in each group of socioeconomic position (SEP): very high SEP (SEP 5), high SEP (SEP 4), middle SEP (SEP 3), low SEP (SEP 2), and very low SEP (SEP 1). Employing the Darden-Kamel CSI, the five clusters of neighborhoods were mapped by SEP status using geographic information system (GIS) techniques (Darden et al, 2010).

The importance of the variables in describing neighborhood socioeconomic characteristics

Each variable examined constitutes a component of the CSI that describes neighborhood *characteristics by socioeconomic status*. The Darden-Kamel CSI recognizes that neighborhoods operate like a social and spatial system, with many variables playing a role in each neighborhood's strengths and weaknesses.

Percentage in poverty

The poverty experienced by the poor is in part due to structural changes in the economy and residential segregation of neighborhoods by class. Poor residents are overrepresented in very low socioeconomic characteristic neighborhoods. They are also overrepresented in the central city.

Unemployment rate

As more jobs moved out of the central City of Detroit to the suburbs, there was a spatial mismatch between where residents lived and where most of their jobs were located. When most jobs are in one geographic area, that is, the suburbs, and the residents are located in a different geographic area, that is, the central city, urban geographers call the concept spatial mismatch. Spatial mismatch impacts the unemployment rates between residents in the central city and residents in the suburbs. However, spatial mismatch does not tell the whole story. Explaining unemployment rate differences by race is more complex. Racial discrimination in employment is still an important factor and spatial mismatch does not adequately take it into account. As a matter of fact, in Detroit, even the few jobs that existed in the central city compared to the many jobs in the suburbs did not ensure employment for city residents. For example, in 2013, a year before bankruptcy ended, only 26.5 percent of jobs within the city were held by people who lived there (Corporation for Skilled Workforce, 2016). Instead, 73.5 percent of the jobs were held by people who lived outside of the city and commuted to work (Corporation for Skilled Workforce, 2016). Workers holding jobs in the city and living in the suburbs created an economic disadvantage for the city's property tax base, thereby impacting the socioeconomic characteristics of neighborhoods in the city. This is because such workers did not pay property taxes to the city. Instead, they paid property taxes to their suburban municipalities where they lived, thereby positively impacting the socioeconomic characteristics of suburban neighborhoods.

Median household income

Income is one of the most important components in the socioeconomic status of racial and ethnic groups, which in ecological theory contributes to racial and ethnic residential segregation by neighborhoods (Massey and Denton, 1993). It is assumed by ecological theory that higher-income groups purchase homes or rent in neighborhoods where lower-income groups cannot afford the same neighborhood, thereby resulting in residential segregation based on income or socioeconomic status.

Occupational status

This variable is a component that often defines socioeconomic status within ecological theory and residential segregation. According to ecological theory, higher-status occupation groups, such as professionals, live in separate neighborhoods from lower-status occupational groups, such as laborers (Darden, 1987b).

Educational attainment

Educational attainment is another important component related to the status of neighborhoods. The education levels of neighborhood residents have been used by social scientists to distinguish the socioeconomic status of racial and ethnic groups in ecological theory (Darden, 1987b; Darden and Kamel, 2000). According to ecological theory, the residential segregation of population groups is linked to differences in the level of education of the groups by neighborhood. Residential segregation and education levels of neighborhoods have certain social consequences. Highly segregated neighborhoods have populations that are less likely to complete high school and even fewer are likely to enter and complete college (Darden and Kamel, 2000).

Median housing value

Similar to the case with income, occupation, and education, past research has demonstrated that as residents increase their socioeconomic status, they are more likely to move to, or reside in, neighborhoods of higher rent or housing cost and separate from neighborhoods of low rent or low housing cost (Darden and Thomas, 2013). Because public schools are funded primarily by property taxes, public schools in neighborhoods of high housing value are more likely to have greater resources to provide children with a high-achieving education than public schools located in neighborhoods of low value-housing (Vojnovic and Darden, 2013).

The percentage of owner-occupied housing units

Homeownership has been linked to the socioeconomic status of residents, which distinguishes them from renters. The extent of homeownership varies by neighborhood. It is more prevalent among neighborhoods in the suburbs than in the central city. Within the residential segregation spatial assimilation theory, homeownership has been considered the ultimate outcome of spatial assimilation, offering the highest quality of life and the greatest benefits, including the greatest access to the highest-achieving public schools (Darden and Thomas, 2013). Homeownership is the largest asset for most Americans regardless of race. According to Wainer and Zabel (2020) homeownership generates positive externalities such as increased exterior maintenance, household and neighborhood stability, greater civic engagement, and increased social capital. According to Shlay (2006), neighborhood improvement that results from homeownership is particularly valuable in low-income neighborhoods.

For most Americans, a home is the single largest asset they own in their lifetime. In 2016, a home accounted for just over half (42.1 percent) of the typical US homeowner's total wealth. But for Black and Hispanic homeowners, their homes have and continue to account for a much larger share of their net worth. For typical Hispanic and Black homeowners, their home accounts for the majority of their wealth (64.7 percent and 55.6 percent, respectively), while a home accounts for just over a third (38.1 percent) for the typical white homeowner (Olsen, 2018). Thus, the gap in homeownership rates between Blacks and whites is very important. Although this chapter focuses on the most recent gap, it is useful to look at the past to see how much progress is needed to close the gap.

The homeownership rate gap was slightly wider in 2016 than it was in 1900. In 1900, 48.1 percent of whites in the United States owned homes while only 20.5 percent of Blacks did—for a homeownership gap of 27.6 percentage points. In 2017, the gap was 30.3 percentage points (Olsen, 2018). Homeownership provides the most common avenue for wealth accumulation (Solomon et al, 2019). According to the Harvard Joint Center for Housing Studies (2018), white renters in the nation had a net worth of $11,070 compared with the net worth of homeowners, which was $384,100.

The net worth of racial minority homeowners was $145,300 compared with renters' net worth, which was only $2,000. Thus, the net worth of minority homeowners—especially Blacks—is initially greater than that of renters. This is because equity homeownership makes up 38 percent of the net worth of white Americans and 66 percent for Black Americans (Brown, 2021: 89).

Median rent

Homeownership notwithstanding, the census data shows that when a family rents, the family does not just rent the apartment, but the entire neighborhood where the apartment is located. The neighborhood can provide benefits provided by taxpayers, such as high-quality public schools that extend beyond the rented apartment. In Metropolitan Detroit, many residents with a moderate income can afford to rent in neighborhoods that have middle to high socioeconomic characteristics, thereby gaining access in theory to high-achieving public schools (Darden and Thomas, 2013). Gross rent includes the monthly contract rent and any monthly payments made for electricity, gas, water and sewer, and any other fuels to heat the house.

Percentage of households with a vehicle available

Scholars of transport geography have argued that steady employment and having an automobile are highly correlated (Grengs, 2010). It has been argued that access to a car, especially in Metropolitan Detroit (DMA), reduces the impact of spatial mismatch (Darden and Thomas, 2013). A car can also reduce the negative effects of food deserts—that is, the lack of supermarkets selling fresh fruits and vegetables in the immediate neighborhood. Food deserts are areas where people have limited access to a variety of healthy foods. This may be due to having a limited income or living far away from sources of healthy and affordable food.

The United States Department of Agriculture (USDA) defines a food desert as an area that has either a poverty rate greater than or equal to 20 percent or a median family income not exceeding 80 percent of the median family income in urban areas. In order to qualify as a food desert, an area must also meet certain other criteria. In urban areas, at least 500 people, or 33 percent of the population, must live more than one mile from the nearest large grocery store (Dutko et al, 2012).

Furthermore, since DMA does not have a rapid public transit system and the city bus service is unreliable, a car is a necessary mode of transportation even for workers within the city, not to mention workers who commute to the suburbs (Grengs, 2010). During 2021, with the availability of a vaccine for COVID-19, the lack of an automobile made equal access to vaccine sites more of a disadvantage for certain population groups, especially those residing in neighborhoods with very low socioeconomic characteristics. Mayor Mike Duggan acknowledged that not every Detroiter has access to reliable transportation, so the city offered rides to COVID-19 testing sites in 2020. He announced a new ride program to the TCF Center for vaccinations. Residents had to request a ride when making their vaccine appointment and could be picked up and dropped off anywhere within the city. Duggan said the cost of transportation was $2 per person, but the fee would be waived for residents who could not afford it (Lewis, 2021).

Using the variables to describe the characteristics of neighborhoods, the social and spatial structure of DMA based on an analysis of the Darden–Kamel CSI shows that there are, in fact, five separate and unequal Detroits, which are divided into separate and unequal clusters of neighborhoods.

Table 3.1 shows Detroit neighborhood characteristics one through five as revealed by the Darden–Kamel CSI. Based on the 2011–15 census data, the poverty rate ranged from 42 percent in SEP 1, where residents in very low socioeconomic characteristic neighborhoods resided, to 3.3 percent in SEP 5, where residents in very high socioeconomic characteristic neighborhoods resided. The unemployment rate ranged from 28.2 percent in SEP 1, where very low socioeconomic characteristic neighborhood residents resided, to 5.5 percent in SEP 5. The inequality was also revealed by the median household income of the residents. In the very low socioeconomic characteristic neighborhoods, the median household income was only $21,888; however, in the very high socioeconomic characteristic neighborhoods, the median household income was $95,035. Inequality was also revealed in the percentage of professional and managerial workers. In the very low socioeconomic characteristic neighborhoods, only 16.4 percent of residents were professionals; however, in the very high socioeconomic characteristic neighborhoods, 55.9 percent of residents were professionals.

Inequality was also revealed in the educational attainment of the population by neighborhoods. In the very low socioeconomic characteristic neighborhoods, only 8.3 percent of the population had a bachelor's degree or higher level of education; however, in the very high socioeconomic characteristic neighborhoods, 54.3 percent had a bachelor's degree or higher. Additionally, inequality was revealed in the housing value of the property. In the very low socioeconomic characteristic neighborhoods, the median housing value was only $58,757; however, in the very high socioeconomic characteristic neighborhoods, the housing value was $202,710. Finally, the homeownership rate varied from 45.8 percent in the very low socioeconomic characteristic neighborhoods to 84.4 percent in the very high socioeconomic characteristic neighborhoods (see Table 3.1).

The census data for the three-county (Wayne, Oakland, and Macomb) DMA for this study were based on a total of 1,098 census tracts.

Table 3.1: Spatial and social structure of Metropolitan Detroit in 2011–15 based on the Darden–Kamel Composite Socioeconomic Index

Mean characteristics of census tracts

Neighborhood index of SEP (quintiles)	Poverty (%)	Unemployment (%)	Median income (US$)	Vehicle ownership (%)	Professional and managerial workers (%)	Bachelor's or higher education (%)	Median house value (US$)	Median monthly rent (US$)	Home ownership (%)
Very high SEP	3.3	5.5	95,035	97.2	55.9	54.3	202,710	1,226	84.4
High SEP	6.2	7.4	63,041	95.2	40.4	32.7	154,441	1,016	74.7
Middle SEP	10.9	9.8	49,598	93.0	31.1	21.7	107,314	901	69.1
Low SEP	24.2	16.5	34,898	86.0	23.0	14.8	78,198	882	55.9
Very low SEP	42.0	28.2	21,888	71.0	16.4	8.3	58,757	784	45.8
All tracts	17.4	13.5	52,815	88.4	33.3	26.3	119,837	960	66.0

Note: SEP = socioeconomic position.

Source: calculated by the authors from the data in the US Bureau of the Census (2011–15) American Community Survey Five-Year Estimates.

The data show that there was clearly extreme inequality in DMA at the time that the 2011–15 census data were collected. The major question this chapter investigates is whether the inequality declined at the time that the 2016–20 census data were collected. Based on the 2016–20 census data, in the very low socioeconomic characteristic neighborhoods, the poverty rate was 36 percent, while this declined to 4.2 percent in the very high socioeconomic characteristic neighborhoods. The unemployment rate was 9 percent in the very low socioeconomic characteristic neighborhoods, while this declined to only 2.4 percent in the very high socioeconomic characteristic neighborhoods. The median household income was $28,454 in the very low socioeconomic characteristic neighborhoods, but the median household income was $112,415 in the very high socioeconomic characteristic neighborhoods. Only 18.9 percent of professional and managerial workers lived in very low socioeconomic characteristic neighborhoods; however, in the very high socioeconomic characteristic neighborhoods, 61 percent of residents were professional and managerial workers.

The median housing value also showed inequality. In the very low socioeconomic characteristic neighborhood the median housing value was $49,450; however, in the very high socioeconomic characteristic neighborhoods, the median housing value was $334,105. Finally, in the very low socioeconomic characteristic neighborhoods, only 27 percent of the residents owned their homes; however, in the very high socioeconomic characteristic neighborhoods, 68 percent of the residents owned their homes (see Table 3.2). A major objective of this chapter is to determine whether the inequality gap between neighborhoods of different socioeconomic characteristics decreased between the 2011–15 and the 2016–20 census years.

The inequality gap between neighborhoods in Metropolitan Detroit in 2011–15 and 2016–20

The analysis of the data shows that the inequality gap decreased in only two socioeconomic areas. These were the poverty rate, which *decreased* from 38.7 percent in 2011–15 to 32 percent in 2016–20. The gap in the unemployment rate *decreased* greatly from 27.7 percent in 2011–15 to 6.6 percent in 2016–20. The gap in other socioeconomic areas *increased*. Gaps in median household income *increased* from $73,147 to $83,961. The gap in the percentage of professional and managerial workers *increased slightly* from 39.5 to 41.6. The gap in the percentage of residents with a bachelor's degree or higher *increased* from 46.0 percent to 50.2 percent. The gap in the housing value *increased substantially* from $143,953 to $284,647. Finally, the gap in homeownership rates *increased* from 38.6 percent to 40.7 percent.

Table 3.2: Spatial and social structure of Metropolitan Detroit in 2016–20 based on the Darden–Kamel Composite Socioeconomic Index

Mean characteristics of census tracts

Neighborhood index of SEP quintiles	Poverty (%)	Unemployment (%)	Median household income (US$)	Vehicle ownership (%)	Professional and managerial workers (%)	Bachelor's or higher education (%)	Median house value (US$)	Median monthly rent (US$)	Homeownership (%)
Very high (SEP 5)	4.22	2.38	112,415	98.76	60.63	59.94	334,105	1,591	67.92
High (SEP 4)	6.93	3.00	75,881	98.62	44.81	37.24	206,641	1,119	66.56
Middle (SEP 3)	9.68	3.47	59,732	97.90	34.23	24.52	146,582	1,001	62.73
Low (SEP 2)	19.19	5.25	44,719	95.28	25.17	16.98	99,757	926	51.47
Very low (SEP 1)	36.27	9.04	28,454	85.87	18.97	9.69	49,458	802	27.19
All tracts	15.24	4.62	64,224	95.29	36.75	29.66	167,242	1,088	55.20

Notes: Based on 1,054 census tracts.

SEP stands for socioeconomic position and is based on the Darden–Kamel CSI.

SEP 5 = very high, SEP 4 = high, SEP 3 = middle, SEP 2 = low, and SEP 1 = very low.

Sources: Darden et al, 2010; US Census Bureau, 2020.

In sum, the inequality gap between neighborhoods in 2011–15 and 2016–20 decreased in two *socioeconomic* areas: poverty and unemployment. However, the inequality gap *increased* in five socioeconomic areas: median household income; percentage of professional and managerial workers; percentage of bachelor's degree or higher educated residents; value of housing; and percentage of homeowners (see Table 3.3). Tables 3.1 and 3.2 show where improvements have occurred between the two periods before and after bankruptcy. Such differences in neighborhood characteristics will be used to explain whether Detroit is moving toward a more inclusive city once the *index of dissimilarity* measures the extent of racial residential segregation between Blacks and whites, and Hispanics and non Hispanic whites over the cluster of neighborhoods.

If Detroit is moving toward being a more inclusive city, there must be evidence of a decline in racial residential segregation by socioeconomic neighborhood characteristics. This can be determined by using census data for the two periods 2011–15 and 2016–20. The method to assess the racial residential segregation is the *index of dissimilarity*. This is the second method used in this chapter. The index of dissimilarity was employed to measure racial and ethnic residential segregation, which is defined as the unevenness in the spatial distribution (that is, residential segregation) of Blacks, whites, and Hispanics over a cluster of census tracts (neighborhoods) with different socioeconomic characteristics.

Table 3.3: The inequality gap between neighborhoods in Metropolitan Detroit in 2011–15 and 2016–20

Socioeconomic variable	2011–15	2016–20	Change in the gap
Poverty rate (%)	38.7	32.0	Decreased
Unemployment rate (%)	27.7	6.6	Decreased
Median household income	$73,147	$83,961	Increased
Percentage of professional and managerial workers	39.5	41.6	Increased
Percentage of residents with a BA degree or higher	46.0	50.3	Increased
Median household value	$143,953	$284,647	Increased
Homeownership rate	38.6	40.7	Increased

Source: calculated by the author from data obtained from US Bureau of the Census American Community Survey 2011–15; 2016–20.

The index of dissimilarity can be stated mathematically as:

$$D = 100 \left(1/2 \sum_{i=1}^{k} |x_I - y_i| \right)$$

where x_I is the percentage of a Metropolitan Area's Black population living in the Detroit Metropolitan Area's very low socioeconomic cluster of neighborhoods (SEP 1) (census tracts) and y_i is the percentage of a Metropolitan Area's white population living in a very low socioeconomic cluster of neighborhoods, k is the number of quintiles cluster of census tracts (neighborhoods), and D is the index of dissimilarity. It is half the sum of the *absolute differences* (positive and negative) between the percentage of the total population of whites and Blacks and Hispanics and non Hispanic whites residing in similar clusters or the same cluster of census tracts.

Racial residential segregation over clusters of neighborhoods based on socioeconomic characteristics

This section examines racial residential segregation based on the 2011–15 census data for Blacks and whites in the DMA. These years occurred mostly before and during bankruptcy. The guiding question here is: what was the extent of Black–white residential segregation during this time in clusters of neighborhoods of different socioeconomic characteristics? A total of 39 percent of all Blacks in the DMA resided in very low socioeconomic characteristic neighborhoods; however, only 4 percent of all whites in the DMA lived in such neighborhoods. A total of 34 percent of all Blacks in the DMA lived in low socioeconomic characteristic neighborhoods; however, only 13 percent of all whites in the DMA lived in such neighborhoods. It is important to note that these two types of neighborhoods are where the majority of Blacks (73 percent) in Metropolitan Detroit lived during this period. This was clear racial separation and inequality in neighborhood lifestyles. Of all the whites in the DMA, only 18 percent lived in similar neighborhoods. In contrast, in neighborhoods that were classified as middle class, only 14 percent of all Blacks in the DMA were residents, while 24 percent of all whites in the DMA were residents.

Only 8 percent of all Blacks in the DMA were residents of high socioeconomic characteristic neighborhoods; however, 28 percent of all whites in the DMA lived in such neighborhoods. Only 5 percent of all Blacks in the DMA were residents of very high socioeconomic characteristic neighborhoods; however, 31 percent of all whites in the DMA lived in such neighborhoods.

Table 3.4: Racial residential segregation between Blacks and whites in neighborhoods of different socioeconomic characteristics in Metropolitan Detroit based on 2011–15 census tract data

American Community Survey Census tract data (ACS) 2011–15		Non Hispanic Black residents	Non Hispanic white residents
SEP	Neighborhood characteristic	%	%
5	Very high	5.05	30.66
4	High	7.97	27.87
3	Middle	14.22	23.88
2	Low	33.82	13.41
1	Very low	38.94	4.19
	Total	100.00	100.00
Dissimilarity Index Score *56.3*			

Notes: An index of dissimilarity of 100 equals complete residential segregation. An index of zero equals no residential segregation. The higher the index, the greater the level of residential segregation.

SEP stands for socioeconomic position and is based on the Darden-Kamel CSI.

Sources: Darden et al, 2010; US Census Bureau American Community Survey 2011–15 Five-Year Estimates.

The *index of dissimilarity* involved calculating the percentage of the absolute differences between where Blacks and whites lived. After making this calculation, I then divided the results by two. The *index of dissimilarity* was 56.3 (see Table 3.4). This means that in order to achieve complete desegregation in Metropolitan Detroit, 56.3 percent of Blacks and whites would have to change neighborhoods of residence—a majority of both racial groups. The conclusion is that Blacks and whites in neighborhoods in Metropolitan Detroit were highly segregated during the 2011–15 period (see Table 3.4).

The new census data, which was released in March 2022, provided me with the opportunity to determine whether during 2016–20 (after bankruptcy), the residential segregation level between Blacks and whites reduced.

Racial residential segregation between Blacks and whites (2016–20)

When Blacks are compared to whites in terms of neighborhood characteristics, the 2016–20 census reveals that 42 percent of all Blacks in the DMA lived in very low socioeconomic characteristic neighborhoods (SEP 1). However, only 4 percent of all whites in the DMA lived in such neighborhoods. In low socioeconomic characteristic neighborhoods (SEP 2), almost twice as many Blacks (29.5 percent) as whites (16 percent) lived in such neighborhoods. Almost twice as many whites (25 percent) as Blacks (13 percent) lived in middle-class neighborhoods (SEP 3). A total of 28 percent of all whites in the DMA lived in high socioeconomic characteristic neighborhoods (SEP 4), but only 9 percent of all Blacks resided in such neighborhoods, while 27 percent of all whites in the DMA lived in very high socioeconomic characteristic neighborhoods (SEP 5), compared to only 6 percent of all Blacks.

The dissimilarity index analysis shows that the residential segregation between Blacks and whites in terms of neighborhoods based on socioeconomic characteristics was 51 percent (see Table 3.5). This means that 51 percent of all Blacks and whites would have to change places of residence in order to desegregate Metropolitan Detroit by neighborhood socioeconomic characteristics. Thus, the results indicate that between 2011–15 and 2016–20, Black–white residential segregation between neighborhoods declined from 55.2 percent to 51 percent, or by 4.2 percentage points. But since the index remains above 50, residential segregations between Blacks and whites in terms of neighborhoods based on characteristics was still considered high in 2020, and over half of the population of Blacks and whites would have to change neighborhoods to completely eliminate the residential segregation.

Table 3.5: Racial residential segregation between Blacks and whites in neighborhoods of different socioeconomic characteristics in Metropolitan Detroit based on 2016–20 census tract data

SEP neighborhood characteristics	Non Hispanic Black residents	Non Hispanic white residents
Very high (SEP 5)	5.95	27.17
High (SEP 4)	9.40	27.59
Middle (SEP 3)	13.07	24.66
Low (SEP 2)	29.49	16.15
Very low (SEP 1)	42.09	4.43
Total	**100**	**100**

Notes: Index of dissimilarity = 51. An index of dissimilarity of 100 equals complete residential segregation. An index of zero equals no residential segregation. The higher the index, the greater the level of residential segregation.

SEP stands for socioeconomic position and is based on the Darden-Kamel CSI.

Sources: Darden et al, 2010; US Census Bureau, 2020.

Residential segregation of Hispanics and non Hispanic whites (2011–15)

In the 2011–15 census years, Hispanics and non Hispanic whites were distributed over neighborhoods of different socioeconomic characteristics in the DMA. A total of 27.7 percent of all Hispanics lived in very low socioeconomic characteristic neighborhoods; however, only 3.3 percent of all whites lived in such neighborhoods. A total of 23 percent of all Hispanics lived in low socioeconomic characteristic neighborhoods compared to only 13 percent of all whites. Hispanics accounted for 20 percent of all residents in middle-class socioeconomic characteristic neighborhoods, compared to 24 percent of all white non Hispanics. A total of 15 percent of all Hispanics and 28 percent of all non Hispanic whites lived in high socioeconomic characteristic neighborhoods. More than twice as many whites (31 percent) lived in very high socioeconomic characteristic neighborhoods compared to Hispanics (14 percent). However, such an uneven distribution of Hispanics and non Hispanic whites resulted in an index of dissimilarity of 34.3 (see Table 3.6). Thus, in order for the Hispanics and non Hispanic whites to be evenly distributed over neighborhoods, 34 percent of each group would have to change neighborhoods.

Table 3.6: Residential segregation between Hispanics and non Hispanic whites in neighborhoods with different socioeconomic characteristics in Metropolitan Detroit based on 2011–15 census tract data

ACS 2011–15		Hispanic residents	Non Hispanic white residents
SEP	**Neighborhood characteristic**	**%**	**%**
5	Very high	14.08	31.29
4	High	15.34	28.35
3	Middle	19.96	24.04
2	Low	22.90	13.04
1	Very low	27.72	3.29
	Total	100.00	100.00

Dissimilarity Index Score *34.3*

Notes: An index of dissimilarity of 100 equals complete residential segregation. An index of zero equals no residential segregation. The higher the index, the greater the amount of residential segregation.

SEP stands for socioeconomic position and is based on the Darden-Kamel CSI.

Sources: Darden et al, 2010; US Census Bureau American Community Survey 2011–15 Five-Year Estimates.

The important research question was whether the level of Hispanic and non Hispanic white residential segregation declined based on the 2016–20 census data.

Residential segregation between Hispanics and non Hispanic whites (2016–20)

Following the 2011–15 census years, I examined whether an equal percentage of all Hispanics lived in neighborhoods with socioeconomic characteristics as an equal percentage of all non Hispanic whites during 2016-20 census years. Table 3.7 indicates that 27 percent of all Hispanics lived in very low socioeconomic characteristic neighborhoods, but only 5 percent of all non Hispanic whites lived in such neighborhoods. Also, 26 percent of all Hispanics lived in low socioeconomic characteristic neighborhoods, compared to only 16 percent of all non Hispanic whites. A total of 17 percent of all Hispanics lived in middle-class socioeconomic characteristic neighborhoods, but only 24 percent of all non Hispanic whites lived there. Hispanics accounted for only 15 percent of the population in high socioeconomic characteristic neighborhoods, while 27.3 percent of all non Hispanic whites lived there. Finally, 14 percent of all Hispanics lived in very high socioeconomic characteristic neighborhoods, compared to 27.5 percent of all non Hispanic whites.

Table 3.7: Residential segregation between Hispanics and non Hispanic whites in neighborhoods with different socioeconomic characteristics in Metropolitan Detroit based on 2016–20 census tract data

ACS 2016–20		Hispanic residents	Non Hispanic white residents
SEP	**Neighborhood characteristic**	%	%
5	Very high	14.01	27.50
4	High	15.46	27.33
3	Middle	17.39	24.35
2	Low	26.31	15.64
1	Very low	26.83	5.17
	Total	100	100
Dissimilarity Index Score 32.3			

Notes: An *index of dissimilarity* of 100 equals complete residential segregation. An index of zero equals no residential segregation. The higher the index, the greater the level of residential segregation.

SEP stands for socioeconomic position and is based on the Darden-Kamel CSI.

Sources: Darden et al, 2010; US Census Bureau, 2020.

As a result of the uneven distribution of Hispanics and non Hispanic whites across the various neighborhoods, the index of dissimilarity was 32.3 (see Table 3.7). The results showed that residential segregation between Hispanics and non Hispanic whites slightly declined from 34 to 32.3. That means that 32.3 percent of all Hispanics and non Hispanic whites would have to move to a different neighborhood in order to reduce the level of residential segregation between them to zero. Hispanics are less residentially segregated from whites than Blacks are.

The discussion now turns to the spatial distribution of Blacks, whites, and Hispanics over the three-county Metropolitan Area derived from GIS mapping techniques.

Mapping the neighborhoods of Metropolitan Detroit based on the Darden-Kamel Composite Socioeconomic Index

Figures 3.1–3.5 show where the neighborhoods that have been discussed are located in Metropolitan Detroit, and the percentage of total Blacks, whites, and Hispanics who live there.

Figure 3.1 shows where the neighborhoods are located in SEP 1, which are the very low socioeconomic characteristic neighborhoods. Most of the 195 neighborhoods (or 93 percent) are located in Wayne County, and 136 are located in the City of Detroit. These neighborhoods are where 42 percent of all Blacks in the DMA reside. As mentioned earlier, these neighborhoods are where only 5.2 percent of all whites and 26.8 percent of all Hispanics in the DMA reside. Thus, both class and racial residential segregation are common features of the DMA. This is because there are so few very low socioeconomic characteristic neighborhoods in the suburbs of Detroit. Such neighborhoods are found in older historical industrial suburbs such as Inkster in Wayne County and Pontiac in Oakland County.

The very low socioeconomic characteristic neighborhoods in Wayne County do not fit the traditional pattern of suburban growth. The population in suburban Inkster evolved as manufacturing workers—many of them Black—moved from Detroit to the Inkster auto plants before 1950. Inkster continued to grow as a smaller, Black satellite municipality outside of Detroit (Darden et al, 1987: 98). Few whites moved there and based on the most recent census, Inkster has a Black population of 73 percent. Pontiac is located 25 miles northwest of Detroit. The industrial suburb evolved from the birthplace of the General Motors truck and motor division. It is a blue-collar industrial suburb that is 48 percent Black and surrounded by white-collar professional neighborhoods that are majority-white. There are also two very low socioeconomic characteristic neighborhood clusters in Macomb County. These suburbs are Sterling

Figure 3.1: Locations of SEP 1 (very low) socioeconomic characteristic neighborhoods

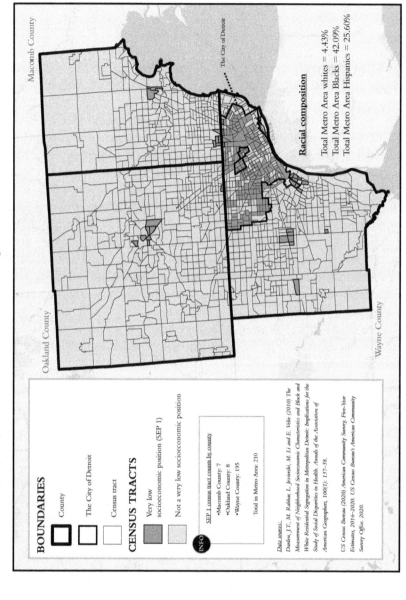

Sources: Esri, HERE, Garmin, FAO, NOAA, USGS, © OpenStreetMap contributors, and the GIS user community.

Heights and Mount Clemens. Mount Clemens is 24 percent Black and used to be a blue-collar industrial suburb.

Figure 3.2 shows the location of low socioeconomic characteristic neighborhoods (SEP 2). A total of 139 (66 percent) are located in Wayne County and 47 (22 percent) are located in Detroit. These are neighborhoods where 29 percent of all Blacks in the DMA reside. They are also where 16 percent of all whites in the DMA and 27 percent of all Hispanics reside. In addition to Wayne County, Macomb County has 50 (or 24 percent) of these types of neighborhoods, with Oakland County containing 22 (or 10 percent).

Figure 3.3 presents the spatial distribution of middle-class neighborhoods. Such neighborhoods are more evenly distributed over the three counties: 95 (45 percent) are in Wayne County; 77 (36 percent) are in Macomb County; and 40 (19 percent) are in Oakland County. Moreover, 13 (6 percent) are in the City of Detroit. Among the three racial groups, 13 percent of all Blacks, 25 percent of all whites, and 17 percent of all Hispanics in the DMA lived in these middle-class neighborhoods (Darden and Rubalcava, 2018).

Figure 3.4 shows the location of high socioeconomic characteristic neighborhoods. Oakland County is where 92 (44 percent) of these neighborhoods are located. Wayne County has 65 (31 percent) of these neighborhoods and Macomb County has 54 (26 percent). The total number of Blacks in the DMA living in such high socioeconomic characteristic neighborhoods is only 9.4 percent, with Hispanics accounting for only 15 percent.

Figure 3.5 shows the location of the very high socioeconomic characteristic neighborhoods, which are disproportionately found in the highly affluent Oakland County.

Conclusion

The social and spatial structures of Metropolitan Detroit based on US census data from 2011–15 and 2016–20 show that neighborhoods are extremely unequal, creating five distinctly different Detroits. One Detroit, where very low socioeconomic characteristic neighborhoods are located (SEP 1), is where residents live a different life and experience different disadvantages than residents living in higher socioeconomic characteristic neighborhoods. There are also low socioeconomic characteristic neighborhoods (SEP 2), which are distinctly different from other neighborhoods, but with socioeconomic characteristics that are not as low as those residents living in very low socioeconomic characteristic neighborhoods. There is also a middle-class (SEP 3) cluster of residents with higher socioeconomic characteristics than those in the SEP 1 and SEP 2 neighborhoods. At a higher level than those in SEP 3 neighborhoods are those neighborhoods with higher socioeconomic characteristics (SEP 4). Finally, there are very

Figure 3.2: Locations of SEP 2 (low) socioeconomic characteristic neighborhoods

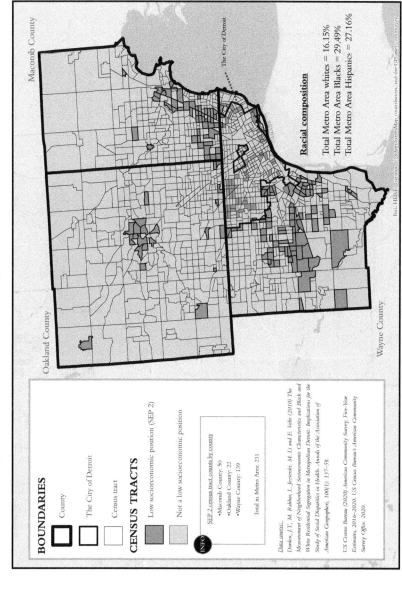

Sources: Esri, HERE, Garmin, FAO, NOAA, USGS, © OpenStreetMap contributors, and the GIS user community.

Figure 3.3: Locations of SEP 3 (middle-class) socioeconomic characteristic neighborhoods

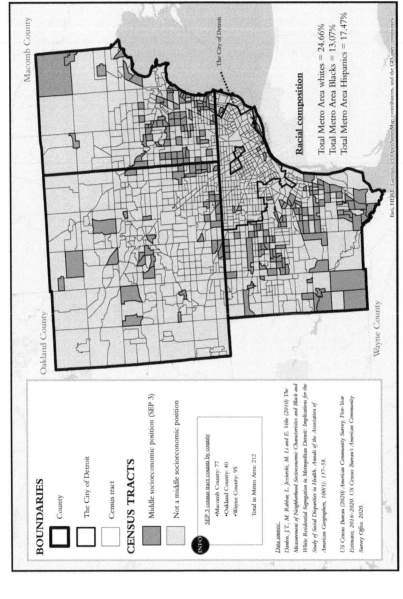

Sources: Esri, HERE, Garmin, FAO, NOAA, USGS, © OpenStreetMap contributors, and the GIS user community.

Figure 3.4: Locations of SEP 4 (high) socioeconomic characteristic neighborhoods

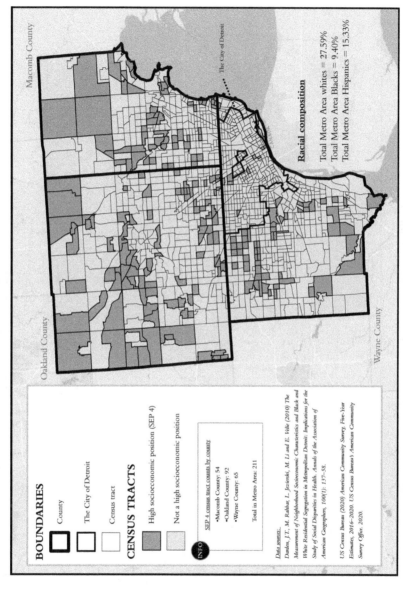

Sources: Esri, HERE, Garmin, FAO, NOAA, USGS, © OpenStreetMap contributors, and the GIS user community.

Figure 3.5: Locations of SEP 5 (very high) socioeconomic characteristic neighborhoods

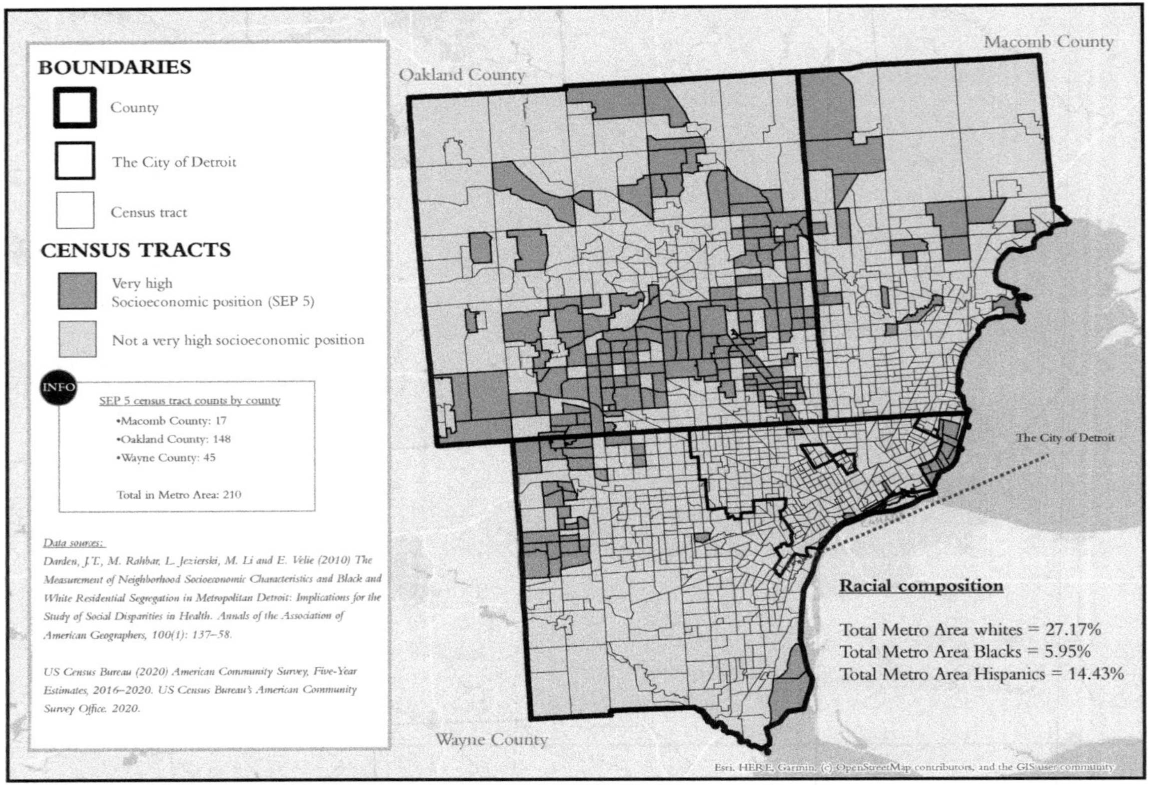

Sources: Esri, HERE, Garmin, FAO, NOAA, USGS, © OpenStreetMap contributors, and the GIS user community.

high socioeconomic characteristic neighborhoods (SEP 5), which are where the most well-off residents reside.

The analysis of the data shows that the *inequality gap* between neighborhoods increased between the 2011–15 and 2016–20 censuses. This inequality has negatively impacted Black and Hispanic residents more than white residents, as Black and Hispanic residents disproportionately reside in neighborhoods with very low and low socioeconomic characteristics. Most whites, on the other hand, live in neighborhoods with high and very high socioeconomic characteristics.

Therefore, the quality of life of residents in Metropolitan Detroit differs by race and ethnicity based on the socioeconomic characteristics of neighborhoods where the racial and ethnic groups disproportionately reside. The analysis of the distribution of racial groups reveals that Black residents lived in neighborhoods separate from and unequal to neighborhoods where whites resided, indicating an index of dissimilarity of 56.3 in 2011–15. The index of dissimilarity declined by only a few percentage points to 51 according to the 2016–20 census data. Hispanics also lived in neighborhoods that were separate from and unequal to neighborhoods where white residents resided. In 2011–15, the index of dissimilarity for Hispanics was 34.3. Based on the 2016–20 data, the index of dissimilarity declined to 32. Thus, both Blacks and Hispanics are residentially segregated from whites, but Blacks are more residentially segregated.

4

Gentrification: A New Method to Measure Where the Process Is Occurring by Neighborhood

Introduction

Gentrification as a concept has not been easy to define. The concept was first introduced by sociologist Ruth Glass in 1964 to describe "working class quarters [that] have been *invaded* by the middle class" (1964: xvii). Glass first defined gentrification as a *process* of change in the social structure of deprived working-class neighborhoods due to the moving in of middle- and upper-class citizens, and the subsequent requalification of the housing stock and displacement of incumbent residents. I notice her use of the same words used by E.W. Burgess (1925) to describe movement of the low-income population into middle-class neighborhoods in the City of Chicago. The concept is also difficult in that there has not been agreement among researchers about its causes and consequences (Vigdor et al, 2002; Freeman, 2005; Lees et al, 2010; Brown-Saracino, 2013).

The objectives

This chapter has several objectives. The first is to determine whether gentrification occurred in Detroit as defined by a new method, the Darden-Kamel Composite Socioeconomic Index (CSI). This defines gentrification as a process that results in a change in *the entire neighborhood* from very low and low socioeconomic characteristics to at least middle, high, or very high socioeconomic characteristics. A second objective is to determine the location of the neighborhoods where gentrification occurred using geographic information system (GIS) techniques to map the location. The final three objectives are connected as follows: to determine whether gentrification resulted in an increase in the white population; to determine whether the white population and the Black population are less residentially segregated in the gentrified census tracts than they were before the tracts became gentrified; and to determine whether the City of Detroit's Private–Public model for economic development leading to gentrification has provided useful assistance to neighborhood residents in their efforts to negotiate with developers in their neighborhoods through the process of "community benefits agreements."

Past studies of gentrification

Over the years, other researchers have agreed with Glass' (1964) definition of the process of gentrification. For example, Clark (2005) wrote that gentrification is a process involving a change in the population of land users such that the new users are of a higher socioeconomic status than the previous users, together with an associated change in the built environment through reinvestment in fixed capital. Smith defined gentrification as "the process by which central urban neighborhoods that have undergone disinvestment and economic decline experience a reversal, reinvestment, and the in-migration of a relatively well-off, middle- and upper-middle-class population" (1996: 198). Although most researchers consider change in the socioeconomic status of the neighborhood residents as gentrification, some authors do not agree that displacement must be part of the definition of gentrification. In other words, gentrification remains a process of change in the socioeconomic structure of the neighborhood, even though displacement may not be part of the socioeconomic change (Ghaffari et al, 2018). How much change is not determined and discussed? Although several scholarly studies were reviewed for this chapter, I present here the most recent important ones. Their contibutions are mentioned in certain sections of the chapter. Examples include Beck (2020) with the focus on policing gentrification (Laniyonu, 2018); City of Detroit (2020) on FY 2024 neighborhood revitalization strategy areas; Ghaffari et al (2018), "Toward a socially acceptable gentrification: A review of strategies and practices against displacement"; Gibbons, Barton, and Brault (2018) on evaluating gentrification's relation to neighborhood and city health; Hutson (2018) on incorporating residents' voices in mitigating the negative impacts of gentrification; Hwang and Ding (2020)," Unequal displacement: gentrification, racial stratification, and residential destinations in Philadelphia"; Looney (2018), "Will Opportunity Zones help distressed residents or be a tax cut for gentrification?"; Martin and Beck (2018), "Gentrification, property tax limitation, and displacement"; Ocbazghi (2019), "Detroit's gentrification is its compromise for economic recovery"; and Schnake-Mahl, Subramanian, Waters' and Arcaya (2020), "Gentrification, neighborhood change, and population health: a systematic review." After reviewing the literature of the most important recent research on gentrification, I presented for the first time a new operational definition of gentrification which is related to the entire neighborhood changing from a lower-level socioeconomic characteristic status to a higher level.

I used the most recent population and economic characteristic census data, and a new method entitled the Darden-Kamel CSI to measure gentrification. The chapter determined whether gentrification occurred in Detroit and, if so, where it occurred by neighborhood using GIS techniques to map the neighborhoods. The Darden-Kamel CSI revealed that gentrification occurred in 12 neighborhoods (census tracts) in Detroit from 2011–15 to 2016–20. This index defined for the first time that gentrification is a process that results in a change in the entire neighborhood from very low and low socioeconomic characteristics to at least middle, high, or very high socioeconomic characteristics.

Most researchers seem to agree that the process of change in a neighborhood is of a higher socioeconomic status, which may or may not result in complete displacement of lower-income residents (see Vigdor et al, 2002). Agreeing with the class-based definition were researchers such as Wyly and Hammel (1999). Other researchers have extended the definition to include not only residential changes but also changes in commercial and retail establishments (Smith, 1996). The process seems to be overwhelmingly class-based. In addition, Shaw (2008) argued that displacement is not necessarily part of the process of gentrification if the original residents cannot afford to move elsewhere or if the higher-income households are able to occupy vacant properties or move into newly constructed developments. Most studies have used a change in median household income and college education to define gentrification, while some authors have used neighborhood-level poverty and housing values (Gibbons, Barton, and Brault, 2018).

Most authors use census data and conclude that *gentrified* neighborhoods are those that saw their median incomes grow from less than 50 percent of the Metropolitan Area's median income to more than 50 percent. On the other hand, according to Freeman (2005), *gentrifying* neighborhoods must be based on a broader set of changes in income, education, and housing. For Freeman, *gentrified* neighborhoods are those that started with median income levels below those for the city as a whole, but where educational levels and housing prices increased to a level higher than those of the city.

Although most researchers consider *change* in the socioeconomic status of the neighborhood residents as gentrification, some authors do not agree that displacement must be part of the definition of gentrification. In other words, gentrification remains a *process* of change in the socioeconomic structure of the neighborhood, even though displacement may not be part of the socioeconomic change (Ghaffari et al, 2017). Researchers have not agreed on how much change is necessary in order for a neighborhood to be gentrified. Some have extended the definition to include not only residential changes but changes in commercial and retail establishments as well (Smith, 1996). However, the process seems to be overwhelmingly class-based.

Gentrification in the United States

Some researchers who have observed gentrification in the US have described it as a process involving increases in the white, young, college-educated population, and expansion into historically Black neighborhoods (Freeman and Cai, 2015). By 2010, more than half of all large US cities had at least one gentrified neighborhood. Gentrification is increasing in cities throughout the US and has garnered substantial ubiquity in the national discussion on urban inequality (Gibbons, Barton, and Brault, 2018).

The process is controversial in part because researchers disagree as to which neighborhoods are gentrified, where gentrification is occurring, and whether low-income existing residents receive any benefits from the process (Been, 2017). A review of the literature suggests that in the US, most researchers do not agree on which neighborhoods have actually gentrified or how to address the negative effects of the gentrification process (Lees and Ley, 2008; Been, 2017).

The significance of this chapter

The significance of this chapter is that it will) provide more knowledge about some unanswered questions: (1) whether the gentrification process offers an opportunity for Detroit to become more inclusive, and achieve more quality, affordable housing (Gould et al, 2013) and more jobs for residents; (2) whether it can improve the socioeconomic characteristics of the neighborhoods where poor residents live, without forcing them to move out due to unaffordable high rents in newly constructed buildings; and (3) whether Detroit can serve as a model for other cities to rebuild neighborhoods to be more racially, ethnically, and class-inclusive, and reverse the exclusive pattern of growth of neighborhoods by class characterized by Burgess (1925), Hoyt (1939), and Harris and Ullman (1945).

In contrast to previous decades, 21st century gentrification has become much more widespread, creating more extreme neighborhood change in a greater number of neighborhoods and impacting many low-income communities of color (Hwang and Lin, 2016). Hwang and Lin state that in the US, in addition to changes in economic class, gentrification often involves a change in a neighborhood's racial and ethnic composition that further alters the characteristics and potentially leads to community tensions and more racial/ethnic conflict.

Other authors who have included the racial component in the gentrification process are Kennedy and Leonard (2001). Some authors consider gentrification as a process of race oppression and colonialism (Martin, 2007). Monroe and Shaw (2011) argue that poor and Black neighborhood residents must be activists and involved in the process in order to avoid such oppression and internal colonialism. Past research is not conclusive as to whether gentrification has a positive or negative effect (or both) on neighborhood residents.

Does gentrification harm or help poor neighborhood residents?

In 1981, Holcomb and Beauregard published "Revitalizing cities," which discussed the "trickle down" economic theory and whether the benefits of gentrification would trickle down to the lower classes in the same way that had been described by some economists in the classic theories of urban spatial structures (see Hoyt, 1939). In addition, Smith (1979) argued that gentrification is usually preceded by filtering, although the process need not occur fully in order for gentrification to ensue. Smith further states that the objective mechanism underlying filtering is the depreciation and devaluation of capital invested in residential inner-city neighborhoods. This depreciation produces the economic conditions that make capital re-evaluation—that is, gentrification—a rational market response to investment. He calls this condition the "rent gap." The rent gap is the disparity between the potential ground rent level and the actual ground rent capitalized under present land use. In the case of filtering, the rent gap is produced primarily by capital depreciation (which diminishes the proportion of the ground rent that can be capitalized) and also by continued urban development and expansion (which raises the potential ground rent level in the inner-city neighborhoods). Gentrification occurs when the rent gap is wide enough that developers can purchase old structures (for example, shells), pay builders' costs, interest, mortgage, and construction costs, and still make a profit (Smith, 1979).

In Glass' (1964) definition of gentrification, public–private partnerships were not mentioned. This led some researchers to associate gentrification with neoclassical residential land use theories (Alonso, 1964). These neoclassical theories imply that gentrification is a natural, inevitable market adjustment process that is part of an apparent middle-class return to the center of the city from the suburbs. According to neoclassical theories, suburbanization reflected preferences for residential space and single-family homeownership (Smith, 1979). These were the major preferences from 1950 until at least the 1970s, when middle-class earnings were rising faster than housing costs. Later, as middle-class earnings started to decline, gentrification became an alternative adjustment to meet preferences for residential space (Smith, 1979). However, Smith argues that the real explanation for gentrification is related to the developers' prospects for profitable redevelopment in neighborhoods once considered not to be profitable. Developers' risks of losing money are reduced by tax incentives from both city and State governments. Although "filter down" economic theory may explain whether developers can make a profit through gentrification, it does not explain whether poor residents also benefit.

Is race a factor in gentrification?

Only a few studies have included the racial and ethnic composition of households in their definitions. Among these exceptions are Levy et al (2007), who define gentrification as the process whereby higher-income households move into low-income neighborhoods, escalating the neighborhoods' property values to the point that displacement occurs (Castagnola, 2015). They further state that in addition to changes in economic class, gentrification often involves a change in a neighborhood's racial and ethnic composition, which further alters its characteristics, potentially leading to community tensions.

According to Kirkland (2008), race is conspicuously absent from many investigations of gentrification and is even missing from most published definitions of the phenomenon. She states that the question of whether race is a factor in gentrification is not settled, but she agrees with other scholars that the general concept of gentrification holds that the people moving into a gentrifying area are usually white, and the residents who move out are typically people of color (Kennedy and Leonard, 2001; Bostic and Martin, 2003).

However, there are areas of "Black gentrification" in which middle-class and upper-class African Americans move back into poor and working-class Black neighborhoods, effecting a socioeconomic transformation but retaining its original racial character (Freeman, 2006; Moore, 2009).

Hwang and Ding (2020) studied the City of Philadelphia and found that financially disadvantaged residents who moved from neighborhoods that were not predominantly Black benefited from gentrification by moving to more advantaged locations, but those moving from once predominantly Black areas did not. They argued that as neighborhoods gentrify, when poor people can no longer remain in their neighborhoods and move, there are fewer affordable neighborhoods. Their findings indicated that there are additional constraints on the Black community when they move, leading them to move to a shrinking set of affordable, yet disadvantaged, neighborhoods within the city. They defined gentrification as areas that experienced a significant increase in terms of either median gross rent or median home value, coupled with an increase in college-educated residents, compared to other areas in the same city.

Beck (2020) defined gentrification as an increase in gentrifying activity, which involved an increase in the non Hispanic white population of a neighborhood and/or an increase in real estate value. To capture the complexity of class status, I constructed an index of class demographics that included four variables by census tract: (1) median household income; (2) the proportion of the tract with a bachelor's degree or higher; (3) the percentage employed as professionals or managers; and (4) the percentage of families not in poverty.

The Detroit Model

As mentioned earlier, in Glass' (1964) definition of gentrification, private–public partnerships were not mentioned. I argue that in order to develop the most important knowledge about the economic redevelopment leading to gentrification in Detroit, an understanding of the private–public partnership relationship is critical. In Detroit, the residential population is overwhelmingly Black and disproportionately poor. The developers are overwhelmingly white, male, and disproportionately middle and upper class. Whether white developers will invest in the downtown or in certain neighborhoods such as the Cultural Center is based on the prospects of earning a profit. White developers' risk of losing money is reduced by the City of Detroit, the State of Michigan and the federal government, all of which provide tax incentives that are significant enough for white developers to take such a risk. Without these incentives, economic redevelopment of the downtown area and such neighborhoods as Corktown would not have occurred.

The poor Black neighborhood residents wanted economic redevelopment in their neighborhoods, but without forcing them to relocate to another neighborhood. The policy and strategy acceptable to residents was the Detroit Model, which included stipulated percentages of affordable housing units for existing low-income residents. Twenty percent was the acceptable percentage. The Model was intended to address the negative effects of gentrification via what has been called "equitable gentrification" (Ghaffari et al, 2018).

The four components of the Detroit Model of the equitable *gentrification* strategy were as follows:

1. Private–Public partnerships negotiated between the city government and developers seeking permits for building or rehabilitation projects located

in specific census tracts (that is, neighborhoods). This component of Detroit's strategy required a certain percentage of units in a development project to be affordable to low-income residents, in exchange for tax advantages or subsidies to the developer. The agreement might also require stipulated percentages of construction and other workers on projects to be Detroit residents.

2. Community benefits agreements: Detroit has 92 neighborhoods, each represented by an association. Some of these associations negotiate privately with developers to establish *community benefits agreements* that require stipulated percentages of units in new or rehabilitated developments to be for low-income residents. They may also require certain percentages of construction and other workers on these projects to be neighborhood residents.

3. Inclusionary housing regulations: in 2017, Detroit's City Council passed an inclusionary housing ordinance that requires developers to provide a stipulated percentage of their developments for low-income and moderate-income residents. The objective of the ordinance is to produce mixed-income housing developments.

4. Enforcing development agreements: Detroit has assigned an enforcement agency with responsibility to ensure that developers comply with the city's affordable housing requirements. The agency can fine noncompliant developers and use the funds to advance affordable housing directly by providing subsidies or other benefits to the most vulnerable residents in very low socioeconomic characteristic neighborhoods.

The economic benefits for white developers versus the benefits of development for the poor Black residents is the focus of this chapter, with an emphasis on neighborhoods and the community benefits agreements after determining whether and where any gentrification occurred in Detroit. Chapter 5 will go on to examine the benefits of the white developers and the tax incentives they received to economically redevelop certain sections of the downtown and certain neighborhoods.

The new method to determine gentrification: the Darden–Kamel Composite Socioeconomic Index

The Darden-Kamel CSI was used to determine whether any gentrification occurred and GIS techniques were used to determine where it occurred. The data used were United States Bureau of the Census American Community Survey Five-Year Estimates (2011–15) compared to United States Bureau of the Census (2016–20) American Community Survey Five-Year Estimates. The geographic unit of analysis was the census tract, which was considered a surrogate for a neighborhood. The Darden–Kamel CSI views census tracts as spatial and social structures that can influence residents' quality of life based on their neighborhood's socioeconomic characteristics. Here I define gentrified neighborhoods as those that change quantitatively from a lower quintile with very low socioeconomic characteristics (SEP 1) and low socioeconomic characteristics (SEP 2) to a higher-level quintile with higher socioeconomic characteristics (SEPs 3–5). I also use the Darden–Kamel CSI to facilitate the mapping of gentrified Detroit neighborhoods using GIS techniques to indicate the location of any gentrified neighborhoods.

Determining gentrification in Detroit

As I indicated earlier, it is my view that gentrification only occurs if an entire neighborhood moves up the socioeconomic ladder to a different socioeconomic status. Based on that definition and the data and analyses, gentrification occurred in only 12 census tracts (see Figure 4.1). There were 210 census tracts that had been analyzed and determined not to have gentrified. Table 4.1 shows the change that occurred in socioeconomic characteristics of the neighborhoods of census tracts that were determined to have been gentrified.

The percentage of bachelor's degree holders increased from 12.4 percent to 18.3 percent, while the percentage of unemployed residents decreased from 21 percent in 2011–15 to 6.8 percent in 2016–20. The percentage of professional and managerial workers increased from 10.7 percent to 19 percent. The median household income increased from $28,467 to $43,631. The median housing value increased from $79,350 to $129,475. The median gross rent increased from $833 to $989. The percentage below poverty decreased from 26 to 12 percent, the percentage of vehicle ownership increased from 50.7 percent to 54.8 percent, and the percentage of homeowners increased from 44 percent to 48 percent.

The change in the socioeconomic characteristics revealed that the entire neighborhood changed, increasing its mobility from very low and low socioeconomic characteristics (SEP 1 and SEP 2) to middle (SEP 3) and high (SEP 4) socioeconomic characteristics. Statistically the change was significant in terms of unemployment, percentage of professional and managerial workers, median household income, and percentage below poverty, all of which had a p-value of 0.0 (see Table 4.1). Where were the gentrified tracts located? I used GIS techniques to map their locations. Figure 4.1 shows that the 12 census tracts that were gentrified were located in the following neighborhoods: Five Points; O'Hair Park; Schaefer 7/8 Lodge; Winship; the Grand River–I96; Detroit Golf and Palmer Park;

Table 4.1: Changes in the socioeconomic characteristics of the neighborhoods of gentrified census tracts in Detroit

Difference in mean neighborhood characteristics across gentrified neighborhoods: Detroit	2015	2020	*p*–value
% bachelor's degree	12.35	18.25	0.225615
% unemployed	21.18	6.84	0.000014
% professional/managerial workers	10.77	19.00	0.002312
Median household income	28,467	43,631	0.001706
$Median home value	79,350	129,475	0.210265
$Median gross rent	833.50	989.67	0.053268
% below poverty level	26.48	11.99	0.000824
% vehicle ownership	50.71	54.86	0.218708
% homeownership	43.89	48.08	0.673785

Note: Mean or average socioeconomic neighborhood characteristics across the following Detroit City census tracts: 501400, 515700, 516000, 516500, 517100, 518000, 534300, 538300, 539300, 539500, 540800, 541800.

Sources: US Census Bureau, *American Community Survey 2011–15 Five-Year Estimates* and *American Community Survey 2016–20 Five-Year Estimates* data, prepared using Social Explorer (https://www.socialexplorer.com/explore-tables).

Cultural Center; Lafayette Park; Rivertown; Gold Coast; Gratiot-Grand; and East English Village. The gentrification map in Figure 4.1 was created from the basemap from ESRI.

Did race matter in the gentrification process?

I also examined whether the census tracts that were gentrified had an increase in the white population, as many past studies had suggested that this occurs when neighborhoods gentrify. The racial composition of census tracts for the 2011–15 census data and the 2016–20 census data were examined. The results revealed that there was an increase in the white population in four of the 12 census tracts, while there was a decrease in the white population in seven tracts and no change in one.

Did gentrification result in more racial residential desegregation?

There are some researchers who believe that gentrification results in more racial residential integration or a reduction in residential segregation. I examined the spatial distribution of the white population and the Black

Figure 4.1: Gentrification in Detroit after bankruptcy

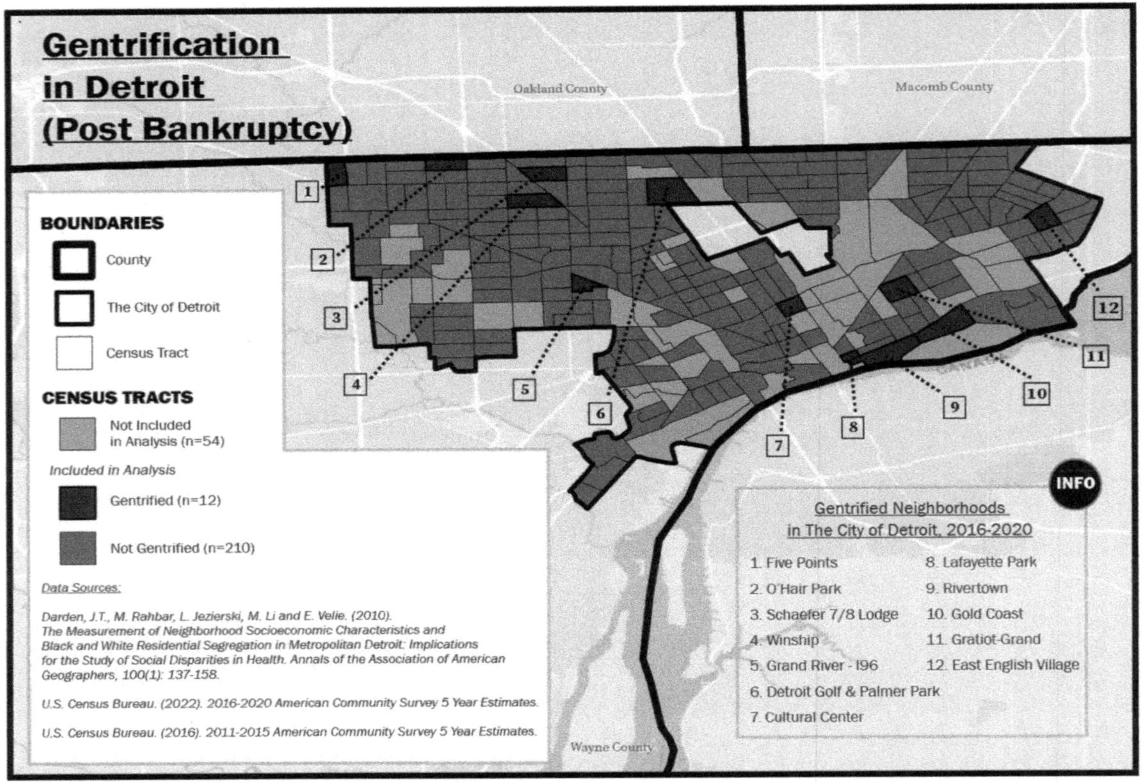

Sources: Esri, HERE, Garmin, FAO, NOAA, USGS, © OpenStreetMap contributors and the GIS user community.

population in the gentrified census tracts. The total population of non Hispanic whites was 2,750 and the total population of non Hispanic Blacks was 25,635. They were not residentially integrated. Based on the index of dissimilarity for the two racial groups in the 2011–15 census data (that is, before gentrification), the index of dissimilarity was 43 (see Table 4.2). This increased to 47 after the census tracts became gentrified, based on the 2016–20 census tract data (see Table 4.3). The total number of non Hispanic whites who experienced gentrification was 4,414, an increase from the previous 2,750. The total number of non Hispanic Blacks that experienced gentrification was 25,117, which marked a slight decrease from 25,635. The analysis clearly indicates that the population of non Hispanic whites did increase in the gentrified tracts. Thus, this analysis of gentrification in Detroit after bankruptcy supports past studies indicating that whites have increased in population in gentrified neighborhoods and Blacks have decreased. Hispanic populations have

Table 4.2: The residential distribution of non Hispanic Blacks and non Hispanic whites in census tracts in 2015 before tracts became gentrified in Detroit

Census tract	Non Hispanic white	% non Hispanic white	Non Hispanic Black	% non Hispanic Black
501400	425	15.43	3,287	12.82
515700	397	14.41	3,016	11.77
516000	59	2.14	1,867	7.28
516500	385	13.97	983	3.83
517100	174	6.32	993	3.87
518000	653	23.70	1,459	5.69
534300	5	0.18	1,484	5.79
538300	110	3.99	1,568	6.12
539300	20	0.73	3,869	15.09
539500	76	2.76	3,083	12.03
540800	41	1.49	2,040	7.96
541800	410	14.88	1,986	7.75
Total	2,755	100.00	25,635	100.00

Source: calculated by the author from data obtained from the 2011–15 and 2016–20 ACS Five-Year Estimate data, prepared using Social Explorer (https://www.socialexplorer.com/expl ore-tables)

Note: The index of dissimilarity between non Hispanic Blacks and non Hispanic whites is 43.

Table 4.3: The residential distribution of non Hispanic Blacks and non Hispanic whites in gentrified census tracts in Detroit in 2020

Non Hispanic white	% non Hispanic white	Non Hispanic Black	% non Hispanic Black	Tracts
435	9.86	2,910	11.59	501400
708	16.05	2,637	10.50	515700
323	7.32	1,957	7.79	516000
807	18.30	1,107	4.41	516500
446	10.11	725	2.89	517100
1,026	23.27	1,398	5.57	518000
0	0.00	1,308	5.21	534300
137	3.11	1,956	7.79	538300
1	0.02	3,750	14.93	539300
57	1.29	3,025	12.04	539500
24	0.54	2,468	9.83	540800
446	10.11	1,876	7.47	541800
4,410	100.00	25,117	100.00	

Note: The *index of dissimilarity* between non Hispanic Blacks and non Hispanic whites is 47.

Source: calculated by the author from data obtained from the 2011–15 and 2016–20 ACS Five-Year Estimate data, prepared using Social Explorer (https://www.socialexplorer.com/expl ore-tables).

also increased in gentrified tracts from 218 before gentrification to 317 after gentrification.

How did the Detroit Mayor and the City Council assist predominately Black and poor neighborhoods to negotiate with white developers in the gentrification process?

Shortly after the city was removed from the restrictions of bankruptcy, Mayor Mike Duggan and the City Council became engaged in activities to economically redevelop neighborhoods. They started to identify neighborhoods for strategic funding and requested approval of funding from the State, the federal government, and the city as early as possible after bankruptcy ended (City of Detroit, 2014b; Duggan and Jemison, 2014).

The Strategic Funding Initiative, also labeled the Strategic Neighborhood Fund (SNF), was launched in 2017 in three neighborhoods and was expanded to seven more in 2018 (City of Detroit, 2022). I will use the SNF in the discussion. With the expansion came investments of $5 million each from seven corporations, each partnering with a specific neighborhood. The SNF had raised more than $50 million for the effort. Along with the Affordable Housing Leverage Fund and Detroit Housing for the Future Fund, the funds supported the revitalization of neighborhoods and both the preservation and building of affordable housing (City of Detroit, 2015).

The City of Detroit requested approval of a Neighborhood Revitalization Strategy (NRS) and the designation of five related Neighborhood Revitalization Strategy Areas (NRSAs), as defined by the Department of Housing and Urban Development (HUD) (Notice CPD-96-01). These NRSAs comprised some of the most distressed residential neighborhoods in Detroit. All qualified for NRSA designation based on the high percentage of low- and moderate-income (LMI) residents, among other factors.

Using all of the tools at its disposal, Mayor Duggan's administration generated enthusiasm for the public–private partnership to work in unprecedented ways in order to revitalize neighborhoods and create jobs for Detroit residents. The Mayor believed that investing a limited number of resources wisely and strategically targeting federal funds within the framework of the city's community revitalization plan would provide an opportunity to increase the numbers of residents able to achieve a higher leverage of private capital. The SNF had the aim of implementing a multi-pronged approach to revitalize and stabilize neighborhoods. There were also other new initiatives such as auctions of publicly owned residential properties, sales of vacant lots, aggressive code enforcement, and an expansive demolition effort to work together to stabilize neighborhoods. The city's new home repair loan program and the continuance of the much-needed emergency repair and lead abatement programs were intended to further the stabilization efforts. These efforts were designed to help low-income families achieve financial stability, access income supports, develop educational and employment opportunities, build wealth, and move up the economic ladder (City of Detroit, 2022). Over 2,000 families were to be offered the opportunity to benefit from the program each year.

The NRS was a new tool implemented by the City of Detroit to improve the plight of the city's LMI population and neighborhoods. Investments included Michigan Hardest Hit funding of $100 million for blight reduction and redevelopment, and NSP funding totaling $110 million to address vacant, foreclosed, and abandoned housing units using a variety of financing mechanisms. The private sector also invested in these targeted Detroit neighborhoods at levels not seen before bankruptcy. There were several "tipping points" that were likely to attract even greater private market investments. The Mayor believed that such "tipping points" would exist in the marketplace where private investment could be attracted with declining levels of tax subsidies as a result of catalytic public investments.

After bankruptcy, the Mayor's office believed the level of decline in housing values and disinvestment in Detroit's neighborhoods required that redevelopment should occur within the context of a comprehensive neighborhood revitalization strategy, and this idea was supported by leveraging *public and private financial financing*. The Mayor's office recognized that significant disinvestment, slum and blighted conditions, declining and undervalued properties, and poverty rates had almost doubled that of the State as a whole (City of Detroit, 2015). Thus, high neighborhood investments and cooperation were necessary from several stakeholders in the city, including the Detroit Land Bank Authority (DLBA) and the Detroit Economic Growth Corporation (DEGC), among other foundations and financial institutions. Additionally, community-based organizations and private businesses also needed to invest in the restoration and revitalization of the city (City of Detroit, 2015). The Mayor's office believed that identified neighborhood boundaries of the NRSAs must be contiguous.

Identified neighborhoods had to be primarily residential and LMI, equal to the "upper quartile percentage" or 70 percent for Detroit. Areas within Empowerment Zones or Enterprise Communities were included automatically. Furthermore, the selected area had to be based on documented input from its stakeholders, including residents, owners/operators of businesses, local financial institutions, nonprofit organizations, and community groups. Documentation had to include a description of the methods used to provide outreach to the groups noted earlier, and a description of how the needs and concerns of the consulted groups (especially residents) had been incorporated into the plan.

According to the Office of the Mayor (2015), the five selected neighborhoods were as follows:

- NRSA 1: *Jefferson-Chalmers neighborhood*. This neighborhood is located along the Detroit River on the east side of Detroit. It boasts 160 acres of waterfront and is located next to Grosse Pointe Park, a suburb of Detroit (City of Detroit, Office of the Mayor, 2020).
- NRSA 2: *Osborn, City Airport, and Morning Side neighborhoods*. This area is located on the City's northeast side. Regent Park and a portion of East English Village are also included in this area.
- NRSA 3: *Historic neighborhoods in southwest Detroit*. Historic neighborhoods are Corktown, Hubbard Farms, and Woodbridge, which were attracting investments particularly from young professionals. They also include neighborhoods such as Springwells Village and Mexicantown, which have retained and are attracting new families.

- NRSA 4: this is located in the center of Detroit. It is anchored by two major institutions, University of Detroit-Mercy to the north and Henry Ford Hospital to the south. It contains the McNichols commercial corridor on the northern boundary, which is characterized by low-density service-related businesses. The New Center commercial district is on its southern boundary. This area was witnessing significant investment with an expansion of Henry Ford Hospital, the M-1 light rail, and Woodward Bus-Rapid-Transit. This area also has historic districts and neighborhoods such as the Boston-Edison District, New Center, and Arden Park, which were seeing increased interest and investment in their markets. It also includes areas such as Hope Village, Dexter-Linwood, and North End, which have high vacancy rates, a concentration of city-owned properties, and significant tax and mortgage foreclosures.
- NRSA 5: this area is located on the northwest side of Detroit. It includes the center core of the historic Grandmont Rosedale neighborhood, and the Brightmoor neighborhood, which has seen a significant decline in population. It is characterized by a stronger market at its core surrounded by distressed markets with a considerable number of publicly owned parcels. A significant concentration of city-owned properties and properties going through the 2014 tax foreclosure auction process were concentrated in the western area (Brightmoor) and the southeastern area of this NRSA. It also contains the Grand River neighborhood commercial corridor in Grandmont Rosedale.

The demographic characteristics at the time of the Neighborhood Funding Strategy

Leading up to and during bankruptcy, the City of Detroit had experienced a severe loss of manufacturing, and more than half of the population had left the city. The city was left with thousands of unoccupied dwellings or numerous homes in need of repair. As a result, according to the US Bureau of the Census, only 54 percent of Detroiters owned their own home. This was a dramatic decline in the homeownership rate that weakened the housing market. The poverty rate in Detroit was 34.5 percent. The median household income was $28,357. Only 7.6 percent of Detroit residents had a bachelor's degree or higher. These stark differences in income and education showed the Mayor and the City Council that if gentrification was to occur, it would not happen without intervention via targeted financial investment to improve economic opportunities for Detroit residents (City of Detroit, 2015). Since the Mayor and the City Council were aware that it would be very difficult to get most of the developers to start redeveloping downtown Detroit and the neglected neighborhoods without tax incentives, they had to persuade neighborhood associations to agree to the tax incentives. This resulted in community benefits agreements for neighborhoods.

Community benefits agreements

Detroit has 92 neighborhoods, each represented by an association. To ensure that each City Council member had a fair share of associations in their districts, the City Council selected some associations to negotiate privately with developers to establish community benefits agreements that required stipulated percentages of units in new or rehabilitated developments to be for low-income residents. Although the City of Detroit played some role in ensuring that poor and long-term residents were provided with a certain amount of affordable housing, some neighborhood groups took it upon themselves to negotiate with developers instead of relying on the city's elected council members. The neighborhood associations could also require certain percentages of construction and other workers on these projects to be neighborhood residents.

The concept of community benefits agreements was born. These are private agreements between a neighborhood (or neighborhoods) and a private developer (or private developers). They grew out of planning theory related to the significance of the participatory process of organized neighborhood groups in making an impact on the decisions of powerful investors. Baxamusa (2008) argues that in order to make participatory processes meaningful, the process must expressly empower communities through grassroots organizing, coalition building, and democratic deliberation.

The demand for community benefits agreements emerged in Detroit after bankruptcy ended on December 11, 2014. Many neighborhood groups wanted a more balanced decision-making process in anticipation of gentrification. They wanted to be sure that developers would not benefit from the very low cost of land and properties in central locations (especially downtown) and exclude neighborhoods elsewhere in the city. They wanted their *fair share* of the investments and employment on projects in their neighborhoods and in the city in general. Since community benefits agreements are private agreements between neighborhoods and developers, they were not necessarily consistent with the city government's overall goals (Baxamusa, 2008). However, the City of Detroit and some of its neighborhoods worked together on community benefits agreements.

The Community Benefits Ordinance

A Community Benefits Ordinance was first approved by voters in 2016. Mary Sheffield, then City Council Pro Tempore and now City Council

President, wanted to lower the investment threshold from $75 million to $50 million to require developers, who receive certain abatements or assistance, to negotiate community benefits with residents. Sheffield, who represents District 5, has demonstrated a track record of service to poor residents and has been committed to addressing their concerns. At the age of 26, she became the youngest Council member ever elected in November 2013, the year of Detroit's bankruptcy. She is a granddaughter of Horace Sheffield, the founder of the Detroit Trade Union Labor Council. This is an important organization that has worked for the inclusion of African Americans in the United Auto Workers Union.

Councilwoman Sheffield sponsored the *inclusionary housing ordinance*. Her website stresses that she is committed to building a "New Detroit" and attracting new residents. However, she wants to also ensure that the city remains committed to residents who stayed during its most difficult times. The residents could count on Councilwoman Sheffield to work in their interests when negotiations took place with developers. In Chapter 5, it will be shown how affluent white developers and poor Black residents have negotiated to redevelop certain areas of the City of Detroit.

Conclusion

The analyses in this chapter using the Darden-Kamel CSI found that gentrification occurred in 12 neighborhoods (census tracts) in Detroit from 2011–15 to 2016–20. The Darden-Kamel CSI defines gentrification as a process that results in a change in the entire neighborhood from very low and low socioeconomic characteristics to at least middle or high or very high socioeconomic characteristics. This chapter has also plotted the locations of the neighborhoods where gentrification occurred using GIS techniques: Five Points; O'Hair Park; Schaefer 7/8 Lodge; Winship; the Grand River–I96; Detroit Golf and Palmer Park; Cultural Center; Lafayette Park; Rivertown; Gold Coast; Gratiot-Grand; and East English Village. Following this, I discussed how gentrification resulted in an increase in the white population and how the white population and the Black population were more residentially segregated in the gentrified census tracts than they were before the tracts became gentrified (Ellen, 2017).

Finally, I outlined how the Detroit Model, which involved a city and private sector relationship to increase neighborhood economic development in the gentrification process, was able to provide useful assistance to predominantly Black and poor neighborhood residents in their efforts to negotiate with white wealthy developers in their neighborhoods through the process of community benefits agreements. These agreements led developers to agree to include 20 percent of their units for LMI renters, thereby reducing the outmigration of some LMI residents from the gentrified neighborhoods. Future evaluations of the influence of the community benefits agreement will be necessary to determine whether it is only wealthy white developers who benefit from gentrification or whether poor Black neighborhood residents also benefit.

5

The Uneven Distribution of Economic Redevelopment: Which Neighborhoods Are Excluded?

Introduction

After emerging from bankruptcy on December 11, 2014, Detroit officials were desperate for investments in rehabilitated apartments and condos to provide economic development in the neighborhoods and businesses downtown so as to increase the tax base. The bankruptcy left the city with numerous deteriorating and abandoned buildings, vacant lots, and very cheap land—an investor's dream (Davey and Walsh, 2014a). Meanwhile, the residents who had remained in Detroit through the bankruptcy period had a 40 percent poverty rate and an unemployment rate twice the state average (US Bureau of the Census, 2016). When Republican Governor Rick Snyder announced that governance was returning to the elected city officials on December 14, 2014, Detroit's Mayor and City Council were given the challenge of rebuilding the city by attracting investments in housing (rehabilitated and new apartments and condos) while ensuring that long-term residents would not experience rents so high that they could not afford to remain in their neighborhoods. Two years after bankruptcy, according to the city's building permit data, several building permits had been issued to developers requesting permission to build apartments and condos in certain neighborhoods, provided Detroit city authorities extend to them the highest tax advantages and subsidies in order to invest. Detroit was governed by a white mayor and a nine-member City Council (seven Blacks, one Hispanic, and one white). In 2016, Detroit's population was 683,443, with Blacks comprising 80 percent, non Hispanic whites 10 percent, Hispanics 8 percent, and Asians 1.4 percent (US Bureau of the Census, 2016).

In this stressful time for Detroit, developers—who were overwhelmingly white and male—saw an opportunity to make a big profit and gain the highest tax advantages and subsidies by agreeing to take part in the economic redevelopment of this predominantly Black city. They started to pressure city officials to award high tax advantages and subsidies without affordable housing agreements in exchange, and city residents pressured City Council members not to agree unless guaranteed numbers of affordable housing units formed part of the deals. There was already a lot of very cheap land, as well as many deteriorating and abandoned buildings and vacant lots before the bankruptcy. However, following bankruptcy, the city bottomed out and the Mayor and the City Council were desperate to redevelop the city. However, the strong pressure from neighborhood groups simultaneously forced city officials not to bargain with developers and to also satisfy the needs of the low-income, predominantly Black residents in the City with a certain percentage of affordable housing. Political consciousness was high among many Black residents in Detroit. The residents wanted the Mayor and the City Council to make sure that they would receive fair treatment from developers.

Mayor Duggan's influence on development

In 2019, Mayor Mike Duggan authorized 19 major project proposals to rehabilitate or build 2,000 residential units, at least 40,000 square feet of office space, and 100,000 square feet of retail space in Detroit. It was the Mayor who granted support for these projects, which totaled $540 million (Pinho, 2019). Economic redevelopment after bankruptcy has not been even. Significant attention has been paid to downtown Detroit compared to neighborhoods. Redevelopment has also been carried out overwhelmingly by white males. Blacks and Hispanics have been largely absent from the process. Chapter 6 will examine the extent of underrepresentation in Black and Hispanic business ownership.

White developers selected by the city for downtown development

Two white developers were selected for the economic redevelopment of Detroit shortly after city officials made the decisions after bankruptcy, having been favored by city officials and given more favorable benefits. The two developers were Dan Gilbert, owner of Quicken Loans, and the Ilitch family. Gilbert was a wealthy white male who owned more than 100 properties with a total investment of more than $5.6 billion.

Dan Gilbert

Gilbert is credited with leading the revival of downtown following the move of Quicken Loans to Detroit from Livonia in 2010, and investing more, for example, $3 billion, to acquire, renovate, and develop 100 city properties.

His companies employed 17,000 people in the city, making them the largest private employer in Detroit. As of 2019, he continued to have another $2.6 billion in development in the works (Dixon, 2019). His developments were tracked in 2023 by the Downtown Detroit Partnership (2023). In order to repay Gilbert, the city's Downtown Development Authority (DDA) sold him via Bedrock Real Estate —a key parcel of land in the city—for $1. Bedrock is a full service commercial real estate firm based in downtown Detroit, specializing in the strategic redevelopment of Midwestern urban cores. At the same time, the board of the Michigan Strategic Fund approved millions in incentives. Gilbert sought reimbursement from the State for sales taxes paid on construction supplies. While most of the tax breaks went toward Gilbert's Hudson and the Monroe block projects downtown, two other Bedrock projects went toward the renovation of the 38-story Book Tower and the 13-story Book Building, and the expansion of Gilbert's Quicken Loans' headquarters building, One Campus Martius. This was further evidence that Gilbert's Bedrock Real Estate Firm was and is the preferred developer by Detroit officials and received more favorable treatment over other developers (Gallagher, 2018b; Dixon, 2019).

Real estate redevelopment in downtown Detroit

Since 2014, the Downtown Detroit Partnership has been tracking the major development projects in downtown Detroit. These are in their most recent report (Downtown Detroit Partnership, 2023). The projects completed since 2018 and the projects still under construction were in its published report on October 3, 2022, titled Downtown Detroit Community and Development Update. Table 5.1 indicates the completed redevelopment projects in Downtown Detroit and the year they were completed. Table 5.2 indicates the projects still under construction as of October 3, 2022.

The State of Michigan wanted to contribute to the projects with transformational Brownfield credits. The credits required legislation. A bill was passed by the Michigan Legislature in 2017, and the Board of the Michigan Strategic Fund approved the deal in 2018 (Dixon, 2019). Bedrock can also seek reimbursement from the State for sales taxes paid on construction supplies. Most of the tax breaks will go toward Hudson's site and the Monroe block projects. The Monroe blocks project will increase the density of the central downtown and will add mostly residential parcels (Tanner and Dixon, 2018). By September 16, 2018, the Detroit Land Bank Authority had celebrated its sale of 10,000 properties, which were vacant lots sold to neighborhood residents (Gallagher, 2018a).

The Detroit Land Bank Authority was started in Flint, Michigan, in 2002 when Dan Kildee, then Geneva County Treasurer and now a US

Table 5.1: Completed redevelopment projects in Downtown Detroit since 2018

Name	Primary type	Year completed
Vinton Building	Residential	2018
1515–1529	Office	2018
David Stott	Residential	2019
Harmonie Social	Retail	2022
The 607	Office	2018
Church of Scientology	Institutional	2018
City Club Apartments	Residential	2021
The 751/Marx	Office	2018
One Campus Martius	Office	2021
Louis Camper	Residential	2019
Shinola Hotel	Hospitality	2018
Philip Houze Apartments	Residential	2018
511 Woodward	Office	2020
The Randolph	Residential	2019
The Farwell Building	Residential	2019
Little Caesars World	Office	2019
Element Detroit	Hospitality	2018
220 – West	Office	2021
The Siren Hotel	Hospitality	2018
Huntington Bank	Office	2021
The Press 321	Residential	2020
Gabriel Houze	Hospitality	2020
Marquette Building	Office	2020
Columbia Street	Office	2020
1225 – Woodward	Office	2021
211 W. Fort	Office	2021
The 1300	Office	2021
The Penobscot	Office	2022

Source: Downtown Detroit Partnership (2023) Downtown Detroit Community and Development Update, October 3, 2022.

Congressman, developed the Geneva County Land Bank Authority in order to provide a way for Geneva County to deal with tax foreclosure property (Gallagher, 2018a). Detroit, like Flint, has acquired vacant and abandoned parcels due to tax foreclosed properties. And Detroit, due to

Table 5.2: Redevelopment projects under construction in Downtown Detroit (projects not completed by October 3, 2022)

Name	Primary type	Year projected completion★
Hudson's Building and Tower	Hospitality	2023
Women's City Club	Office	2021
The Residences	Residential	2023
Root Book Tower	Hospitality	2022
Detroit Life Building Office	Residential	2021
The Park Avenue Building	Residential	2024
Cambria Hotel Detroit	Hospitality	2022
Book Building	Residential	2022
Cambria/Walker	Office	2022
The Exchange	Residential	2023
The Joe Parking	Transportation	2023
Michigan and Church Street	Residential	2024
Isaac Agree Synagogue	Office/event space	2021
Book Depository	Office	2022
The Louis	Residential	2024
Lafayette West	Residential	2023
City Modern	Residential	Not listed
Michigan Central (consists of four buildings: The Station, Bagley Mobility Hub, Book Depository, and Factory)	Multiple Use	2023

Note: ★ Construction had not been completed by the year indicated, according to the Downtown Detroit Partnership, October 3, 2022 data.

Source: Downtown Detroit Partnership (2023) Downtown Detroit Community and Development Update, October 3, 2022.

the largest bankruptcy in American history, has the largest number of foreclosed properties of any other US cities its size. Yet the Detroit City Council first rejected the creation of a land bank due to their reluctance to give control of city-owned properties to an independent agency. It was not until 2014, after the city had experienced bankruptcy, that the City Council finally agreed to the establishment of a Land Bank Authority. Supporting the idea of a land bank, Mayor Duggan sought to empower the Land Bank Authority, and the City Council agreed to transfer the city's 50,000 vacant parcels into Detroit Land Bank Authority (DLBA) control in 2014 (Gallagher, 2018a).

The mission of the DLBA is to return vacant properties to productive use. It oversees side lot sales and online sales through programs such as Own It Now and Rehabbed & Ready. It also oversees contracting and billing for $265 million in federally funded home demolitions (Frank, 2019). By 2018, the DLBA's inventory stood at 95,000 vacant parcels that were under its control, which accounted for 25 percent of all the parcels in the city. This was the largest inventory of publicly held land in any city in the US (Gallagher, 2018a). The inventory included not only vacant lots but also abandoned residential structures and even old industrial structures abandoned by the land bank due to the nonpayment of property taxes (Gallagher, 2018a).

The DLBA also facilitated the purchase of side vacant lots for as little as $100 (Gallagher, 2018a) and auctioned off houses online via its website Buildingdetroit.org. Bidding began at $1,000 at 9 am and concluded at 5 pm, with the highest bidder gaining the property. Buyers would have six months after closing on the property to rehab and occupy the property or it would revert back to the DLBA. Under the DLBA buyback program, the renters or owners living in the property prior to foreclosure who make monthly reports to cover the property taxes to buy the home can own it for only $1,000 (Gallagher 2018a). As of 2018, the DLBA had auctioned off 866 houses, sold 1,906 properties, and also sold 10,000 side lots (Gallagher 2018b).

The Detroit Land Bank Authority, homeownership, and foreclosures

The DLBA is a public authority that owns and manages approximately 100,000 parcels of property in the City of Detroit, making it the city's largest landowner (City of Detroit Open Data Portal, 2021). As of May 15, 2019, the DLBA owned 91,669 properties, which were divided into four categories: (1) owned vacant land; (2) owned vacant lots for sale; (3) owned structures; and (4) owned structures for sale (City of Detroit Open Data Portal, 2021).

How the Detroit Land Bank Authority auctions off homes

In order to purchase a home from the DLBA, the purchaser can bid for it. The bidder must be a Michigan resident, a non Michigan resident who will live in the property after rehab, or a company or organization authorized to do business in Michigan. The following rules also apply:

- The bidder cannot have unpaid delinquent property taxes on properties located in Wayne County or have lost property to back taxes in Wayne County in the last three years (Detroit is a city within Wayne County).

- The bidder cannot have material unresolved blight or code violations in the City of Detroit.
- If the bidder uses a legal entity to purchase the property, they must be authorized by that entity to acquire property on its behalf.
- A bidder is ineligible to purchase a property from the DLBA if they or the entity they are purchasing under are currently involved in a bankruptcy proceeding.
- A bidder is ineligible to purchase a property from the DLBA if they or the entity they are purchasing under have an Internal Revenue Service (IRS) lien filed against them.
- A bidder cannot bid on more than one property at a time (that is, bidders cannot bid on an auction property and make an offer on an Own It Now home at the same time).
- The bidder is limited to the purchase of one auction or Own It Now property until that first purchased property achieves compliance. Compliance includes the property being brought up to code and being occupied within six months (or nine months for homes located in a historic district). Once the purchaser has demonstrated the ability to meet the terms of the purchase agreement by successfully bringing the property up to code and having the property occupied, the purchaser may be eligible to purchase additional properties. The purchaser can purchase one property per calendar month up to a total of nine properties in a 12-month period from the last date of transfer. However, the purchaser will not be able to purchase any additional properties if any property that was previously purchased is not in compliance with all the requirements outlined in the purchase agreement. It should be noted that, for the purposes of this rule, any property that is purchased may be deemed to be out of compliance at any time, regardless of the six-month (or nine-month) deadline. This rule is applied to all purchasers that have won previous auction bids and have not completed the rehabilitation of at least one property and have failed to get it occupied within the required time period.
- In addition, the DLBA reserves the right to exclude participants with a history of delinquent taxes.
- The DLBA posts daily auctions on vacant homes that need extensive renovation. Auctions start on most homes at $1,000. The DLBA rents vacant lots that can be bought as well as move-in-ready homes through its *Rehabbed and Ready Home* program (https://buildingdetroit.org).

From January 1, 2015 (when the city regained control after bankruptcy) to May 15, 2019, 536 homes had been listed for auction by the DLBA under its Own It Now policy. There were seven homes for sale under the DLBA's *Rehabbed and Ready Home* Program policy, with prices ranging from $89,900 to $210,000.

Race matters in the home purchase process

Race is an important factor in terms of the ability to purchase a home. Despite the fact that the population of Detroit is 80 percent Black, the mortgage banks are owned and controlled by whites. Thus, the ability to have a mortgage loan and to purchase a piece of property was—and still is—affected by the race of the applicant. White applicants in 2017, while representing only 10 percent of the population, received nearly half of the home mortgage loans in which the race of the applicant was indicated (Gallagher and Lynch, 2022). The data from the Federal Home Disclosure Act (HMDA) showed that few Black people were given mortgages in Detroit: white applicants were approved for 44 loans (41.2 percent) of the 1,072 mortgage loans approved in the city in 2017; only 461 mortgage loans (43 percent) were approved for Black applicants. Yet Blacks represented 80 percent of the population in Detroit (a detailed analysis will be presented in Chapter 9 showing more recent Black, white and Hispanic differential mortgage denial rates in Detroit).

Between 1999 and 2019, at least 145,000 Detroit properties had been put up for sale in auction. More importantly, an estimated 50,000 properties were occupied at the time of foreclosure, that is not paying the monthly mortgage payment when due (Gross, 2019). Owners are notified by the Wayne County Treasurer's office at least two months in advance that properties are at risk of tax foreclosure. Those who receive notice are invited to come to the Treasurer's office for a hearing. The hearings allow struggling taxpayers to enroll in a payment plan. Foreclosure occurs only after three years of unpaid property taxes (Gross, 2019). If the taxpayer pays a percentage of what is owed, they can redeem the property. If that does not occur, the property will receive a judgment of foreclosure on March 31 and is put up for auction in September or October of the same year (Lee, 2015).

The New Employees Mortgage Discount Program was implemented by Mayor Duggan in June 2015. It was limited to DLBA houses that were obtained by bonds, via auctions of foreclosed homes. The program was intended to serve city workers, retirees, and their immediate families (Lee, 2015) in terms of providing an incentive for city employees to return from the suburbs and live in Detroit (Lee, 2015). According to the Mayor: "if we can't force employees to live here, we shouldn't want to. What we can do and are doing, is making Detroit the place that they want to live" (Lee, 2015).

Developers and redevelopment of neighborhoods and the Inclusionary Housing Ordinance

In order to monitor the behavior of developers who wanted to redevelop neighborhoods, Detroit City Council President and ProTempore at the time Mary Sheffield considered it necessary to write an Inclusionary

Housing Ordinance. The Ordinance was designed to address the *inequality in landlord–tenant disputes*. Landlords—most of them white and affluent—were represented by legal counsel and had more power in the disputes than tenants, most of whom were Black and poor, and were not usually represented by legal counsel. The Ordinance required all residents have the ability to counsel with an attorney prior to any conviction. All residents at or below 20 percent of the federal poverty level would receive legal representation throughout the settlement process (City of Detroit, 2019). Sheffield argued that the Ordinance would have a positive impact by helping to stabilize families and neighborhoods, prevent blight, and keep neighborhoods safe.

Budget priorities of President Sheffield

Mary Sheffield was and continues to be a strong advocate for funding the needs of impoverished residents in neighborhoods outside of Downtown and midtown Detroit, as well as those elsewhere in the City. As the Detroit City Council President, she supports policies that ensure the following:

- Detroit residents receive at least 51 percent of the jobs associated with all contracts.
- The hiring of three full-time employees with duties to monitor the income verification requirements outlined in the Inclusionary Housing Ordinance.

Additionally, she introduced legislation that resulted in a Workforce Development Ordinance. This ordinance applied to all publicly funded construction projects, which would be required to hire at least 51 percent of workers from the City of Detroit. This ordinance carries a financial penalty that requires developers who violate the policy to pay into a workforce training fund.

Some redevelopment activities in selected neighborhoods

Although economic redevelopment of neighborhoods occurred in certain neighborhoods in the city, I have selected some of the most well-known neighborhoods for discussion here (see Table 5.3).

Brush Park development

As the rent to live in a development in Downtown Detroit started to increase by 37 percent between 2016 and 2017, Dan Gilbert promised that 20 percent of the rental units at his Brush Park development would offer

Table 5.3: Detroit development projects by neighborhoods

Location	Number	Percentage of Detroit
Central Business District (CBD)	34	45.9
Midtown	23	31.0
New Center	6	8.1
Corktown	4	5.4
Brush Park	2	2.7
Eastern Market	2	2.7
Rivertown	2	2.7
Lafayette Park	1	1.4
Total	**74**	**100**

Source: calculated by the author from data obtained from CBRE Research (2017).

units at affordable housing rates, and another 60 of the 410 residences for sale would be set aside for low-income residents as defined in relation to Detroit's median income (Afana, 2016). New construction mixed-use, mixed-income development in Brush Park (known as Brush Watson) was expected to break ground in 2020 (Jibrell, 2019). An update is provided by the Downtown Detroit Partnership Report (2023).

Corktown development

Corktown is a historic neighborhood located just west of Downtown Detroit. It is the oldest neighborhood in the city (Marklew, 2018) and was recognized as an Irish immigrant neighborhood in 1850. In 2018 it was selected for redevelopment by the Henry Ford Company, with the company promising to invest $740 million (Walsh, 2018). The company will invest in the 1.2 million square foot surrounding area, including the vacant 104-year-old Michigan Central Station. Ford's investment is expected to create and preserve 200 units of affordable housing units (Pinho, 2019). Ford also promised a philanthropic fund to help revitalize Michigan Avenue, a corridor seen by some as having the best location for attracting investment outside of its Corktown investment (Frank, 2019). Ford, the Detroit City Council, and Mayor Duggan also agreed that the company would invest an additional $10 million in workforce education and training.

Fear of displacement by residents of Corktown

The overarching concern of many residents in Corktown and the broader southwest Detroit region was whether the property values and rent would increase to a level that they could not afford, forcing them to move to another neighborhood. Such fears usually occur when there is gentrification of poor neighborhoods.

The Oakman Boulevard neighborhood

A $26 million affordable housing development in Detroit's Oakman Boulevard neighborhood was completed in July 2019 (Jibrell, 2019). The two-phase development, led by Harper Woods-based American Community Developers Inc., is a blend of new construction and rehabilitated units. American Community as a developer has more than 2,700 affordable apartments in the city.

Opportunity Zones in Detroit

In 2017, President Donald Trump and the Republicans created a tax advantage for large investors called Opportunity Zone tax incentives. These incentives were designed to benefit the affluent, enabled investors to defer and reduce capital gains (Carrns, 2019). Thus, the primary beneficiaries of the Opportunity Zone federal program are investors, who are overwhelmingly white. The program is considered to be the most significant tax break for large investors in decades (Carrns, 2019). Minimum investments are often $50,000–$100,000.

The implementation of the program

If an investment remains in the Opportunity Zone fund for five years, the investor will reduce the taxable gain by another 5 percent. Furthermore, any profit in the opportunity fund is tax-free if the investor remains in the fund for ten years. However, the investor must pay taxes on the initial gain rolled into the fund no later than December 31, 2028, regardless of whether they stay in the fund (Carrns, 2019). The program allowed investors to postpone federal taxes on recent capital gains until the end of 2016. They could also reduce the taxable portion of those gains by as much as 15 percent after seven years (Carrns, 2019). Also, they could eliminate taxes on additional gains from investing in the fund itself if they held the investment for ten years. If the investor has investments that have appreciated, they can defer capital gains taxes by selling the investment and reinvesting the money into an opportunity fund within six months. For example, if an investor sold stock for $500,000 and $300,000 of it was a gain, only $300,000 must be rolled into the opportunity fund. The remaining $200,000 can be used as the seller chooses (Carrns, 2019).

Table 5.4: The location of Opportunity Zones by neighborhood socioeconomic characteristics based on the Darden-Kamel Composite Socioeconomic Index

Socioeconomic position (SEP) rank for census tracts in city of Detroit	Number of eligible Opportunity Zones
Very high	0
High	4
Low	12
Very low	43
NQ = not quantified	5
Total	**64**

Note: * NQ = not quantified by Darden-Kamel Composite Socioeconomic Index (CSI). The total traits designated for Metropolitan Detroit were 120; 64 are in Detroit; 59 were analyzed using the Darden-Kamel Composite Socioeconomic Index; Five could not be analyzed by census tracts.

Source: calculated by the author from data obtained from US Census Bureau (2011–15) ACSS Year Estimates.

The intended target neighborhoods for zone investments

Based on each State's recommendations, the US Department of Treasury has designated more than 8,700 eligible census tracts in the US. In theory, these neighborhoods were those with the greatest need for capital and would benefit from investments like those via new businesses, upgraded apartment buildings, retail shops, and hotels.

Opportunity Zone tracts in Metropolitan Detroit (Wayne, Oakland, and Macomb)

There were a total of 120 opportunity tracts in Metropolitan Detroit. Of those, 64 are in Detroit, 24 are in Wayne County outside of Detroit, 17 are in Macomb County, and 15 are in Oakland County. Although Macomb County is working class, Oakland County is one of the most affluent counties in the US. The zones in Wayne County are located in the City of Detroit (64 tracts) and suburban Wayne (24 tracts) (see Table 5.5).

The socioeconomic characteristics and racial composition of the Opportunity Zones

In order to determine the socioeconomic characteristics of the tracts selected by the State of Michigan for investment, I applied the Darden-Kamel CSI to set the socioeconomic quintile for each tract. The results revealed that the number of census tracts in the lowest quintile (SEP 1) is 39 in Wayne County. These neighborhoods are the most in need of redevelopment via investment. However, Wayne County also has 15 census tracts that are in the second quintile (SEP 2) and 15 census tracts in the third quintile (SEP 3). These tracts are low (SEP 2) to middle class (SEP 3), according to the Darden-Kamel CSI. Even more surprising is that two census tracts are in the fourth quintile (SEP 4). These are both located in the City of Detroit. Most of the tracts in Macomb County—nine—are in the second quintile (SEP 2). Oakland County has a similar pattern to Macomb County, with nine of its tracts in the second quintile (SEP 2) (see Table 5.5).

In terms of racial composition, the population of the Opportunity Zones in Wayne County consists of 128,722 Blacks, 83,615 whites, 16,921 Hispanics, 8,419 Asians, and 12,743 of other races, for a total of 250,420. Of the potential beneficiaries, 51.4 percent are Black, 33 percent are white non Hispanics, 6.8 percent are Hispanic, 3.4 percent are Asian, and 5.1 percent are other races. In the suburban Macomb County, the potential beneficiaries consist of 34,928 whites, 11,352 Blacks, 1,756 Hispanics, 763 Asians, and 2,370 other races, for a total of 51,169. Thus, racially, the major beneficiaries of the Opportunity Zone tax reductions consisted of a population that was 68 percent white, 22 percent Black, 4 percent Hispanic, 2 percent Asian, and 4 percent other races (see Table 5.6).

In Oakland County, there were 15 Opportunity Zone tracts. Two of the tracts were considered very low (SEP 1) in terms of neighborhood characteristics based on the Darden-Kamel CSI. These tracts were located in Pontiac. Pontiac is an industrial suburb of Detroit that is located in the affluent Oakland County, but two of the neighborhoods qualified as Opportunity Zones because of their very low socioeconomic characteristics.

Of the remaining tracts, nine were ranked in the second quintile of socioeconomic status (SEP 2) according to the Darden-Kamel CSI. They were located in such 10,000 or more population municipalities as Southfield, Oak Park, Hazel Park, and Madison Heights. However, among the other census tracts that qualified as Opportunity Zones were two that ranked high (SEP 4) in terms of socioeconomic status according to the Darden-Kamel CSI. These were located in Rochester and Troy. In terms of racial composition of all Opportunity Zones, six of the 15 tracts were majority-white and seven were majority-Black. The highest percentage of Hispanics (20 percent) lived in an Opportunity Zone in Pontiac, located in the affluent Oakland County.

The weakness of the Opportunity Zone legislation

The legislation that created the Opportunity Zones does benefit the developers who are overwhelmingly white. However, the legislation does not guarantee any measurable benefits to local residents, who are

Table 5.5: Opportunity Zones in Metropolitan Detroit (Wayne, Oakland, and Macomb Counties)

Municipality	Tracts percentage of total	SEP level of neighborhood characteristics by Quintile
Wayne County		
Dearborn	3	2
Dearborn Heights	2	2
Detroit	70	1, 2, 3, 4
Ecorse	1	1
Hamtramck	1	1
Highland Park	1	2
Inkster	1	1
Lincoln Park	1	2
Redford Charter Township	3	2
River Rouge	1	2
Romulus	2	2, 3
Taylor	3	2, 3
Van Buren Charter Township	1	3
Wayne	1	2
Westland	2	2
Subtotal	93	
Oakland County		
Wixom	1	2
Pontiac	4	1, 2
Waterford	1	2
Southfield	3	2, 3
Oak Park	1	2
Ferndale	1	3
Hazel Park	1	2
Madison Heights	1	2
Rochester Hills	1	4
Troy	1	4
Subtotal	15	
Macomb County		
Sterling Heights	2	3
Charter Township	2	2

Table 5.5: Opportunity Zones in Metropolitan Detroit (Wayne, Oakland, and Macomb Counties) (continued)

Municipality	Tracts percentage of total	SEP level of neighborhood characteristics by Quintile
Clinton Charter Township	1	2
Mount Clemens	1	1
Roseville	4	2, 3
Eastpointe	2	2
Warren	4	2
Easter Township	1	NA
Subtotal	17	
Grand total	**125**	

Source: calculated by the author from data obtained from City of Detroit and US Bureau of the Census (2011–15) ACSS Year Estimates.

Table 5.6: The racial composition of Opportunity Zones in Metropolitan Detroit (Wayne, Oakland, and Macomb Counties)

Race	Number	Percentage of total populations by race living in Opportunity Zones
Black	166,365	46.3%
Hispanic	22,635	6.3%
Asian	11,031	3.1%
White	141,225	39.3%
Other	18,400	5.1%
Total		100%

disproportionately Black and Hispanic. There is also no guarantee that the residents will receive employment or local services or affordable housing. Tax benefits are for the investors, not the residents (Looney, 2018).

According to Looney (2018), there is no evidence that the design of Opportunity Zones will be effective as a redevelopment tool for local residents in neighborhoods. The tax subsidies provided to developers are based on capital appreciation and not on employment. There are no provisions in the legislation to prevent the displacement of low-income residents or to require developers to provide a certain percentage of affordable housing. Thus, the Opportunity Zones could have the unintended consequence of displacing local residents in favor of high-income newcomers (Looney, 2018).

It is not known whether poor residents in Detroit and its suburbs will benefit or be displaced. Moreover, since some Opportunity Zones are in Detroit's suburbs (including the affluent Oakland County), investors might select census tracts that are characterized as high in socioeconomic status, such as Rochester Hills and Troy. These two census tracts are 98 and 71 percent white respectively.

The Opportunity Zone legislation has been criticized as a tax break for the rich (Looney, 2018; Ernsthausen and Elliott, 2019). It has been argued that it will not benefit poor neighborhoods via revitalization and redevelopment. This is because there is no enforcement and monitoring legislation to oversee results related to investment in affordable housing and job creation in poor neighborhoods (Ernsthausen and Elliott, 2019). While poor residents of Detroit were hoping to benefit economically from the Opportunity Zone legislation passed in 2017, the Trump administration instead loosened regulation in 2019 to benefit a wider group of wealth investors (Tankersley, 2019).

Wealthy investors are benefiting from the rule that conveys tax advantages to investors, who take the proceeds of a capital gain through the sale of a stock or a business. The legislation has no legal guidelines to ensure the investments actually benefit low-income neighborhoods and low-income residents. According to Tankersley (2019), this is a fundamental flaw in the Opportunity Zone legislation (Costello, 2019). Since 2017, when the legislation was introduced, there has been no evidence to support the idea that low-income residents of Detroit are benefiting in terms of gaining access to more affordable housing through redevelopment. So, who benefits?

Who benefits from the Opportunity Zone legislation?

An important question that most Detroit residents want to know is who is the primary beneficiary of the Opportunity Zone legislation? Is it the poor neighborhood residents of Detroit? Or is it the affluent living elsewhere? The Opportunity Zone legislation had the objective in theory to benefit the poorest neighborhoods via new investments, but studies suggest that Opportunity Zones seem to be benefiting wealthy white investors at the expense of poor Black and Hispanic neighborhoods (Ernsthausen and Elliot, 2019).

One wealthy developer who won big was Dan Gilbert, the billionaire developer who bought 100 properties. The properties are managed by Gilbert's own developer, Bedrock Detroit. The primary beneficiaries of the Opportunity Zone federal program are investors, not poor residents. According to *ProPublica*, Gilbert was given tax incentives for wealthy areas of Downtown Detroit, where he owns billions worth of property (Ernsthausen and Elliott, 2019). Three downtown areas were selected as Opportunity Zones under the legislation signed by then President Trump.

Using the Quicken Loans company, Gilbert gave $750,000 to Trump's inaugural fund. Gilbert had also built a relationship with Ivana Trump, who appeared at one of Gilbert's Detroit buildings in 2017 for a panel discussion. Again according to Ernsthausen and Elliot of *ProPublica* (2019), the Opportunity Zones where Gilbert owns property became eligible due to his close association with Trump; these zones did not meet the eligibility criteria.

The few studies that have been done on the impact of Opportunity Zones in the two years since the legislation was passed reveal that Opportunity Zones provided benefits to wealthy investors (Theodos, Hangen, Gonzalez and Meixell, 2020). For every low-income census tract that was selected for Opportunity Zone legislation, another three tracts were not selected. Real Capital Analytics examined the sale of development sites and properties scheduled for redevelopment in the three types of census tracts. If sales activity increased in both designated Opportunity Zones and census tracts that were ripe for redevelopment, then both areas should have seen more sales activity as cities grew and populations expanded.

Are Opportunity Zones for billionaires?

The research thus far suggests that Opportunity Zones are not benefiting poor residents in Detroit. The question of whether the Opportunity Zone legislation was intended for billionaires continues to be asked by Detroit residents, City Council members, community leaders, and researchers. Even the *New York Times* asked the question in an editorial (*New York Times*, 2019).

It is true that the legislation lets the wealthy avoid capital gains taxes by investing in projects owned by companies located in designated geographic areas. First, the purpose is to provide an incentive for wealthy investors to invest in neighborhoods that developers may have avoided. Second, the legislation lets the federal government give States significant discretion in selecting the census tracts from a list of low socioeconomic characteristic census tracts. This resulted in some politicians choosing neighborhoods that were already experiencing development (*New York Times*, 2019).

The *New York Times* noted that the Trump administration's interpretation of the legislation enabled the inclusion of a limited number of higher-income neighborhoods (tracts) adjacent to low-income tracts (*New York Times*, 2019). These include the tracts in Downtown Detroit owned by Gilbert that were discussed earlier. The billionaire beneficiaries are not required by the legislation to report the value of the tax breaks they receive or the value of the projects they develop. According to the *New York Times* (2019), this makes it impossible to assess the merits of the investment program. Another question that most Detroit residents have about the legislation is whether investors include a representative sample of Blacks and Hispanics in a city that is overwhelmingly Black.

Do Opportunity Zones exclude minority investments?

According to *Crain's Detroit Business* database, minority Depository Institutions and Community Development Banks are excluded from qualifying for tax benefits available to other businesses under the *Federal Tax Cuts and Jobs Act of 2017*. According to Barth and Kelley (2019), these nonprofit minority organizations are also excluded from the current designation of qualified Opportunity Zone investments. Barth and Kelly argue that banks are the cornerstone of economic revival and that the exclusion of these community-focused institutions impedes the ultimate success of Opportunity Zone initiatives.

Conclusion

This chapter has demonstrated that after emerging from bankruptcy on December 11, 2014, the Mayor and the City Council were desperate for investments in rehabilitated apartments and condos in order to provide economic development in the neighborhoods, as well as investments in businesses downtown in order to increase the tax base. Bankruptcy had left Detroit with numerous deteriorating and abandoned buildings, vacant lots, and very cheap land. The developers who took advantage of the situation were almost completely white males who bought the land at cheap prices and started the redevelopment, focusing disproportionately on downtown areas.

Midtown was another area that experienced redevelopment in Detroit following the bankruptcy. The challenges of advancing redevelopment in neighborhoods instead of downtown and midtown, and the development of more affordable housing, led the Detroit City Council to pass an inclusionary *housing* ordinance that required developers to provide a stipulated percentage of their developments for low- and moderate-income residents. The ordinance mandated those developers who received city-owned property at less than the true market value and/or public funding to set aside 20 percent of their units for residents, making no more than 80 percent of the Metropolitan Area's median income. Investors were reluctant to invest in the redevelopment of neighborhoods without strong incentives, such as tax breaks and other advantages from the city, the State, and the federal government. Examples of neighborhoods that were subject to redevelopment and did get affordable housing units have been summarized in this chapter. The chapter has also discussed the importance of the DLBA to redevelopment in neighborhoods.

Finally, this chapter examined whether poor residents in Detroit benefited economically from the Opportunity Zone legislation passed by Congress in 2017 and whether the investors who received so much in incentives from the government (Federal, State, and Local) agreed to include a proportionate percentage of Black developers from Detroit. The evidence relating to all of these issues reveals that the city, after bankruptcy, has not achieved the goal of an "inclusive city" as measured in terms of whether Blacks and the poor in Detroit are receiving an equal share of the economic benefits of redevelopment. The results of studies on the Opportunity Zone legislation have shown that it was affluent white developers who received most of the benefits from the legislation, not the poor Black and Hispanic residents living in the City of Detroit.

6

Black and Hispanic Underrepresentation in Business Ownership in a Majority-Black City

Introduction

Before and during bankruptcy, Black and Hispanic business owners were extremely underrepresented compared to their populations in the City of Detroit. This chapter examines both Black-owned and Hispanic-owned businesses.

Black-owned businesses nationwide: previous studies

As far back as 2007, I conducted research on Black business development in Michigan (Darden, 2007). Past research revealed that Black-owned firms in Detroit and other cities in Michigan were suffering from limited market size, as was the case in the US as a whole. In other words, most Black-owned businesses relied on Black consumers to remain in business. Other researchers came to the same conclusion (Fairlie and Robb, 2007a).

According to Bates (1993), such racially restrictive markets were due to racial residential segregation and discrimination. He noted that white merchants continued to open stores in Black neighborhoods, but Black merchants were historically excluded from white neighborhoods. The typical Black business was characterized as a small business concentrated in predominately Black neighborhoods. The socioeconomic characteristics of the Black neighborhoods were very low. Throughout the early period, before the *Civil Rights Acts* of the 1960s and based on data going up to 2002, Black-owned businesses continued to experience limited access to capital, which influenced the size, location, and type of such businesses. This lack of capital also influenced the type of Black-owned business. Research revealed that firms in construction, manufacturing, and wholesale trade usually required a larger amount of capital than small personal service businesses and retail establishments (Ong, 1981). As a result, fewer Blacks are represented in these types of firms (Darden, 2007).

Research also suggests that the limited access of Blacks to capital is related to the higher loan denial rates Black business owners have experienced even after controlling for differences in creditworthiness (Cavalluzzo et al, 2002). It has also revealed that Black business owners were required to pay higher interest rates or put down more collateral than white business owners (Fairlie and Robb, 2007a). The limited access to capital forced Blacks into types of businesses with higher turnover rates, such as small retail (Reynolds and White, 1997; Robb and Fairlie, 2007b). Bates (1997) noted that fewer Black-owned businesses compared to white-owned businesses obtained a larger supply of capital to open manufacturing and wholesale businesses, which have lower turnover rates. Also, a lower supply of human capital influences failure rates and reduces the amount of profits (Darden, 2007). The previous research has shown that Black-owned firms are more likely to be found in personal service businesses—which usually have worse outcomes on average than other firms—compared to white-owned firms (Fairlie and Robb, 2007a).

Other researchers have attributed the low level of Black business ownership compared to white business ownership to a lack of parental self-employment (Bates, 1997; Fairlie, 1999; Hout and Rosen, 2000; Robb, 2002). Black business owners have less of the inheritance of the family business and intergenerational transfer of business skills (Dunn and Holtz-Eakin, 2000). Fairlie and Robb (2007b) explored the role that intergenerational links in self-employment play in contributing to racial differences in such small business outcomes as size, profits, and sales. They concluded that the inability of Blacks to acquire general and specific business human capital through exposure to businesses owned by family members may contribute to their limited success in business ownership (Fairlie and Robb, 2007b). Fairlie (1999) and other researchers (Hout and Rosen, 2000) concluded that a potential business owner who had a self-employed parent had a higher probability of becoming self-employed than a potential business owner with a nonself-employed parent.

Nationwide, Blacks, or African Americans, owned approximately 124,551 businesses, with about 28.5 percent (35,547) of these businesses in the healthcare and social assistance sector, the highest percentage of any minority group according to the *2019 Annual Business Survey*. According to the Brookings Institution, Black-owned firms with paid employees generate over $103 billion in revenue annually (Perry and Romer, 2020).

Authors Andre Perry and Carl Romer of the Brookings Institution used the US Census Bureau's *2018 Annual Business Survey* (ABS) to analyze data at the national and metropolitan levels in order to compare Black and non Black-owned businesses. They published a 2020 report entitled "To expand the economy, invest in Black businesses," which focused on examining equity. This was determined by comparing the total Black population in the US in terms of percentage with the total Black business ownership as a percentage. The data showed that Black people comprise approximately 14.2 percent of the US population, but Black-owned businesses comprise only 2.2 percent of all businesses. The business survey data show that there is another racial disparity. According to the *2018 Annual Business Survey* (ABS), only 4.2 percent of Black-owned businesses had employees, compared to 20.6 percent of white-owned businesses, a ratio of 4.9, which means that the white-owned businesses are four times more likely than Black-owned businesses to have employees.

Perry and Romer state that the US has not yet experienced an economy that is inclusive. This is measured by parity: if Black-owned employee businesses reached a similar percentage to non Black employee-owned businesses, parity would be reached. It also considers that equity and inclusiveness would also be achieved. The authors stated that if Black-owned businesses with employees equaled the percentage of Blacks in the US population, that would be parity. There are 124,551 Black-owned businesses, accounting for 2.2 percent of all employer businesses. If Black businesses accounted for 14.2 percent of employer firms (equivalent to the Black population), there would be 806,218 more Black businesses and parity would be reached (Perry and Romer, 2020).

Perry and Romer (2020) argued that the underrepresentation of Black businesses is due to structural barriers underscoring America's tumultuous history of structural racism. They argue that one of the principal barriers to the growth and development of Black-owned businesses is that Black households have been denied equal opportunities for wealth accumulation. The median Black household's wealth ($9,000) is nearly one-15th that of non-Black households ($134,520). According to their data and analysis of *2018 Survey of Income and Program Participation* (SIPP) data, the second barrier is that Blacks have less than whites in terms of startup capital because of historic discrimination in housing and mortgage lending (Immergluck, 2002). Such discrimination reduced the Black homeownership rate compared to the white rate and equity. According to their analysis of the *American Business Survey*, 90 percent of new businesses among all races do not receive any outside investment; most potential business owners use the equity in their homes to start their firms (Perry and Romer, 2020).

A third barrier is that Black-owned businesses experience higher loan denials and pay higher interest rates than white-owned businesses, even after controlling for differences in creditworthiness, and receive less capital than similarly situated white owners (Bates and Robb, 2015a; Hoffman, 2018).

A fourth barrier is that Black-owned business owners have fewer resources. Recent data from the Federal Reserve's Survey of Consumer Finances, which was examined by Kim et al (2021), show an enormous racial wealth gap, with

Black families having both median and mean wealth less than 15 percent of that of whites. This racial disparity appears to have been largely unchanged since at least the 1960s. Because Black owners tend to have fewer resources, both personally and through family and friends, they are more dependent on outside funding, yet they do not receive it due to racial discrimination (Lederer et al, 2020). Black-owned businesses tend to operate with less finance and employ fewer workers than those owned by whites (Kim et al, 2021).

Kim et al (2021) found that the racial financing gap is most pronounced at startup and tends to narrow with the firm's age. At any age, Black-owned firms are less likely to receive bank loans, more likely to refrain from applying because they expect denial, and more likely to report that lack of finances reduces their profitability (Baradaran, 2017; Kim et al, 2021). Concerning employment, the authors found that Black-owned firms have on average about 12 percent fewer employees than those owned by whites.

Characteristics of Black-owned businesses nationwide

Kim et al (2021) presented recent data indicating that non Hispanic Blacks own only 1.72 percent of employer firms in the US, while non Hispanic whites own 84 percent, non Hispanic Asians own 9 percent, and Hispanics own 5 percent. Black owners tend to be younger than whites: 26 percent of Blacks are less than 45 years old, compared with 20 percent of whites, while 32 percent of Blacks and 52 percent of whites are aged 55 or over (Kim et al, 2021).

Black owners are more likely to be the sole owner of businesses than whites. For each variable, the difference in sole ownership is more than ten percentage points. Conversely, Blacks are much less likely to be members of multi-owner teams. For teams of two to four owners, the percentage for Blacks is 29 percent compared to 38 percent for whites, and whites are nearly twice as likely to own firms with more than four owners. Whites are also more likely to have prior business experience: 32 percent compared to 27 percent for Blacks. As revealed in earlier studies and earlier data, Black business ownership is relatively much higher in the healthcare sector: 27 percent of business owners are Black compared to 10 percent who are white. White ownership is more common in construction, manufacturing, and wholesale and retail trade (Kim et al, 2021).

This is the situation nationwide. I will now turn to discuss the situation in Metropolitan Detroit.

Black business ownership in Metropolitan Detroit

One of the most commonly used databases to examine Black business ownership in the US and in Metropolitan Detroit and the City of Detroit is the Census Bureau's *Survey of Business Owners*. This survey defined Black-owned businesses as firms in which African Americans (Blacks) hold 51 percent or more of the stock or equity in the business. Although all businesses are important, the focus in this chapter is on businesses with paid employees. Similar to the pattern of ownership nationwide, the kinds of businesses owned by Blacks in Metropolitan Detroit showed that the businesses were highest in the healthcare and social assistance industries, at 18 percent. Services, excluding public administration, was another kind of business where Blacks owned 10 percent or more of businesses. The kinds of businesses owned by Blacks differed from those owned by whites. Black-owned businesses were very underrepresented in construction, real estate, rental and leasing, retail trade, and professional, scientific, and technical services.

The extreme underrepresentation of Blacks in the construction sector has not changed. Based on the *2014 Survey of Business Ownership*, there were only 123 Black-owned firms with paid employees in construction compared to 6,918 white-owned firms in construction in Metropolitan Detroit. As was the case in 2007, the two kinds of businesses in which Black business ownership with paid employees was highest were in the healthcare and social services sector (Darden, 2007). Generally, businesses with paid employees are larger and generate higher sales and receipts. For example, in 2002, 84 percent of the total sales and receipts for Black-owned firms were generated by those with paid employees. In order to determine how extreme Black underrepresentation is, it must be measured.

One way to measure Black business underrepresentation is to use the Black business participation rate (BPR). The BPR is measured as the number of Black-owned firms divided by the number of Blacks in the county or city multiplied by 1,000. According to the data from the *Survey of Business Owners* for 2002, in Metropolitan Detroit the Black BPR was highest in the Macomb (63.06) and Oakland (54.6) Counties, whereas it was only 26.6 in Wayne County (Darden, 2007: 74). In 2002, the City of Detroit had 1,199 firms with paid employees. The Black population in 2002 was 775,772. When the number of Black-owned firms with paid employees was divided by the Black population multiplied by 1,000, the result was a BPR for Detroit of 1.55 (Darden, 2007: 77).

The state of Black-owned businesses in Metropolitan Detroit more recently

Based on recent data, Blacks are disproportionately more likely to own smaller businesses and pay more for access to capital, due in part to systemic racial discrimination. In 2012, just 2.8 percent of the estimated 50,000 Detroit firms owned by non white people had employees, compared to 45 percent of firms owned by whites (US Bureau of the Census, 2015).

New businesses owned by Black owners are more likely to be discouraged from applying for loans and more likely to have their applications denied by banks compared to white owners (Bates and Robb, 2015a; Orozco et al, 2020; Kim et al, 2021).

It will also be shown later on in this chapter that more Paycheck Protection Program (PPP) loans went to white business owners than to Black and Hispanic owners.

Data from the most recent survey on Black-owned businesses in Metropolitan Detroit with paid employees

The objective of this section is to assess the extent of underrepresentation of Blacks in the field of business ownership in Detroit, focusing on Black businesses with paid employees rather than on Black businesses with sole proprietors. This is because the former are usually large firms that have an impact on employment because they have jobs in which the population of the City of Detroit are employed. After Detroit's bankruptcy ended on December 11, 2014, some key questions that this chapter will answer are as follows:

(1) How many Black-owned businesses with paid employees were there?
(2) How many employees were working in Black-owned businesses?
(3) Were there additional Black businesses with paid employees founded or created after bankruptcy?
(4) To what extent were Black businesses with paid employees located in the City of Detroit compared to the Detroit suburbs?
(5) What were the types of businesses with paid employees that Black owners operated?
(6) Where were the municipalities located where Black and Hispanic businesses received Paycheck Protection Program (PPP) loans to maintain their businesses during the COVID-19 pandemic?

Data

The data were obtained from *Crain's Detroit Business* database (https://www.crainsdetroit.com/data-lists/2020-book-lists). The list is an approximate compilation of the largest such businesses in Wayne, Oakland, and Macomb Counties, which combined comprise Metropolitan Detroit for the purposes of this chapter. The percentage of the company that is African American-owned may not be solely held by a majority owner. It is not a complete listing, but is the most comprehensive list currently available. The *Crain's* estimates are based on industry analyses and benchmarks, news reports, and a wide range of other sources. Unless otherwise noted, the information was provided by the company. I examined the characteristics of Black-owned businesses with paid employees first, followed by the examination of Hispanic-owned businesses with paid employees. Data on the businesses that received PPP loans and the municipalities where they were located were obtained from United States Small Business Administration Paycheck Protection Program Report Approvals 5-31-2021.

Characteristics of Black-owned businesses with paid employees

According to *Crain's Detroit Business* database, there were 32 large Black-owned businesses with paid employees in the Detroit Metropolitan Area (that is, Wayne, Oakland, and Macomb Counties) in January 2021. Data were provided on the revenue of 19, or 59 percent, of these businesses in 2020. The revenue ranged from $12 million for Jenkins Construction to $2876.3 for the Piston Group. For the 20, or 63 percent, of the businesses that provided data on the number of local employees for January 2021, the number of employees ranged from nine for ScriptGuideRX to 1,700 for Advantage Living Centers. Data were provided for the location of all 32 Black-owned businesses. Only 16, or 50 percent, of the Black-owned businesses with paid employees were located in the City of Detroit in January 2021. Six, or 19 percent, were located in suburban Southfield, including the largest Black-owned business with paid employees (the Piston Group). The remaining ten, or 31 percent, of the Black-owned businesses with paid employees were located in the following Detroit suburbs: St. Clair Shores, Royal Oak, Grosse Pointe Park, Farmington Hills, Taylor, Woodhaven, Wixom, Livonia, and Troy (see Table 6.1).

All but one of the Black-owned businesses with paid employees were established before Detroit's bankruptcy. One objective of this section is to assess whether there was an increase in the number of Black-owned businesses with paid employees after bankruptcy. The one Black-owned business with paid employees that was established in 2017 (after bankruptcy) was ACE Petroleum. The company's founder and Black CEO Moses Shepherd started the company to capitalize on the scant number of minority gas suppliers operating in the nation's $147 billion oil and gas market. ACE Petroleum is a certified Minority Business Enterprise by the Michigan Minority Supplier Development Council and National Minority Supplier Development Council (McKinney, 2020). It provides gasoline, diesel, ethanol, and biodiesel fuel to businesses and government entities. ACE Petroleum's clients include Barton Malow Co. in Southfield, Michigan, and Detroit-based Ideal Contracting. ACE Petroleum obtained a $27 million contract with Detroit to supply fuel services for the city's police cars, fire trucks, buses, emergency medical vehicles, and other transportation units. The five-year contract calls

Table 6.1: The largest African American-owned businesses ranked by 2020 revenue

Employer	# of employees	Type of business	Location	2020 revenue in US$ million
Piston Group	865	Automotive supplier	Southfield	$2,876.3
Bridgewater Interiors	1,294	Epsilon Technologies	Detroit	$1,567.6
Detroit Manufacturing Systems	1,219	Full module assemblies	Detroit	$642.4
Prestige Automotive	150	Automotive dealership	St Clair Shores	$308.6
Royal Oak Ford	253	Automotive dealership	Royal Oak	$241.9
Global Automotive Alliance	171	Warehousing, assembly	Detroit	$229.1
Devon Industrial Group	68	Construction management	Detroit	$168.0
Chemico	89	Chemical manufacturing	Southfield	$158.0
Epitec, inc	1,050	IT, engineering	Southfield	$131.6
James Group	260	Supply chains and logistics	Detroit	$117.0
Avis Ford	119	Automobile dealership	Southfield	$112.9
Advantage Living Centers	815	Skilled nursing homes	Southfield	$109.1
Scriptguiderx	23	Pharmacy benefits	Grosse Pointe Park	$104.3
MPS Group	162	Waste management	Farmington Hills	$102.0.
Bill Perkins	69	Automobile dealership	Taylor	$97.7
MCL Jasco, Inc	167	Automotive, energy industries	Detroit	$90.5
Michael Bates Chevrolet	NA	Automobile dealership	Woodhaven	$78.0
WJR Consulting	NA	IT staffing and consulting	Southfield	$47.9
First Independence Bank	32	Living trust services	Detroit	$36.5

(continued)

Table 6.1: The largest African American-owned businesses ranked by 2020 revenue (continued)

Employer	# of employees	Type of business	Location	2020 revenue in US$ million
Walker–Miller	119	Energy waste reduction	Detroit	$29.7
MIG East LLC DBA/ MIG Construction	26	General construction	Detroit	$26.2
Tag Holdings LLC	39	Manufacturing	Wixom	$22.8

Source: Crain's Detroit.com/data. *Crain's Detroit Business: The Book 2022,* December 2021.

for ACE Petroleum to provide Detroit with over two million gallons of fuel per year (McKinney, 2020).

ACE Petroleum has steadily grown. The company reported it had $6 million in revenue for 2019 and projects revenue of $15 million in 2020. The data is not readily available to indicate whether ACE Petroleum reached the $15 million in 2020. Crain's Detroit Business Book (2021) only provided data on the highest-ranked Black-owned businesses based on revenue in 2020. ACE Petroleum was not listed. Shepherd says his firm is now pursuing other fuel contracts with large municipalities, companies, and corporations nationwide (McKinney, 2020). The company's number of employees has quadrupled, growing from three in 2017 to 12 in 2020. Before launching his new company, Shepherd started ACE Investment Group LLC in 2003. This firm focuses on buying properties in Detroit and is now among the city's largest Black-owned apartment operators with more than 1,000 units. Both of Shepherd's businesses are housed in a 13,000 square foot building he owns in Detroit. He plans approximately $600,000 in renovation work. ACE Investment Group LLC bought three apartment communities in northwest Detroit containing a total of 144 units for $3.6 million in 2018, adding to the more than 1,000 rental units Shepherd manages in the city (Frank, 2018). He wants to replace the roof on one, install new boilers in two, and put in electric security gates in all three (Frank, 2018).

The type of Black-owned businesses with paid employees

Many Black-owned businesses with paid employees were focused on automotive supplies, automotive assemblies, and automotive dealerships. For example, the Piston Group, the largest Black-owned auto supplier not just in Southfield, a Detroit suburb, but also in the US, is engaged in automotive subsidiaries manufacture modules, assemblies, seating components, climate control systems, and parts sequencing for automakers (Walsh, 2018). The

Piston Group is one of the fastest-growing companies in Michigan: its revenue increased from $570 million in 2012 to $2.9 billion in 2020, and it now has more than 10,000 employees across its four subsidiaries (Nagl, 2022).

These types of businesses accounted for at least 28 percent of the Black-owned businesses with paid employees. Six (19 percent) of the Black-owned businesses were general contractors, or were involved in construction management and professional design: MiG East Construction, Devon Industrial Group, White Construction Company, KEO and Associates, Jenkins Construction, and Hamilton Anderson Associates. All of the Black-owned construction businesses are located in the City of Detroit. The small number of Black-owned businesses in construction may be a factor in the limited participation and underrepresentation of Black-owned businesses in the economic redevelopment of Detroit. Such economic redevelopment has been overwhelmingly undertaken by white contractors. One exception has been Hamilton Anderson Associates, which has been substantially involved in the $55 million expansion of the Motown Museum's Plaza, which will be tiled with granite pavers and adorned with benches and a new line of trees on the property's West Side (McCollum, 2021). The fully expanded complex will ultimately comprise 50,000 square feet, including new exhibits, a theater, meeting rooms, and a working studio. The construction was expected be completed in 2022 (McCollum, 2021).

The most recent data on the largest Black-owned businesses in Detroit and its suburbs

Crain's Detroit Business provided data on the largest African American-owned businesses based on the 2020 revenue. The data are provided in Table 6.1, which shows that the Piston Group ranked first with revenue of $2,876.3. The company is located not in Detroit but in Southfield, a predominantly Black suburb on the border of Detroit. It has 865 employees and is an automobile supplier (Crain's Detroit Business, 2021). Crain's Detroit Business listed the 22 largest African American-owned businesses. The business with the lowest revenue was TAG Holdings with a revenue of $22.8. Among the 22 largest African American-owned businesses listed, only (41 percent) are located in the City of Detroit. The biggest share in Detroit of the businesses are located in the suburb of Southfield with 27.2 percent and the rest are distributed in Grosse Pointe Park, Farmington Hills, Taylor, Woodhaven, Wixom, Royal Oak, and St. Clair Shores.

Twenty of the largest African American-owned businesses provided employment for 6,938 workers. Two of the businesses did not provide data on their number of employees. The most common types of business were automotive suppliers and automotive dealerships. There is only one large African American-owned bank—First Independence Bank, which was founded on May 14, 1970 as a result of the civil disorders in Detroit in 1967 (Darden and Thomas, 2013; First Independence Bank, 2022). Those who established the bank saw the need for Blacks to own a bank in order to help address the financial needs of Blacks in the city where they were discriminated against by many white-owned banks. It was the only Black-owned bank in Detroit listed in Crain's Detroit Business Book in 2021. In 2021, it was also the seventh-largest Black-owned bank in the US (First Independence Bank, 2022).

Today—including credit unions—there are only 44 Black-owned financial institutions in the US. Of these, about half are Black-owned banks and half are not-for-profit credit unions. By and large, Black-owned banks tend to be community institutions, offering the same services as major financial institutions with a greater focus on specific neighborhoods. As such, they are a great resource for Black business owners (Perry and Romer, 2020). Taken together, they have approximately $6.82 billion in assets in total.

Black-owned auto dealerships and the significance of suburban location

Location matters in terms of the size of Black-owned auto dealerships. According to Crain's Detroit Business 2021 list of the largest local auto dealers (regardless of race) in Wayne, Oakland, and Macomb Counties, there were six Black auto dealers among all of the largest local auto dealers. Based on revenue, they are as follows: Elder Automotive Group located in Troy, with a revenue in 2021 of $353.1 million; Prestige Automotive located in St. Clair Shores, with a revenue of $341.3 million; Royal Oak Ford located in Royal Oak, with a revenue of $267.5 million; Avis Ford located in Southfield, with a revenue of $137.1 million; Bill Perkins Automotive Group located in Taylor, with a revenue of $101.8 million; and Michael Bates Chevrolet located in Woodhaven, with a revenue of $86.2 million. It is important to note that all of the largest locally owned Black auto dealerships are located in the Detroit suburbs and not in the City of Detroit.

Summary

Black-owned businesses are still extremely underrepresented in Detroit after the city's bankruptcy. Only one new Black-owned business was founded after bankruptcy ended in 2014. Only 32 large African American-owned businesses existed in Wayne, Oakland, and Macomb Counties, with half of them located in the City of Detroit. Most of the businesses were associated with and dependent on the auto industry to a certain extent. Very few were in the construction industry. Where the information was provided, Black-owned businesses with paid employees had a total of 8,674 employees in January 2021 (see Table 6.1).

What Black business owners want from the Mayor of the City of Detroit

Following the re-election of Mayor Duggan, Blacks and other leaders indicated that they wanted a seat at the table for Black-owned construction contractors. They also wanted a continued focus on rebuilding Detroit's manufacturing base. Michigan Minority Contractors Association Executive Director Jason Cole was interviewed by Frank and Livengood of *Crain's Detroit Business* (Frank and Livengood, 2021). He said his members wanted: (1) an economic disparity study that shows who does and does not get a seat at the table on government contracts that help businesses grow; (2) a prompt payment ordinance to ensure contractors and subcontractors do not have to wait for their money; and (3) not charging Black-owned companies to get certified as a minority business with the government. He also stated that contracting is especially important for wealth building and employment, since the City of Detroit is declining (Frank and Livengood, 2021: 27)—its population fell by 10.5 percent between 2010 and 2020 (US Bureau of the Census, 2022).

The Duggan administration agreed with the Detroit City Council resolution that listed an array of commitments across city departments. One of these commitments was to hire small Detroit-based contractors. Some actions have been taken—for example, 30 out of 39 demolition contractors and all 23 contracts for cleaning out salvageable houses have gone to small or microbusinesses; moreover, 36 and 23 respectively are Detroit-based and around half are Black-owned (Frank, 2021: 26).

Chris Rizik, CEO and Fund Manager of Renaissance Venture Capital, said that Detroit needs to increase the resources aimed at identifying, mentoring, and providing seed capital to promising entrepreneurs of color (Frank, 2021: 27). Lisa Johanon, Housing Director of the Central Detroit Christian Community Development Corporation, wanted the Mayor and the City Council to prioritize affordable housing for low-income families (Frank, 2021: 27). Donna Givens Davison, President and CEO at Eastside Community Network, agreed that low- and moderate-income residents in Detroit cannot find affordable quality housing in the city. She said there has not been a single-minded focus on adequate housing for low-income people (Frank, 2021: 27).

Hispanic-owned businesses nationwide

This section begins with a nationwide assessment. Most of the information on the nationwide Hispanic-owned businesses versus white-owned businesses was derived from the 2020 State of Latino Entrepreneurship Report by Orozco et al (2020). The Stanford University Business School Report examined the impact of Latino-owned employer businesses in the US economy and compared their experiences to those of non Hispanic white-owned employer firms in the US. The report uses "Latino" instead of "Hispanic." However, to be considered for the Latino business owner sample, respondents had to answer these questions in the affirmative: are you a business owner with 50 percent or more ownership and are you of Latino or Hispanic origin? (If yes to the second question, the respondent had to simultaneously specify country/ancestry) [Orozco et al, 2020].) Latino business owners are of any race and for the white business owner sample, respondents had to indicate they were not Latino. The report focuses on Hispanic/Latino business owners, but also a comparison group of non Hispanic white business owners in order to identify similarities and differences in their experiences.

The authors collected a sample of 3,500 white-owned businesses and 3,500+ Latino-owned businesses. The focus was on employer firms, which are those with at least one paid employee other than the owner. These businesses are poised to have the greatest impact on the economy and job creation. This focus on employer firms aligns with the approach taken by the US Bureau of the Census in its *Annual Business Survey*. According to the report, in the US as a whole, the number of Latino-owned businesses has grown by 34 percent since 2010 compared to just 1 percent for all other small businesses. Among these industries, the growth rate is highest in the following sectors: (1) construction; (2) finance and insurance; (3) transportation and warehousing; and (4) real estate.

Like Black-owned employer businesses, Latino-owned employer businesses are significantly less likely than white-owned employer businesses to have loan applications approved by national banks.

Only 20 percent of Latino-owned businesses that applied for national bank loans over $100,000 obtained funding, compared to 50 percent of white-owned businesses. If loans of all sizes are considered, 51 percent of Latino-owned businesses were approved for all or most of the loans they requested from national banks, compared to 77 percent of white-owned businesses. Loan approvals from national banks are 60 percent lower for Latinos (Orozco et al, 2020: 4).

Although the report focuses on the growth rate at the national level, it emphasizes the growth for States. In Michigan, the growth rate in the number of Latino-owned employer businesses from 2012 to 2017 was 18 percent (Orozco et al, 2020). These data are supported by the US Bureau of the Census's *2018 Annual Business Survey* and *2012 Survey of Business Owners*. Latinos are starting businesses across all industries; however, employer businesses are seeing the highest growth in the nonservice sectors.

Hispanic-owned businesses in Metropolitan Detroit

The US Bureau of the Census for 2020 reported the following racial breakdown of the population: 70.1 percent white, 22.8 percent Black/African

American, 3.3 percent Asian, 0.3 percent Native American, 0.02 percent Pacific Islander, 1.2 percent from other races, and 2.2 percent from two or more races. Hispanics or Latinos of any race comprised 6.2 percent of the population of Metropolitan Detroit and 7.6 percent of Detroit's population was Hispanic or Latino.

According to the US Bureau of the Census, many lived in southwest Detroit, also known as Mexicantown, a vibrant community less than two miles from downtown (Darden and Thomas, 2013).

The state of Hispanic-owned businesses in Metropolitan Detroit more recently

Like the pattern in the US as a whole, Hispanics are disproportionately more likely to own smaller businesses and pay more for access to capital than non-Hispanic white-owned businesses, due in part to systemic racial discrimination (US Bureau of the Census, 2015). Like Black business owners, new businesses owned by Hispanics are more likely to be discouraged from applying for loans and are more likely to have their applications denied by banks compared to non Hispanic white owners (Bates and Robb, 2015a).

Data from the most recent survey on Hispanic-owned businesses in Metropolitan Detroit with paid employees

Like Black-owned businesses, the objective of this section is to assess the extent of underrepresentation of Hispanic business ownership with paid employees. After Detroit's bankruptcy ended on December 11, 2014, I had the same questions for Hispanic business owners as I had for Black-owned businesses:

(1) How many Hispanic-owned businesses with paid employees were there?
(2) How many employees were working in Hispanic-owned businesses?
(3) Were there additional Hispanic businesses with paid employees founded or created after bankruptcy?
(4) To what extent were Hispanic businesses with paid employees located in the City of Detroit compared to the Detroit suburbs?
(5) What were the types of businesses with paid employees that Hispanic owners operated?

Data

The data were obtained from *Crain's Detroit Business* data (https://www.crainsdetroit.com/data-lists/2020-book-lists). The list is an approximate compilation of the largest such businesses in Wayne, Oakland, and Macomb

Counties. The percentage of the company that is Hispanic-owned may not be solely held by a majority owner. It is not a complete listing, but is the most comprehensive list currently available. The *Crain's* estimates are based on industry analyses and benchmarks, news reports, and a wide range of other sources. Unless otherwise noted, the information was provided by the company. I examined the characteristics of Hispanic-owned businesses with paid employees.

Characteristics of Hispanic-owned businesses with paid employees

According to *Crain's Detroit Business*, there were eight large Hispanic-owned businesses with paid employees in the Detroit Metropolitan Area (that is, Wayne, Oakland, and Macomb Counties) in January 2021. Data were provided on the revenue of five of those businesses in 2020, which ranged from $37.2 million for Aztec Manufacturing Corporation to $319.2 million for the Elder Automotive Group. Seven of the nine businesses provided data on the number of employees as of January 2021. The number of employees ranged from 33 at Three Star to 364 at the Ideal Group. For the location of the Hispanic-owned businesses, data were provided for five. Only two of the Hispanic-owned businesses were located in the City of Detroit. The others were located in the following suburbs of Detroit: Troy, Warren, Westland, Dearborn, and Pontiac (see Table 6.2).

Only one of the Hispanic-owned businesses with paid employees was founded after bankruptcy: Performance Driven Workforce, which

Table 6.2: The largest Hispanic-owned businesses ranked by 2020 revenue

Employer	# of employees	Type of business	Location	2020 revenue
The Diez Group	NA	Aluminum, steel sales	Dearborn	$1,265.0
Elder Automotive Group	NA	Automobile dealership	Troy	$319.2
The Ideal Group Inc	364	General contracting	Detroit	$237.5
Global Parts	14	Manufacturing, engineering	Westland	$71.0
Gonzalez Design Group	NA	Design engineering	Pontiac	$57.2
PMA Consultants LLC	40	Project and construction	Detroit	$48.6

Source: Crain's Detroit.com/data. *Crain's Detroit Business: The Book 2022*, December 2021.

was founded in 2015. The first Hispanic-owned company with paid employees—Elder Automotive Group, located in Troy, a suburb of Detroit—was founded in 1967. There was one Hispanic business that opened in 1971. It was Sanders PMA Consultants, which was located in Detroit. The Ideal Group and Three Star opened in 1979. In 1983, Aztec Manufacturing Corporation opened. It was located in Romulus, a suburb of Detroit. During the 1990s, Gutierrez ICR Services opened in Warren, a suburb of Detroit, and Goodman Insurance opened up in 1997 in Troy, another suburb of Detroit. There was an 18-year gap in Hispanic business development, which lasted from 1997 to 2015. The types of businesses owned by Hispanics included automobile dealership, general contracting, program project and construction management, industrial repair services, auto repairs, manufacturing, and insurance.

The most recent data on the largest Hispanic-owned businesses in Detroit and its suburbs

Crain's Detroit Business (2021) provided the most recent data on the largest Hispanic-owned businesses with paid employees in Detroit and its suburbs, and listed the largest businesses based on their 2020 revenue. According to its ranking, the largest Hispanic-owned business is the Diez Group with a revenue in 2020 of $1,265. The company, which focuses on aluminum and steel sales, and processing, is located not in Detroit but in suburban Dearborn, which borders the City of Detroit. The company did not provide data on its number of employees. The largest Hispanic-owned business with the lowest revenue ($40.2) is Gutierrez ICR Services, which engages in industrial repair services and automation. This company also did not provide data on its number of employees. Only two of the six largest Hispanic-owned businesses are located in Detroit. The rest are located in the following suburbs: Dearborn, Troy, Westland, Pontiac, and Warren. The three businesses that provided data on the number of employees showed a total of 418 employees working in the largest Hispanic-owned businesses (see Table 6.2).

Summary

Hispanic-owned businesses with paid employees are still extremely underrepresented in Detroit after bankruptcy. Only one new Hispanic-owned business was founded after bankruptcy ended in 2014. Only two large Hispanic-owned businesses existed in Wayne, Oakland, and Macomb Counties, and only two were located in the City of Detroit. Most of these businesses were associated with and dependent on the auto industry. Few were involved in the construction or the manufacturing sectors.

Analyses of Paycheck Protection Program loans to Black-owned, white-owned, and Hispanic-owned businesses

The PPP is an emergency disaster loan program offered through the Small Business Administration (SBA). It was first implemented in 2020 to aid businesses impacted by the COVID-19 pandemic as part of the *CARES Act*, which was passed in March 2020. The PPP loans to Michigan business owners, which ended on May 31, 2021, totaled 176,993 and the net loan amount was $8,418,112,644. White business owners received the largest percentage of the loans. Based on the United States Small Business Administration Paycheck Protection Program Report (2021), white business owners received 917,340 loans, while Black business owners received 825,959—a difference of 91,381. There was also a difference in the total net amount received: white business owners received $43,538,074,339, while Black business owners received $16,115,604,264—a difference of $27,422,470. Although JPMorgan Chase approved the largest loan amount ($12,189,061,552), the largest number of loans (494,415) was approved by Prestos CDFI, LLC. Capital Plus Financial provided 472,036 loans, Harvest Small Business 429,098 loans, and Banworthy Capital 334,434 loans.

Which businesses located in municipalities in Metropolitan Detroit received PPP loans?

Data provided by United States Small Business Administration Paycheck Protection Program Report Approvals (2021) indicated where the businesses were located by municipality in Metropolitan Detroit. The data do not indicate the race of the business owner. However, one can check the names of the Black and Hispanic business owners against the *Crain's Detroit Business* database, which lists Black and Hispanic businesses, and the municipality where they are located. For the demographic groups that received PPP loans, see Table 6.3.

There were 45 businesses that received PPP loans and they were located in a number of Detroit suburban municipalities; most were not Black- or Hispanic-owned. Municipalities containing one business that received PPP loans were Birmingham, Canton, Center Line, Dearborn, Farmington Hills, Flat Rock, Mount Clemens, Novi, Pontiac, Roseville, St. Clair Shores, Taylor, Utica, Van Buren, and Warren. Municipalities containing two businesses that received loans were Farmington, Rochester Hills, and Sterling Heights. Municipalities containing four businesses that received loans were Livonia and Southfield. The municipalities with businesses that received the largest number of businesses were Detroit (nine) and suburban Troy (seven). Of the 45 businesses, one is Hispanic-owned (Ideal Contracting

Table 6.3: Demographic groups for 2021 PPP Loans Paycheck Protection Program Report

Race of applicant	Number of loans approved	Net amount
Black/African American	825,959	$16,115,604,264
White	917, 340	$43,538,074,339
Difference	*−91381*	*$27,422,470*
Hispanic/Latino	252,517	$9,013,651,378
Difference	*−664,823*	*−$46,598,439*

Source: United States Small Business Administration Paycheck Protection Program Report Approvals, May 31, 2021.

Company), which is engaged in commercial and institutional building construction. It is located in the City of Detroit, received $10 million, and maintained 417 jobs. One company, Detroit Manufacturing Systems, which was engaged in motor vehicle seating and interior trim manufacturing, was Black-owned: it received $8,185,662 and maintained 500 jobs. The suburban city of Southfield, which is predominantly Black, was a municipality where four PPP loans were received by businesses. One of these was EPIC, which is Black-owned and is involved in job displacement. It received $10 million and maintained 500 jobs.

Conclusion

Before and during bankruptcy, Black and Hispanic business owners were extremely underrepresented compared to their populations in the City of Detroit. This chapter has examined Black-owned businesses followed by businesses owned by Hispanics.

The kinds of businesses owned by Blacks differed from those owned by whites. The data were obtained from *Crain's Detroit Business* database, the *Survey of Business Owners*, and the United States Small Business Administration Paycheck Protection Program Report. Black-owned businesses were very underrepresented in construction, real estate, rental leasing, retail trade, and professional, scientific, and technical services. On the other hand, compared to white-owned firms, Black-owned businesses were overrepresented in the healthcare and social assistance sectors, and other services, except public administration. The extreme underrepresentation of Blacks in construction has not changed. Based on the *2014 Survey of Business Ownership*, there were only 123 Black-owned firms with paid employees in construction compared to 6,918 white-owned firms in Metropolitan Detroit.

Based on recent data, Blacks are disproportionately more likely to own smaller businesses and pay more for access to capital, due in part to systemic racial discrimination. According to the *Crain's Detroit Business* database, there were 32 large Black-owned businesses with paid employees in the Detroit Metropolitan Area (that is, Wayne, Oakland, and Macomb Counties) in January 2021. The revenue ranged from $12 million for Jenkins Construction to $2,876.3 for the Piston Group. Only 16, or 50 percent, of the Black-owned businesses with paid employees were located in the City of Detroit in January 2021. Six, or 19 percent, of the businesses were located in suburban Southfield, including the largest Black-owned business with paid employees (the Piston Group). The one Black-owned business with paid employees that was established—that is, after bankruptcy ended in 2014—was ACE Petroleum. Black-owned businesses are still extremely underrepresented in Detroit after bankruptcy. Only one new Black-owned business was founded after the city's bankruptcy ended in 2014. Only 32 large African American-owned businesses existed in Wayne, Oakland, and Macomb Counties with half of the businesses located in the City of Detroit. Most of the businesses were associated with and dependent on the auto industry to a certain extent. Very few were in the construction industry. Where this information was provided, Black-owned businesses with paid employees had a total of 8,674 employees in January 2021.

Hispanics are disproportionately more likely to own smaller businesses and pay more for access to capital than non Hispanic white-owned businesses, due in part to systemic racial discrimination (US Bureau of the Census, 2015). Like Black business owners, new businesses owned by Hispanics are more likely to be discouraged from applying for loans and are more likely to have their applications denied by banks compared to non Hispanic white owners.

Most of the PPP loans were given to white-owned businesses. The municipalities receiving the largest number of businesses were Detroit that received nine and suburban Troy that received seven. Of the 45 businesses that received the PPP loans, only one is Hispanic-owned: Ideal Contracting Company. It is engaged in commercial and institutional building construction. It is located in Detroit. It received $10 million and maintained 417 jobs. One company was Black and is located in Detroit: Detroit Manufacturing Systems. It received $8,185,662 and maintained 500 jobs. It is engaged in motor vehicle seating and interior trim manufacturing. Thus, neither Black-owned businesses or Hispanic-owned businesses reduced the Black and Hispanic disparity in business ownership and became more representative after bankruptcy.

7

Racial Inequality in Student Academic Achievement Levels: A Neighborhood Solution to the Problem

Introduction

Since the City of Detroit came out of bankruptcy on December 11, 2014, a major question of many Black parents living in the city—where their children *must* attend schools—is whether their children, who are attending racially segregated schools, are receiving an equal education to white students living in Wayne County (outside of the city), Macomb County, and Oakland County. The objective of this chapter is to answer this question using the most appropriate data and methods. Much data were obtained from the *Educational Opportunity Project* at Stanford University (Reardon et al, 2022). The researcher there used public school test scores in grades 3–8 from 2008–9 through 2017–18 to create the first comprehensive database on educational opportunity in the US. For this chapter, the data used from the Stanford project database focus on overall average district test scores for Black, white, and Hispanic students. Student scores are compared to the national average test scores.

Calculating the national average test scores

The *Educational Opportunity Project* first calculated the mean test score in each school, district, county, metropolitan statistical area, commuting zone, and State for all students and by student subgroups (gender, race/ethnicity, and economic disadvantage). Low test scores indicated low educational opportunity and high test scores indicated high educational opportunity. The *Educational Opportunity Project* data also revealed learning rates, which explore how much students learn each year, to see how the nation's schools are contributing to educational opportunity and trends in test scores. In turn, these scores revealed how much average test scores are changing each year and provided an insight into where educational opportunities are improving or declining. The following section indicates overall average test scores, test scores for Black, white, and Hispanic students for a racial comparison, and poor and nonpoor students for a class comparison for Detroit and selected suburban school districts. I begin with the Detroit public schools community district.

Detroit public schools community district

Overall average test scores: −2.68
Black students: −2.76; white students: −2.51; Hispanic students: −2.31; poor students: −2.78; nonpoor students: −1.98

Educational opportunity overview

Based on the data that compare all districts in the US, the *Educational Opportunity Project* concluded that the Detroit school district is a district where test scores are lower than the US average and test scores have been declining over time. The socioeconomic status of the Detroit school district is far below the national average. Compared to school districts with a similar socioeconomic status, the test scores in the Detroit school district are lower and have been declining faster than test scores in other districts. The *Educational Opportunity Project* concluded that the district shows declining educational opportunity for students. Test scores *decreased* by an average of 0.09 grade levels each year from 2009 to 2018. Average scores have *decreased* by 0.07 grade levels, less than those of districts with a similar socioeconomic status. The *Educational Opportunity Project* concluded that the average student test scores are influenced by home environments, early childhood experiences, community resources, and schools. The trend or change in average student test scores from one year to the next is a good indicator for Detroit parents to know whether educational opportunities are improving or declining in Detroit.

Where the trend is positive, students' opportunities to learn are improving. The opposite is also true. The trend in Detroit is negative. In terms of learning rates, students learn 1.7 percent less each grade than the US average. Opportunities may improve over time because of changes in school quality or changes in family resources, home environments, early childhood experiences, and/or community resources.

Another database—the Public School Review online database—was used to compare the suburban districts selected with the Detroit district, with additional variables to those of the *Educational Opportunity Project* at Stanford. For the 2021–2 school year, there were 109 public schools serving

49,593 students in the Detroit Public Schools Community School District. There were 40,728 Black students (82 percent), 6,598 Hispanic students (13 percent), and only 1,199 white students (3 percent). Public schools in this district have an average math proficiency score of 12 percent (versus the Michigan public school average of 39 percent) and a reading proficiency score of 18 percent (versus the 49 percent Statewide average).

The Detroit public schools community school district is ranked in the bottom 50 percent of all 864 school districts in Michigan (based on combined math and reading proficiency testing data) for the 2018–19 school year. The district's graduation rate of 76 percent has decreased from 78 percent since the 2018–19 school year. Revenue per student of $9,413 in this school district is less than the state median of $14,094. The school district revenue per student has grown by 6 percent over four school years. The school district's spending per student of $8,792 is less than the state median of $13,691 and has stayed relatively flat over four school years (Public School Review, 2022).

I now focus on a number of school districts in suburban Detroit to see how educational opportunity varies between school districts and whether the Detroit public schools community school district is unequal to the suburban school districts, thereby denying students in the Detroit school district an equal education after bankruptcy. The school districts selected were those in municipalities of 10,000 population or more and where at least 20 Black and Hispanic applicants had applied for a home mortgage loan to purchase a home in the school districts in 2015 and 2020 (Consumer Financial Protection Bureau, 2015, 2020).

The Black and Hispanic applicants were applying to these suburban districts over other suburban districts. Home mortgage applications indicate their *preferences* for the school district and their desire for homeownership there. In Michigan, unless school districts participate in a school of choice program, students must attend the school in the district where they live— that is the law.

Selected suburban Detroit school districts

Allen Park school district

Overall average test scores: −0.11
Black students: −1.93; white students: +0.01; Hispanic students: −0.8; poor students: +0.02; nonpoor students: +0.02

Educational opportunity overview

In the Allen Park district, the test scores are roughly the same as the US average.

Test scores are relatively stable over time. Unlike the Detroit school district, the socioeconomic status of the Allen Park district is above average. Compared to districts with a similar socioeconomic status, the test scores are lower and learning rates are lower. However, the test scores are staying roughly the same over time. Compared to the Detroit school district, overall test scores are higher for students from each of the three racial groups. Black, white, and Hispanic students have higher average test scores. Test scores are also higher for both poor and nonpoor students. *Home Mortgage Disclosure* data, which provide data on whether an applicant who applies for a mortgage loan is denied or approved to purchase a home, showed that 22 Black home seekers and 74 Hispanic home seekers applied for mortgage loans to live in Allen Park in 2015, and 75 Black and 144 Hispanics applied for mortgage loans in 2020. The school district had 3,105 white students (81 percent), 492 Hispanic students (13 percent), and 94 Black students (3 percent). The revenue per student of $11,689 in this school district is less than the state median of $14,094 and has stayed relatively flat over four school years.

The Allen Park school district is ranked within the top 50 percent of all 864 school districts in Michigan (based on combined math and reading proficiency testing data) for the 2018–19 school year. The school district's graduation rate of 87 percent has increased from 85 percent over five school years (see http://www.appublicschools.com). For the 2021–2 school year, there were six public schools serving 3,820 students in the Allen Park school district. The district's average testing ranking is 7/10, which is in the top 50 percent of public schools in Michigan. Public schools in this district have an average math proficiency score of 38 percent (versus the Michigan public school average of 39 percent) and a reading proficiency score of 50 percent (versus the 49 percent statewide average) (Allen Park Public Schools, n.d.). The scores are much higher than the 12 percent for math and 18 percent for reading in the Detroit school district.

Dearborn school district

Overall average test scores: –0.65
Black students: –2.03; white students: –0.42; Hispanic students: –1.15; poor students: –1.07; nonpoor students: + 0.76

Educational opportunity overview

In the Dearborn school district, test scores are lower than the US average; however, learning rates are faster than the US average. Test scores are improving over time. The district's socioeconomic status is about average compared to districts with similar test scores socioeconomic status, and learning rates are higher.

Based on *Home Mortgage Disclosure* data from 2015, 49 Black home seekers and 53 Hispanic home seekers applied for mortgage loans to live in Dearborn in 2015. In 2020, 246 Black home seekers and 216 Hispanic home seekers applied for mortgage loans in Dearborn. For the 2021–2 school year, there were 38 public schools serving 20,814 students in the Dearborn school district. The school district had 19,574 white students (94 percent), 610 Black students (3 percent), and 385 Hispanic students (2 percent).

Geographically, the Dearborn school district borders the Detroit school district. The district's average testing ranking is 7/10, which is in the top 50 percent of public schools in Michigan. Public schools in the district have an average math proficiency score of 40 percent (versus the Michigan public school average of 39 percent) and a reading proficiency score of 47 percent (versus the 49 percent statewide average). The graduation rate is 96 percent compared to the state average of 85 percent (http://www. appublicschools.com). The revenue per student of $13,488 in this school district is less than the state median of $14,094 and has stayed relatively flat over four school years. The district's spending per student of $12,801 is less than the state median of $13,691, but has grown by 7 percent over four school years.

Eastpointe school district

Overall average test scores: −2.67
Black students: −3.06; white students: −1.44;
poor students: −2.86; nonpoor students: −1.91

Educational opportunity overview

Test scores in the Eastpointe school district are lower and learning rates are slower than the US average at 23 percent. Test scores have been declining over time. Socioeconomic status is below the national average. Compared to districts with a similar socioeconomic status, test scores are lower, learning rates are lower, and test scores have been declining faster.

Despite low test scores, according to the *Home Mortgage Disclosure Act* data, 355 Black home seekers, but only four Hispanic home seekers, applied for mortgage loans to purchase a home in Eastpointe in 2015. In 2020, 638 Black home seekers and 24 Hispanic home seekers applied for mortgage loans. School data provided by the Public School Review show that for the 2021–2 school year, there were 809 Black students (79 percent), 464 white students (16 percent), and 11 Hispanic students (1 percent). The demographic composition of the district is very different from the state demographic distribution by race.

Eastpointe is ranked in the bottom 50 percent of all 694 school districts in Michigan (based on combined math and reading proficiency testing data) for the 2018–19 school year. The school district's graduation rate of 67 percent is less than the Michigan average of 86 percent and has decreased from 71 percent over five school years. Public high schools in Eastpointe have an average math proficiency score of 9 percent (versus the Michigan public high school average of 36 percent) and a reading proficiency score of 16 percent (versus the 49 percent statewide average). These scores are even lower than the scores for the Detroit school district. Eastpointe borders the City of Detroit. The revenue per student of $13,466 in this district is less than the state median of $14,094, but has grown by 11 percent over four school years. The school district's spending per student of $12,276 is less than the state median of $13,691 and has stayed relatively flat over four school years (Public School Review, 2022). The data clearly shows that not all suburban Detroit school districts score highly in terms of academic achievement.

Lincoln Park school district

Overall average test scores: −1.82
Black students: −2.59; white students: −1.54; Hispanic students: −1.92; poor students: −2.01
Lincoln Park school district did not provide data on non poor student test scores.

Educational opportunity overview

Test scores in the Lincoln Park school district are lower and learning rates are lower than the US average. Test scores have been declining over time. Socioeconomic status is below the national average.

Despite these results, according to the *Home Mortgage Disclosure* data, 58 Black home seekers and 106 Hispanic home seekers applied for mortgage loans to purchase a home in the Lincoln Park school district in 2015. In 2020, 139 Black home seekers and 269 Hispanic home seekers applied for mortgage loans. For the 2021–2 school year, there were ten public schools serving 4,816 students in the Lincoln Park school district. The district had 2,033 Hispanic students (42 percent), 1,914 white students (40 percent); and 579 Black students (12 percent). The district's average testing ranking is 3/10, which is in the bottom 50 percent of public schools in Michigan.

Public schools in the Lincoln Park school district had an average math proficiency score of 19 percent (versus the Michigan public school average of 39 percent) and a reading proficiency score of 32 percent (versus the 49 percent statewide average). The district is ranked in the bottom 50 percent of all 864 school districts in Michigan (based on combined math and reading proficiency testing data) for the 2018–19 school year. The district's graduation rate of 78 percent has decreased from 79 percent over five school years. The revenue per student of $14,586 is higher than the state median of $14,094 and has grown by 6 percent over four school years. The district's spending per student of $13,871 is higher than the state median of $13,691 and has grown by 5 percent over four school years (Public School Review, 2022).

Livonia Public School district

Overall average test scores: +0.59
Black students: −1.72; white students: +0.8; Hispanic students: +0.19; poor students: −0.79; nonpoor students: +1.19

Educational opportunity overview

Test scores in the Livonia Public School district are higher; however, test scores have been declining over time compared to the US average. Socioeconomic status is above average. Compared to districts with a similar socioeconomic status, test scores are lower, learning rates are roughly equal, and test scores are falling more quickly.

According to the *Home Mortgage Disclosure Act* data, 139 Black home seekers and 84 Hispanic home seekers applied for mortgage loans to live in the Livonia school district in 2015. In 2020, 237 Black home seekers and 160 Hispanic home seekers applied for mortgage loans. For the 2021–2 school year, there were 27 public schools serving 14,029 students in the district. The district had 10,910 white students (78 percent), 1,286 Black students (9 percent), and 678 Hispanic students (5 percent). The district's average testing ranking is 9/10, which is in the top 20 percent of public schools in Michigan.

Public schools in the Livonia Public School district have an average math proficiency score of 51 percent (versus the Michigan public school average of 39 percent) and a reading proficiency score of 59 percent (versus the 49 percent statewide average). The district's graduation rate of 94 percent has increased from 91 percent over five school years. The revenue per student of $14,736 is higher than the state median of $14,094 and has stayed relatively level over four school years. The district's spending per student of $15,321 is higher than the state median of $13,691, but has declined by 5 percent over four school years.

Novi Community School district

Overall average test scores: +2.38
Black students: −0.55; white students: +2.14; Hispanic students: +0.58; poor students: N/A; nonpoor students: −0.19

Educational opportunity overview

Test scores in the Novi Community School district are higher and learning rates are faster than the US average. Test scores are improving over time. Socioeconomic status is far above the national average. Compared to districts with a similar socioeconomic status, test scores are roughly equal, learning rates are roughly equal, and test scores are staying roughly the same.

According to the *Home Mortgage Disclosure Act* data, 134 Black home seekers and 53 Hispanic home seekers applied for mortgage loans to live in Novi in 2015. In 2020, 227 Black home seekers and 175 Hispanic home seekers applied for mortgage loans. For the 2021–2 school year, there were 12 public schools serving 6,552 students in the district. The district had 2,748 white students (42 percent), 511 Black students (8 percent), and 218 Hispanic students (3 percent). The district's average testing ranking is 10/10, which is in the top 1 percent of public schools in Michigan.

Public schools in the Novi Community School district have an average math proficiency score of 76 percent (versus the Michigan public school average of 39 percent) and a reading proficiency score of 73 percent (versus the 49 percent statewide average) (Public School Review, 2002). The district is ranked in the top 5 percent of all 864 school districts in Michigan (based on combined math and reading proficiency testing data) for the 2018–19 school year. Its graduation rate of 95 percent has decreased from 96 percent over five school years.

Oak Park school district

Overall average test scores −2.59
Black students: −2.59; white students: −2.45; Hispanic students: N/A; poor students: −2.65; nonpoor students: −2.22

Educational opportunity overview

Test scores in the Oak Park school district are lower and learning rates are slower than the US average. Test scores have been declining over time. Socioeconomic status is below the national average. Compared to districts with a similar socioeconomic status, test scores are lower, learning rates are lower, and test scores have been declining faster.

Regardless of the test scores, according to the *Home Mortgage Disclosure* data, 341 Black home seekers and nine Hispanic home seekers applied for mortgage loans to live in Oak Park in 2015. In 2020, 433 Black home seekers and 29 Hispanic home seekers applied for mortgage loans. For the 2021–2 school year, there were eight public schools serving 5,109 students in the district. The district had 4,927 Black students (97 percent), 150 white students (3 percent), and 13 Hispanic students (0.25 percent). The district's average testing ranking is 1/10, which is in the bottom 50 percent of public schools in Michigan.

Public schools in the Oak Park school district have an average math proficiency score of 11 percent (versus the Michigan public school average of 39 percent) and a reading proficiency score of 20 percent (versus the 49 percent statewide average). The math scores are similar to the 12 percent math scores for the Detroit school district. The reading scores are only slightly higher than the 18 percent for Detroit. The district's graduation rate of 61 percent has increased from 58 percent over five school years. The revenue per student of $12,229 in the district is less than the state median of $14,094 and has stayed relatively flat over four school years (Public School Review, 2002). The district's spending per student of $11,438 is less than the state median of $13,691, but has grown by 5 percent over four school years.

Pontiac City school district

Overall average test scores: −2.59
Black students: −2.95; white students: −1.73; Hispanic students: −2.17; poor students and nonpoor students: +0.61

Educational opportunity overview

Test scores in the Pontiac City school district are lower and learning rates are slower than the US average. Test scores have been declining over time. Socioeconomic status is far below the national average. Compared to districts with a similar socioeconomic status, test scores are lower, learning rates are lower, and test scores have been declining faster.

Regardless of these test scores, according to the *Home Mortgage Disclosure Act* data, 293 Black home seekers and 62 Hispanic home seekers applied for mortgage loans to purchase a home in Pontiac in 2015. In 2020, 387 Black home seekers and 98 Hispanic home seekers applied for mortgage loans. For the 2021–2 school year, there were 11 public schools serving 4,175 students in the district. The district had 2,190 Black students (52 percent), 1,358 Hispanic students (33 percent), and 323 white students (8 percent). The district's average testing ranking is 2/10, which is in the bottom 50 percent of public schools in Michigan.

Public schools in Pontiac have an average math proficiency score of 13 percent (versus the Michigan public school average of 39 percent) and a reading proficiency score of 20 percent (versus the 49 percent statewide average). These scores are similar to those in the Detroit school district.

Thus, if parents moved to Pontiac from Detroit, this would be unlikely to result in an improvement in their children's test scores. The district's graduation rate of 64 percent has increased from 55 percent over five school years (Public School Review, 2022), but is even lower than that for Detroit (76 percent). The revenue per student of $17,474 is higher than the state median of $14,094 and has stayed relatively flat over four school years. The district's spending per student of $18,264 is higher than the state median of $13,691 and has stayed relatively flat over four school years.

Romulus Community School district

Overall average test scores: −1.34
Black students: −1.54; white students: −0.7; Hispanic students: −1.48; poor students: −1.72; nonpoor students: −0.2

Educational opportunity overview

Test scores in Romulus Community School district are lower and learning rates are slower than the US average. Test scores have been declining over time. Socioeconomic status is below the national average. Compared to districts with a similar socioeconomic status, test scores are lower, learning rates are lower, and test scores have been declining faster.

Regardless of these data, according to the *Home Mortgage Disclosure Act* data, 284 Black home seekers and 14 Hispanic home seekers applied for mortgage loans to purchase a home in Romulus in 2015. In 2020, 541 Black home seekers and 30 Hispanic home seekers applied for mortgage loans. For the 2021–2 school year, there were eight public schools serving 2,737 students in the district. The district had 1,960 Black students (72 percent), 115 Hispanic students (4 percent), and 567 white students (21 percent). The district's average testing ranking is 3/10, which is in the bottom 50 percent of public schools in Michigan.

Public schools in the Romulus Community School district have an average math proficiency score of 23 percent (versus the Michigan public school average of 39 percent) and a reading proficiency score of 31 percent (versus the 49 percent statewide average). The district is ranked in the bottom 50 percent of all 864 school districts in Michigan (based on combined math and reading proficiency testing data) for the 2018–19 school year. The district's graduation rate of 65 percent has decreased from 71 percent over five school years. The revenue per student of $15,628 is higher than the state median of $14,094 and has grown by 10 percent over four school years. The district's spending per student of $12,684 is less than the state median of $13,691 and has declined by 11 percent over four school years (Public School Review, 2022).

Roseville Community School district

Overall average test scores: −1.62
Black students: −2.44; white students: −0.7; Hispanic students: −1.48;
poor students: −1.72; nonpoor students: −0.2

Educational opportunity overview

Test scores in the Roseville Community School district are lower and learning rates are slower than the US average. Test scores have been declining over time. Socioeconomic status is below the national average. Compared to districts with a similar socioeconomic status, test scores are lower, learning rates are lower, and test scores have been declining faster.

Despite this, according to *Home Mortgage Disclosure Act* data, 133 Black home seekers and 24 Hispanic home seekers applied for mortgage loans to purchase a home in Roseville in 2015. In 2020, 308 Black home seekers and 37 Hispanic home seekers applied for mortgage loans. In the 2021–2 school year, there were 11 public schools serving 4,720 students in the district. The district had 2,588 white students (55 percent), 1,593 Black students (34 percent), and 98 Hispanic students (2 percent). The district's average testing ranking is 2/10, which is in the bottom 50 percent of public schools in Michigan.

Public schools in the Roseville Community School district have an average math proficiency score of 19 percent (versus the Michigan public school average of 39 percent) and a reading proficiency score of 31 percent (versus the 49 percent statewide average). The district is ranked in the bottom 50 percent of all 864 school districts in Michigan (based on combined math and reading proficiency testing data) for the 2018–19 school year. The district's graduation rate of 86 percent has stayed relatively flat over five school years. The revenue per student of $12,889 in this district is less than the state median of $14,094, but has grown by 5 percent over four school years. The district's spending per student of $12,441 is less than the state median of $13,691 and has stayed relatively flat over four school years (Public School Review, 2022).

Southfield Public School district

Overall average test scores: −1.61
Black students: −1.69; white students: +0.26; Hispanic students: −1.42;
poor students: −1.98; nonpoor students: −0.8

Educational opportunity overview

Test scores in the Southfield Public School district are lower and learning rates are slower than US average. Test scores have been declining over time.

Socioeconomic status is about average. Compared to districts with a similar socioeconomic status, test scores are lower, learning rates are lower, and test scores have been declining faster.

Despite this, according to the *Home Mortgage Disclosure Act* data, 1,434 Black home seekers and 15 Hispanic home seekers applied for mortgage loans to purchase a home in Southfield in 2015. In 2020, 1,893 Black home seekers and 132 Hispanic home seekers applied for mortgage loans. Southfield is located on the border of the Detroit school district. In the 2021–2 school year, there were 14 public schools serving 6,131 students in the district. The district had 5,781 Black students (94 percent), but only 154 white students (3 percent) and 83 Hispanic students (1 percent). The district's average testing ranking is 3/10, which is in the bottom 50 percent of public schools in Michigan.

Public schools in the Southfield Public School district have an average math proficiency score of 20 percent (versus the Michigan public school average of 39 percent) and a reading proficiency score of 36 percent (versus the 49 percent statewide average). The district is ranked in the bottom 50 percent of all 864 school districts in Michigan (based on combined math and reading proficiency testing data) for the 2018–19 school year. The district's graduation rate of 88 percent has decreased from 93 percent over five school years. The revenue per student of $16,548 is higher than the state median of $14,094 and has stayed relatively flat over four school years. The district's spending per student of $15,470 is higher than the state median of $13,691 and has stayed relatively flat over four school years (Public School Review, 2022).

Taylor school district

Overall average test scores: −1.18
Black students: −1.88; white students: −0.82; Hispanic students: −1.15; poor students: −1.51; nonpoor students: −0.16

Educational opportunity overview

Test scores in the Taylor school district are lower but learning rates are faster than the US average. Test scores have been improving over time. Socioeconomic status is below the national average. Compared to districts with a similar socioeconomic status, test scores are lower, learning rates are higher, and test scores are improving faster.

The educational data show that test scores are lower than average in the US, but they are improving faster; Black home seekers may have been influenced by that. *Home Mortgage Disclosure Act* data show that 119 Black home seekers applied for mortgage loans to purchase a home in this school district in 2015. In 2020, 292 Black home seekers and 142 Hispanic home seekers applied for mortgage loans. For the 2021–2 school year, there were 14 public schools serving 6,280 students in the district. The district had 3,360 white students (54 percent), 1,850 Black students (30 percent), and 555 Hispanic students (9 percent). The district's average testing ranking is 3/10, which is in the bottom 50 percent of public schools in Michigan.

Public schools in the Taylor school district have an average math proficiency score of 20 percent (versus the Michigan public school average of 39 percent) and a reading proficiency score of 31 percent (versus the 49 percent statewide average). The district is ranked in the bottom 50 percent of all 864 school districts in Michigan (based on combined math and reading proficiency testing data) for the 2018–19 school year. The district's graduation rate of 65 percent has decreased from 69 percent over five school years. Its graduation rate is lower than the Detroit graduation rate of 76 percent. The revenue per student of $13,811 in the district is less than the state median of $14,094, but has grown by 9 percent over four school years. The district's spending per student of $13,638 is slightly less than the state median of $13,691, but has grown by 5 percent over four school years (Public School Review, 2022).

Troy school district

Overall average test scores: +2.4
Black students: −0.32; white students: +1.92; Hispanic students: +0.78; poor students: −0.1; nonpoor students: +2.74

Educational opportunity overview

Test scores in the Troy school district are higher and learning rates are faster than the US average. Test scores have been improving over time. Socioeconomic status is far above the national average. Compared to districts with a similar socioeconomic status, test scores are roughly equal, learning rates are roughly equal, and test scores are staying roughly the same.

The Troy school district has a very high level of academic achievement. This may have influenced the 871 Black applicants who applied for mortgage loans in 2015 to purchase a home to live in Troy. There were fewer than 20 Hispanic applicants. In 2020, 120 Black home seekers and 163 Hispanic home seekers applied for mortgage loans. For the 2021–2 school year, there were 22 public schools serving 12,464 students in the district. The district had 6,708 white students (54 percent), 607 Black students (5 percent), and 437 Hispanic (4 percent). The district's average testing ranking is 10/10, which is in the top 1 percent of public schools in Michigan.

Public schools in the Troy school district have an average math proficiency score of 71 percent (versus the Michigan public school average of 39 percent) and a reading proficiency score of 77 percent (versus the 49 percent statewide average). The district is ranked in the top 5 percent of all 864 school districts in Michigan (based on combined math and reading proficiency testing data) for the 2018–19 school year. The district's graduation rate of 92 percent has increased from 91 percent over five school years. The revenue per student of $15,020 is higher than the state median of $14,094 and has grown by 8 percent over four school years. The district's spending per student of $14,735 is higher than the state median of $13,691 and has grown by 5 percent over four school years.

Warren Consolidated School district

Overall average test scores: −0.87
Black students: −2.16; white students: −0.69; Hispanic students: −0.82; poor students: −1.61; nonpoor students: +0.18

Educational opportunity overview

Test scores in the Warren School district are lower and learning rates are slower than the US average. Test scores have remained relatively stable over time. Socioeconomic status is about average. Compared to districts with a similar socioeconomic status, test scores are lower, learning rates are lower, and test scores have stayed roughly the same.

Despite this, according to the *Home Mortgage Disclosure Act* data, 286 Black home seekers applied for mortgage loans to purchase a home in the district in 2015. There were fewer than 20 Hispanic applicants. In 2020, there were 894 Black home seekers and 130 Hispanic home seekers who applied for mortgage loans. For the 2021–2 school year, there were 25 public schools serving 13,873 students in the district. The district had 9,618 white students (69 percent), 1,782 Black students (13 percent), and 217 Hispanic students (2 percent). The district's average testing ranking is 5/10, which is in the bottom 50 percent of public schools in Michigan.

Public schools in the Warren Consolidated School district have an average math proficiency score of 32 percent (versus the Michigan public school average of 39 percent) and a reading proficiency score of 47 percent (versus the 49 percent statewide average). The district is ranked in the bottom 50 percent of all 864 school districts in Michigan (based on combined math and reading proficiency testing data) for the 2018–19 school year. The district's graduation rate of 88 percent has increased from 80 percent over five school years. The revenue per student of $13,875 in the district is less than the state median of $14,094, but has grown by 5 percent over four school years. The district's spending per student of $15,776 is higher than the state median of $13,691 and has grown by 14 percent over four school years (Public School Review, 2022).

Summary

The Stanford method compares average test scores in the nation with test scores in school districts across the country. The districts I selected had a population of at least 10,000 and at least 20 Black and Hispanic applications were made to financial institutions to purchase a home in the district in 2015 and 2020 based on the *Home Mortgage Disclosure Act* data.

A total of 14 suburban school districts were examined in Wayne, Oakland, and Macomb Counties to compare them with the Detroit school district. The districts were very diverse in test scores and racial composition. The number of districts where scores were above the national average was three. They ranged from 42 percent white to 78 percent white. One school district that had an average test score that was the same as the US average had a white population of 94 percent. Of the 11 districts that had test scores below the national average, six districts were majority-Black and four were majority-white. One had a Hispanic population of 42 percent.

In the three test score comparisons, racial composition seemed to have been a factor influencing the test scores. The test scores differed by the race of the students. No district had Black students who tested above the average test scores for the US. Although below the national average, Black students tested highest in Troy (which is 54 percent white) with a test score of –0.32. Black students tested lowest in the suburban school district of Eastpointe, a district that borders Detroit, where the average test scores were –3.06 compared to –2.76 for Detroit. The Black population of Eastpointe is 79 percent compared to 82 percent in Detroit.

Unlike Black students, white students had test scores above the national average in five school districts (Novi, Troy, Livonia, Southfield, and Allen Park). Race appears to be an issue here: three of the five school districts were predominantly white, and one was predominantly Black (Southfield, which borders Detroit). White student test scores ranged from +2.14 in Novi to –2.51 in Detroit. There were three districts in which the average test scores of Hispanic students were above the national average: Troy (+0.78), Novi (+0.58), and Livonia (+0.19). Hispanic student test scores ranged from +0.78 in Troy to –2.31 in Detroit. Troy is 4 percent Hispanic and Detroit is 13 percent Hispanic.

The racial segregation of school districts

Black and white students, and Hispanic and white students, are segregated by school district.

When the three racial student groups are distributed over school districts, the results reveal that they are not evenly distributed. Black students are very overrepresented in Detroit and very underrepresented in Dearborn, Livonia, and Warren. Based on the index of dissimilarity (where an index of zero = no segregation and the higher the index, the higher the degree of Black and white student segregation), the degree of Black versus white segregation is 82. This is very high since an index of 100 = complete segregation. Hispanic students are overrepresented in the school districts of Detroit, Lincoln Park, Pontiac, and, to a lesser degree, Southfield. On the other hand, Hispanics are underrepresented in Dearborn, Warren, and Livonia. School district segregation measured by the Black and white students between Hispanic and white students revealed a figure of 70. Thus, Hispanic students are not as segregated from non Hispanic white students as Black students are.

The race of students matters in terms of which district they attend school. White students attend districts that are ranked higher in terms of test scores and resources received from the State of Michigan than districts attended by Black and Hispanic students. Since students must attend school districts where they live and white students are more likely to live in neighborhoods with school districts that are higher in socioeconomic characteristics compared to Black and Hispanic students, students are racially segregated in separate and unequal schools.

Table 7.1 shows the extent of separate and unequal student attendance in Metropolitan Detroit. Notice the unequal percentage of all white students attending school in the very high socioeconomic characteristic (SEP 5) neighborhoods, and the high level of Black and Hispanic students attending

Table 7.1: Black and white students attend schools in separate and unequal neighborhoods in Metropolitan Detroit

SEP	Percentage of white students	Percentage of Black students	Absolute difference
5	22.2	4.4	17.8
4	30.1	10.9	19.2
3	29.1	17.9	11.2
2	15.3	33.9	18.6
1	3.3	32.8	29.5
Total	100	100	96.3

Note: 96.3 divided by 2 is 48.15 or the index of dissimilarity on residential segregation in neighborhood characteristics where Black and white students attend school.

Sources: Michigan Department of Education Racial Census Report by School Districts for 2020–1; United States Bureau of the Census (2022) *American Community Survey Five-Year Estimates, 2016–20.*

Table 7.2: Hispanic and white students attend schools in separate and unequal neighborhoods in Metropolitan Detroit

SEP	Percentage of white students	Percentage of Hispanic students	Absolute difference
5	22.2	7.7	14.5
4	30.1	13.2	16.9
3	29.1	24.4	4.7
2	15.3	19.0	3.7
1	3.3	35.7	32.4
Total	100	100	72.2

Note: 72.2 divided by 2 is 36.1 or the index of dissimilarity on residential segregation in neighborhood characteristics where Hispanic and white students attend school.

Sources: calculated by the author from data obtained from Michigan Department of Education Racial Census Report by School Districts for 2020–1; United States Bureau of the Census (2022) *American Community Survey Five-Year Estimates, 2016–20.*

school in the very low (SEP 1) and low socioeconomic characteristic (SEP 2) neighborhoods.

The decision to attend the districts where the best schools are located is not one each Black and Hispanic parent can make; such a decision is made by the State of Michigan's Department of Education with the support of the Michigan Legislature and the Governor. These policy makers have restricted students, regardless of school quality, to attending schools in the districts where their parents live.

This was also supported by the decision of the US Supreme Court in the *Milliken v. Bradley* case in 1974, which involved a fight for equal access to quality schools due to inequality between the schools in the City of Detroit and those in the suburbs. The schools were unequal in terms of academic achievement and school resources but the court wanted to know whether the suburban school districts were responsible for school segregation. Each predominantly white suburb concluded that it was not responsible. Yet most Black parents in Detroit had been prevented from living in Detroit's suburbs due to racist housing discrimination by many white real estate brokers, white apartment managers, white builders, and white mortgage lenders. As a result, a State of Michigan policy that Black students still had to attend school in their neighborhood resulted in segregated and unequal school quality and resources (Nieuwenhuis, Kleinepier and van Ham, 2021).

The 1974 Supreme Court decision and the State of Michigan's policy restricting Black and Hispanic students to attending school in the neighborhood where they live have contributed to the continued racial segregation of schools and racial inequality in access to resources today in Metropolitan Detroit (Darden et al, 1987; Darden and Thomas, 2013; Nadworny and Turner, 2019). The analysis conducted thus far here has supported this conclusion, showing that white students are disproportionately enrolled in districts that score higher on tests.

The racial segregation of Black and Hispanic students in Macomb County

According to the Michigan Department of Education (2021), there were 80,194 white students (67 percent), 22,506 African American students (18.6 percent) and 4,322 Hispanic students (3.6 percent) in Macomb County. If the distribution of African American and Hispanic students was even across the school districts, each district would have 18.6 percent of African American students and 3.6 percent of Hispanic students. A higher percentage than this indicates the degree of racial segregation. According to the Michigan Department of Education Racial Census Report by school districts, African American students are overrepresented in the school districts and academies, shown in Table 7.3 (note that the percentages are over 18.6 percent).

Black students are underrepresented in other Macomb County school districts and academies. As a result, the racial segregation between Black and white students as measured by the index of dissimilarity is 49.7.

Table 7.3: Schools/academies where Black students are overrepresented in Macomb County District

District/academy	Black students (%)
Fitzgerald Public School district	22.6
Macomb Academy	23.2
Connor Creek Academy	98.1
Huron Academy	25.9
Arts Academy in the Woods	33.6
Mount Clemens Montessori Academy	28.6
Prevail Academy	65.5
Academy of Warren	96.9
Research Charter Academy	86.0
Macomb Montessori Academy	90.8
Rising Stars Academy	28.5
Center Line Preparatory Academy	76.6

Source: Michigan Department of Education (2021).

Racial segregation between Hispanic students and non Hispanic white students

Hispanic students represent 3.6 percent of all students in Macomb County. They are overrepresented in the school districts and academies, shown in Table 7.4.

As a result of Hispanic students' overrepresentation in these districts and academies and their underrepresentation in other districts and academies, the Hispanic student segregation of non Hispanic white students in Macomb County was 16.5 in 2021 based on the index of dissimilarity. The level of segregation was less than the segregation of Black students from white students (Michigan Department of Education, 2021).

The racial segregation of Black students from white students in Oakland County

According to the Michigan Department of Education Racial Census Report by School Districts for 2020 (Michigan Department of Education, 2021), there were 35,804 Black students in Oakland County. Black students accounted for 20 percent of students in the Oakland County districts. If Black students were evenly distributed over the districts, each district would have

Table 7.4: Schools/academies where Hispanic students are overrepresented in Macomb County District

District/academy	Hispanic students (%)
Centerline Public School district	4.7
Clintondale Community School district	55.8
Chippewa Valley School district	11.3
Fitzgerald Public School district	39.7
Fraser Public School district	14.4
Lakeshore Public School district	14.7
Lakeview Public School district	13.4
L'Anse Ceruse Public School	14.6
Mount Clemens Public School district	8.3
New Haven Public School district	17.7
Richmond Public School district	5.9
Romeo Public School district	9.0
Prevail Academy	6.5

Source: Michigan Department of Education (2021).

20 percent Black students; a higher percentage than this would mean that the district would be somewhat segregated. According to the Michigan Department of Education Racial Census Report, Black students were overrepresented—that is, they exceeded 20 percent in the districts and academies, shown in Table 7.5.

Due to Black student overrepresentation in these school districts and academies, and the underrepresentation in other school districts and academies in Oakland County, the racial segregation of Black students as measured by the index of dissimilarity was 65, which is considered to be high.

Table 7.5: Schools/academies where Black students are overrepresented in Oakland County District

District/academy	Black students (%)
Ferndale school district	62.6
Pontiac school district	51.3
Southfield school district	94.2
Avondale school district	27.4
Clarenceville school district	35.2
Hazel Park school district	40.0
Madison school district	46.7
West Bloomfield school district	36.0
Great Lakes Academy	81.6
Oakside Scholars Charter Academy	45.3
Dr. Joseph Pollack Academic Center of Excellence	98.2
Walton Charter Academy	36.0
Advanced Technology Academy	74.4
Arts and Technology Academy of Pontiac	78.4
Bradford Academy	98.4
Laura's Academy	93.0
Life Skills Center of Pontiac	73.5
Crescent Academy	98.6
Great Oaks Academy	85.0
Michigan Mathematics and Science Academy	79.4
Faxon Academy	67.7
Momentum Academy	33.0
Oakland FlexTech High School	22.0

Source: Michigan Department of Education (2021).

The racial segregation of Hispanic students from non Hispanic white students in Oakland County

Hispanic students account for 7 percent of the students in Oakland County. As such, a higher percentage than this would indicate a certain degree of segregation. According to the Michigan Department of Education Census of Students in School Districts by race for 2020 (Michigan Department of Education, 2021), Hispanic students are overrepresented in the school districts and academies, shown in Table 7.6.

Due to the overrepresentation of Hispanic students in certain districts and academies, as mentioned earlier in Oakland County, and their underrepresentation in other districts and academies, the segregation of Hispanic students from non Hispanic white students based on the index of dissimilarity is 50, which is lower than the segregation of Black students from non Hispanic white students in Oakland County.

The racial segregation of Black students from white students in Wayne County

According to the Michigan Department of Education Racial Census Report by School Districts for 2020 (Michigan Department of Education, 2021), there

Table 7.6: Schools/academies where Hispanic students are overrepresented in Oakland County District

District/academy	Hispanic students (%)
Pontiac school district	35.4
Avondale school district	11.1
Oxford school district	8.2
Farmington school district	24.9
Lamphere school district	9.7
Walled Lake Consolidated School district	8.8
Great Lakes Academy	10.5
Oakside Scholars Charter Academy	33.3
Walton Charter Academy	51.5
Advanced Technology Academy	20.6
Arts and Technology Academy of Pontiac	17.9
Life Skills Center of Pontiac	14.2
Momentum Academy	55.5
Waterford Montessori Academy	11.7

Source: Michigan Department of Education (2021).

were 110,497 Black students in Wayne County, representing 41.4 percent of all students. There were 114,151 non Hispanic white students, representing 42.7 percent of all students in Wayne County. As such, the County had a small difference in the total number of Black and white students. The key question related to equity and equal opportunity in education is the extent of racial segregation of Black and white students throughout Wayne County. If the percentage of Black students exceeds 41.4 percent in districts and academies (which is what they represent in the county), this overrepresentation will result in a degree of segregation. According to the Michigan Department of Education Racial Census of Students by School Districts (Michigan Department of Education, 2021), Black students are overrepresented in the districts and academies, shown in Table 7.7.

As a result of such a high level of Black overrepresentation (especially in academies) and underrepresentation in other districts and academies, Black students are very highly segregated from white students in Wayne County. The level of school segregation based on the index of dissimilarity is 77.2, which is very high.

The racial segregation of Hispanic and non Hispanic white students in Wayne County

According to the Michigan Department of Education Racial Census Report by School Districts for 2020 (Michigan Department of Education, 2021), there were 23,558 Hispanic students, representing 8.8 percent of the students in Wayne County; as such, a percentage higher than 8.8 in a school district would reflect overrepresentation of Hispanic students or segregation. The Michigan Department of Education Racial Census of Students by School Districts (Michigan Department of Education, 2021) show that Hispanic students were overrepresented in the school districts and academies, shown in Table 7.8.

Due to the overrepresentation of Hispanic students in these school districts and academies and their underrepresentation in other school districts and academies, Hispanic students are racially segregated in Wayne County. The level of school segregation based on the index of dissimilarity is 55. This is a moderate level of segregation that is lower than the very high index of dissimilarity for Black students in Wayne County (77.2).

Selected highly segregated school districts and charter schools in Wayne County and the academic consequences

The most segregated school district is Detroit public schools community school district, which is located in the City of Detroit. It has 50,644 students in grades PK, K–12 with a student-teacher ratio of 16 to 1. According

Table 7.7: Schools/academies where Black students are overrepresented in Wayne County District

District/academy	Black students (%)
Detroit Public School district	81.6
Detroit Public Safety Academy	98.4
James and Grace Lee Boggs School	58.0
Vista Meadows Academy	87.7
University YES Academy	98.7
Global Heights Academy	70.6
Regent Park Scholars Charter Academy	96.6
Jalen Rose Leadership Academy	99.5
American International Academy	96.6
New Paradigm Glazer Loving Academy	96.9
Pathways Academy	99.0
Detroit Innovation Academy	99.7
Cornerstone Health and Technology School	98.7
Madison Carver Academy	98.8
WAY Academy	58.2
MacDowell Preparatory Academy	99.4
Rutherford Winans Academy	98.4
Highland Park Public School Academy System	98.9
Michigan Educational Choice Center	96.0
Capstone Academy Charter School	69.8
Grand River Academy	78.0
Cornerstone Jefferson – Douglas Academy	98.8
Sigma Academy for Leadership	100
Early Middle College	100
Plymouth Educational Center Charter School	100
Martin Luther King Education Center Academy	98.9
Eaton Academy	99.0
Commonwealth Community Development Academy	100
Academy for Business and Technology	82.9
Chandler Park Academy	99.7
Marvin Winans Academy for the Performing Arts	99.4
Detroit Community School District	99.6

(continued)

Table 7.7: Schools/academies where Black students are overrepresented in Wayne County District (continued)

District/academy	Black students (%)
Henry Ford Academy	57.5
Detroit Academy of Arts and Sciences	99.5
Dove Academy of Detroit	99.5
Barack Obama Leadership Academy	99.6
George Crockett Academy	100
Summit Academy North	55.3
Voyageur Academy	77.0
Hope Academy	99.1
Weston Preparatory Academy	98.9
Detroit Edison Public School Academy	97.9
David Ellis Academy	100
Detroit Service Learning Academy	99.8
Old Redford Academy	99.1
Joy Preparatory Academy	98.6
West Village Academy	84.1
George Washington Carver Academy	99.2
Metro Charter Academy	80.2
Warrendale Charter Academy	92.8
Detroit Merit Charter Academy	94.1
Detroit Enterprise Academy	95.4
American Montessori Academy	57.9
Detroit Premier Academy	91.2
Covenant House Academy in Detroit	83.2
David Ellis Academy West	98.6
Taylor Exemplar Academy	47.6
Clara B. Ford Academy	52.1
Flagship Charter Academy	95.0
Ace Academy	63.2

Source: Michigan Department of Education (2021).

Table 7.8: Schools/academies where Hispanic students are overrepresented in Wayne County District

District/academy	Hispanic students (%)
Detroit Public School district	13.8
Allen Park Public School district	15.0
Dearborn Heights school district	20.9
Garden City Public School district	12.0
Grosse Pointe Public School district	15.9
Hamtramck Public School district	11.6
Lincoln Park Public School district	12.7
Livonia Public School district	9.9
South Redford Public School district	76.0
Taylor Public School district	29.6
Wayne-Westland Public School district	35.1
Van Buren Public School district	42.8
Detroit Achievement Academy	75.3
University Preparatory Science and Math Academy	96.4
University Preparatory Academy	96.6
University Preparatory Art and Design	97.9
WAY Academy	9.4
New Paradigm College Preparatory	54.2
Quest Charter Academy	41.3
Escola Avancemos Academy	
Highland Park Public School Academy	98.9
Michigan Educational Choice Center	96.0
Capstone Academy Charter	69.8
Tipton Academy	39.2
Taylor Preparatory High School	42.0
Grand River Academy	78.0
Cesar Chavez Academy	93.1
Dearborn Academy	31.4
Voyageur Academy	18.6
Hope Detroit Academy	87.9
Creative Montessori Academy	18.8
Trillium Academy	11.5
Covenant House Academy in Detroit	12.2

Source: Michigan Department of Education (2021).

to state test scores, only 12 percent of students are proficient in math and 18 percent are proficient in reading. As this chapter has shown, when most suburban districts were examined, race was a factor in terms of achievement. White students scored high on tests. In the Detroit school district, 82 percent of the students are African American, but only 2.5 percent are white. The overall grade academically is C-. The graduation rate is 76 percent. The district's spending per student was $13,886, which is higher than the $12,239 national average. No data existed on the teachers who were in their first and second years of teaching. The neighborhood where the school district is located indicates that the median income was $24,981, which is lower than the national average of $62,843. The median rent is $646 compared to the national average of $1,062; however, the median housing value is $218,100 compared to the national average of $217,500.

The City of Detroit also has several charter schools. Two typical charter schools in the Detroit area will be discussed here. One is Detroit Merit Academy, which is 94.3 percent Black and 0.4 percent white in terms of its students. The overall grade academically is C+. The test scores show that 26 percent of students are proficient in math and 39 percent are proficient in reading. The teachers are less experienced than teachers in many suburban schools. There are about 55 other charter schools that are majority-Black and these have similar characteristics. Those most closely related to the Detroit Merit Academy are Detroit Enterprise Academy (95.4 percent Black), George Crockett Academy (100 percent Black) and Dove Academy of Detroit (99.5 percent Black) (Niche.com). Among the lowest-ranked academies is Barack Obama Leadership Academy, which is 99.6 percent Black. It is a public charter school located in Detroit. It has 391 students in grades K–8 with a student–teacher ratio of 65 to 1. According to state test scores, 3 percent of students are proficient in math and 7 percent are proficient in reading. The teachers are not as experienced as many in suburban schools. Charter schools that have similar academic characteristics to the Barack Obama Leadership Academy are Hope Academy (99.1 percent Black) and the Detroit Academy of Arts and Sciences (99.5 percent Black).

Conclusion

The evidence seems to be clear that racial segregation of Black students at the elementary level and at higher grade levels (especially in Wayne County) is denying Black students an equal education to that of white students in the Detroit Metropolitan Area. Thus, in terms of the education of students, Detroit after bankruptcy has not achieved a level of racial equity, equal opportunity, and inclusion. The race of students is still the dominant factor in educational quality in Wayne County, where the City of Detroit is located. The State of Michigan has failed to provide Black students with an equal education after the *Brown v. Board of Education* decision in 1954. It was the conclusion of the US Supreme Court that: (a) racial segregation impacts Black students by labeling them as inferior; (b) the existence of a racially segregated school system operates to injure Black students; and (c) once the state has successfully established and institutionalized racial segregation, the institution is self-perpetuating and need not be maintained (Lawrence, 1977; Darden and Thomas, 2013). The evidence was overwhelming in the Darden and Thomas (2013: 74) analyses that the State of Michigan, through its actions or inaction, enabled or allowed a racially segregated public school system in the city of Detroit. The recent analysis presented here shows that the system of racial segregation continues. Hackworth concluded that political control over the State's education systems was a factor in the conservative support for charter public schools for students in Detroit instead of equal funding for public schools in Detroit and the suburbs (Hackworth, 2019: 117–33). Kang (2020) also discussed the reasons behind conservative Republican support for charter schools in Detroit as Black political officials who were mostly Democratic and Black lost control of the city and school board. This led to the teachers and administrators conceding control to the private interests and the privatization of the public schools via the charter schools becoming the dominant educational system to educate the students in Detroit. Kang highlighted the role played by the conservative Republican Secretary of Education Betsy DeVos in the Detroit charter school movement under the Trump administration.

I argue that the solution is not to produce more charter schools, as the quality of these schools is not significantly different from noncharter schools. The solution, based on the data, must be related to the residential location of Black students in the same neighborhoods and attending the same school as white students.

These conclusions are consistent with the findings of the Stanford University Educational Opportunity Project, which concluded that average student test scores are influenced by the home environment, early childhood experiences, community resources, and schools. The trend or change in average student test scores from one year to the next indicates whether educational opportunities are improving or declining in Detroit. Where the trend is positive, students' opportunities to learn are improving, but the opposite is also true. The trend in Detroit is negative. In terms of learning rates, students learn 1.7 percent less each grade than the US average. Opportunities may improve over time because of changes in school quality or changes in family resources, home environments, early childhood experiences, and/or community resources (Rouse and Barrow, 2006).

According to the authors of the Stanford University Educational Opportunity Project, racial segregation is strongly associated with the magnitude of achievement gaps in the third grade and the rate at which gaps grow from the third to the eighth grades. The association of segregation with achievement gaps is completely accounted for by racial differences in school poverty (that is, "racial economic segregation"). Racial segregation appears to be harmful because it concentrates Black students and, to a lesser extent, Hispanic students in high-poverty schools, that is, schools located in neighborhoods with very low socioeconomic characteristics with students experiencing family poverty and the schools receiving less in resources. They are less effective in providing students with the academic assistance needed for social mobility than lower-poverty schools (Reardon et al, 2021, 2022).

8

Unequal Exposure to Crime in the City of Detroit: A New Method to Measure Exposure by the Characteristics of Neighborhoods

Introduction

The neighborhood effects conceptual framework

This chapter argues that *place* matters in understanding why crimes occur in some neighborhoods more than others. Many years ago, urban researchers at the University of Chicago examined the correlation between characteristics of neighborhoods and delinquency (Burgess, 1916; Shaw, 1929b). This chapter examines crime incidents as the unequal *exposure* of certain neighborhoods to crimes based on neighborhood socioeconomic characteristics and on the theoretical concept of "neighborhood effects" advanced by Black sociologist William J. Wilson, who was a professor at the University of Chicago. He linked crime incidents to certain neighborhoods that experienced *concentrated poverty* (Wilson, 1987). According to him, crimes are directly related to neighborhood characteristics where residents in concentrated poverty reside (Kim, LaGrange, and Willis, 2013). He defined *concentrated poverty* as neighborhoods (census tracts) where 40 percent or more of the residents residing there were poor. Wilson (1987) also found that a high percentage of the Black population of Chicago compared to the white population was restricted to residence in such concentrated poverty neighborhoods. Wilson's ideas can be traced back to classic ecological theories that indicated that neighborhoods with high poverty close to commercial and industrial districts exhibited the highest levels of delinquency and criminality (Shaw and McKay, 1942).

Researchers who have studied crimes and neighborhoods in cities have consistently shown that crimes are not randomly distributed, but tend to be concentrated in certain neighborhoods (Johnson, 2010). Poverty and crime are associated and exhibit spatial clustering (Peterson and Krivo, 2010). The pattern of where crimes are concentrated is so common in cities that Wilcox and Eck (2011) have concluded that the same concentration is the pattern for all cities. Weisburd (2015) agrees. Earlier studies have noted that criminal behavior varies according to sex, age, and, most importantly, *socioeconomic characteristics*. The argument put forward in this chapter is that crimes do not occur evenly in the City of Detroit; they tend to concentrate in neighborhoods with very low socioeconomic characteristics. The ideas expressed here are supported by other researchers who have studied the distribution of crimes in cities. For example, Graif et al (2014) argued that structural conditions like neighborhood poverty contributed to delinquency and crime.

Graif et al (2014) argue that the unequal spatial distribution of crime can be examined with appropriate data to make an analysis that tests the link between the concentration of crime and the concentration of poverty. America has higher documented crime rates in neighborhoods where levels of socioeconomic disadvantage are greatest. Hipp and Kim (2017) examined crime rates by census tracts in large and smaller cities and found that the observed effects of socioeconomic disadvantage on crime rates vary across local neighborhood clusters (Hipp, 2022). Thus, researchers should take this into account when developing theoretical explanations and empirical models of how socioeconomic characteristics shape crime rates (Hipp, 2010).

The influence of distance and knowledge of nearby neighborhoods matter

Research has also shown that those who commit most criminal acts are more likely to commit them the least distance from where they live. In relation to burglary, offenders are said to be more likely to commit crimes in their own neighborhoods or in their former neighborhoods. Potential offenders develop knowledge of the risks and rewards associated with neighborhoods and choose to offend in nearby neighborhoods that provide ecological advantages (Vandeviver and Bernasco, 2017). According to researchers (Chopin et al, 2020), as a result of the offender's *spatial knowledge* of such locations, crime is predicted to occur when their space awareness intersects with opportunities to engage in crime. Recent studies supporting this theory indicate that offenders are more likely to engage in crimes close to their home and in neighborhoods that offer the opportunity for the least consequences, that is, the lowest chance of repercussions. Chopin et al (2020) examined where sexual homicides occur. Their study was based on a national dataset (N = 173) that focused on extra-familial sexual homicides. The results show the validity of the distance decay function, with over 70 percent of homicides occurring within 10 km of the offender's residence. There is also increasingly strong evidence that indicates that individuals commit crime not far from their current (and previous) place of residence and that their journey is affected by different types of geographical barriers (Townsley and Sidebottom, 2010).

According to Johnson and Summers (2015), crime is spatially concentrated. However, most research relies on information about where crimes occur, without reference to where offenders reside. The study by these authors examines how the characteristics of neighborhoods and their proximity to offender home locations affect offender spatial decision making. Using a discrete choice model and data for detected incidents of *theft from vehicles*, they tested predictions from two theoretical perspectives: crime pattern and social disorganization theories. They found that juvenile delinquents commited crimes close to where they lived. Some researchers have argued that crime patterns follow the principle of structured human behavior and offenders tend to minimize journey time to commit their crime in order to maximize the rewards at their intended destination (Bernasco, 2010). The research undertaken by Nordquist (2019) has been used to explain why the distances offenders travel to commit crimes are usually relatively short (for example, see Bernasco, 2010). Crime is spatially concentrated. Lee et al (2017) identified 44 studies that empirically examined crime concentration at places and provided quantitative information sufficient for analysis. They found that crime is concentrated in relatively few places. Crime is also concentrated among victims based on where they live in terms of neighborhood socioeconomic characteristics. In other words, residents most exposed to crimes live in neighborhoods with similar socioeconomic characteristics as the person who commits the crimes.

The *principle of least effort* explains why offenders choose to commit crimes near where they live. This principle proposes an explanation for this: people will only travel as far as is necessary (Zipf, 1949; Nordquist, 2019). The principle means, for example, that a person (including a potential offender) will strive to minimize the *probable average rate of their work expenditure* (over time), and in so doing, they will be minimizing their *effort*. Congruent with the principle of least effort is the *concept of distance decay*, or the inverse spatial relationship between activity (legitimate or otherwise) and distance. It takes more effort financially to travel further, meaning potential offenders are more likely to commit crimes closer to their homes. The potential offenders must feel safe and unlikely to be perceived as an outsider. They will be comfortable enough to commit the crime in their familiar neighborhood where the risk is known and perceived as lowest. Also, low-density, very high socioeconomic characteristic neighborhoods may have limited access to transportation, making the effort to travel to commit a crime less feasible or not worth the extra effort, since the offender may also be viewed as an outsider and therefore perceived as a higher risk (Bernasco, 2010).

Offenders may also be more likely to target disadvantaged neighborhoods because they are more likely to live in such neighborhoods. Bernasco (2010) found that the odds of an area being selected as a target are significantly greater if the suspect currently lives there or has lived there in the recent past. If potential offenders live in a very low socioeconomic characteristic neighborhood, which is usually residentially segregated from very high socioeconomic characteristic neighborhoods, they may be less familiar with the very high socioeconomic characteristic neighborhoods that are not nearby, thus supporting the *least effort principle* (Andersen and Shen, 2019). Indeed, a large body of work has established that offenders do not travel far from their residences to commit crimes.

According to the geometry of crime, offenders are expected to commit their offenses within their awareness space. The expectation has been confirmed in the context of offenders committing robberies, residential burglaries, thefts from vehicles, and assaults, doing so close to home or previous residences (Bernasco, 2010). Also, researchers have used *rational choice theory* (a fundamental tenet of classical criminology) to explain why potential offenders commit specific crimes. According to *rational choice theory*, individuals evaluate their choice of actions in accordance with each option's ability to produce advantage. Potential offenders engage in a specific crime because it can be rewarding; the central premise of this theory is that people are rational beings whose behavior can be controlled or modified by fear of punishment. In this way, it is believed that offenders can be persuaded to desist from offending by intensifying their fear of punishment. Sanctions should be limited to what is necessary to deter people from choosing to commit crime (Siegel and McCormick, 2006).

Neighborhood air pollution and crime incidents

Although there have been few studies of cities in the US, there is at least one study in London that relates air pollution in neighborhoods to crime in those neighborhoods. The authors of this study examined whether short-term exposure to elevated levels of ambient air pollution affects crime in London (Roth et al, 2019). London is similar to many major cities around the world in terms of its pollution and the social and economic characteristics of its neighborhoods. The authors found that air pollution has a positive and statistically significant impact on overall crime and on several major crime categories, including those with economic motives. Importantly, the effect also occurs at pollution levels, which are unevenly distributed across income groups. Their study divided London into wards (which are spatial units similar to census tracts, but slightly larger). They focused on daily variation in pollution levels (and crime) and found that, overall, the larger effects of pollution on crime seem to occur mainly at the bottom of the income distribution. This suggests that despite relatively low exposure, the effect of pollution on crime is large in less wealthy wards. Their results had policy implications: reducing air pollution in cities may be an effective measure to reduce crime and air pollution forecasts could be used to improve the crime problem (Roth et al, 2019). Air pollution is more prevalent in Detroit's very low socioeconomic characteristic neighborhoods and so are crime incidents.

Foreclosures and crime

Detroit has had a high number of foreclosures, most occurring in neighborhoods that are very low in socioeconomic characteristics (Eisenberg et al, 2019). Gould et al (2013) investigated what effects foreclosed properties might have on their surrounding neighborhoods and on criminal activity in particular. However, their study was based on data in New York and not Detroit. They found that additional foreclosures on a block led to additional total crimes. These effects appear to be greatest when foreclosure activity was measured by the number of foreclosed properties that were on their way to an auction or had reverted to bank ownership.

Health and wellbeing in neighborhoods and crime

Health researchers Kawachi et al (1999) argue that major theoretical and empirical developments in the field of criminology suggest that the same social environmental factors that predict *geographic variation* in crime rates may also be relevant in terms of explaining geographic variations in health and wellbeing. The purpose of the authors' research paper was to present a conceptual framework for investigating the influence of the social context on community health, using crime as the indicator of collective wellbeing. They argued that two sets of societal characteristics influence the level of crime: the degree of relative deprivation in society (for instance, measured by the extent of income inequality) and the degree of cohesiveness in social relations among citizens (measured, for instance, by indicators of social capital and collective efficacy). They tested their conceptual framework using state-level ecological data on violent crimes and property crimes in the US (Blakely and Woodward, 2000). They found that crimes (homicide, assault, and robbery) were consistently associated with relative deprivation (income inequality) and indicators of low social capital. Among property crimes, burglary was also associated with deprivation and low social capital. Neighborhoods with high crime rates also tended to exhibit higher mortality rates from all causes, suggesting that crime and population health share the same social origins. They concluded that crime is thus a mirror of the quality of the social environment (Kawachi et al, 1999). I am in strong agreement with their conclusions.

Other authors argue that it has been a long tradition in criminological research that crime is most prevalent in societies that permit large disparities in the material standards of living of their citizens (Hsieh and Pugh, 1993). The fact that crime is high in the most disadvantaged neighborhoods in the City of Detroit compared to more affluent neighborhoods is consistent with the same type of large disparities. My research shows that the residents with the worst health also live in neighborhoods with very low socioeconomic characteristics. These neighborhoods are also where the most crime incidents occur in Detroit. However, the data in this chapter will show that some residents in the City of Detroit have little exposure to crime, while others have disproportionate exposure to crimes. The characteristics of the neighborhoods where residents live matter.

Neighborhoods with the lowest socioeconomic characteristics have the highest incidence of crimes. Those populations that live in the neighborhoods with the lowest socioeconomic characteristics have the *greatest exposure* to crime. On the other hand, those populations that live in neighborhoods with the highest socioeconomic characteristics have the *least exposure* to the crime incidents. This relationship is the major focus of this chapter. Previous studies have found that the link between crime and neighborhood disadvantage has been measured by the percentage of households living under the poverty threshold, with various types of crime ranging from burglaries (Nobles et al, 2016) to homicides (Kawachi et al, 1999). Other aspects of neighborhoods that are often used as indicators of disadvantage are housing tenure and unemployment. Findings from the US suggest that the share of renters in an area is positively associated with crime rates in very low and low socioeconomic economic characteristic neighborhoods, but not in very high socioeconomic characteristic neighborhoods.

The final work that is relevant to this chapter focuses specifically on residential segregation and crime (Krivo et al, 2015). The analyses in this paper were based on all 8,895 census tracts within a sample of 86 large US cities. The authors used multilevel models of crime that incorporated measures of local segregation between Blacks and whites. The results revealed that white–Black local segregation is associated with lower levels of violent and property crime. Low–high-income local segregation is connected with higher neighborhood crime. All the studies discussed in this section are important in order to better understand the connection between the neighborhood socioeconomic characteristics where crimes occur and the neighborhood socioeconomic characteristics where residents live who are most exposed to crimes.

Data sources

The data used in this chapter were obtained from the *City of Detroit Open Data Portal Datasets* on crimes by year. These data reflect reported criminal offenses that have occurred in the City of Detroit. Offense data were extracted from the Detroit Police Department's records management system. This dataset contains the most recent data available and is updated whenever the Detroit Police Department (DPD) sends official crime records to the Michigan Incident Crime Reporting (MICR) or the National Incident Based Reporting systems. It should be noted that some incidents involve the commission of multiple offenses, such as a domestic assault where property is also vandalized. Accordingly, the data describe all offenses associated with all reported incidents. This chapter will assess crimes that occurred in Detroit before bankruptcy (that is, between January 1, 2011 and December 31, 2014) and crimes that occurred in Detroit after bankruptcy (2016–20), with the aim to see what changes occurred.

The *Detroit Open Data Portal* provided a database on incidents that occurred between January 1, 2011 and December 31, 2014 (Detroit's bankruptcy ended on December 11, 2014). This makes the database very useful in terms of assessing the categories of criminal incidents before and during bankruptcy. The report that was issued on January 1, 2011 indicated that 234,978 incidents of crime had been recorded by December 31, 2014. These were divided into the following categories:

Type of crime	Percentage of total
Larceny	29.89
Burglary	24.01
Stolen vehicle	20.58
Aggravated assault	15.92
Robbery	9.01
Homicide	0.59
Total	*100*

Source: Detroit Open Data Portal.

The average number of larcenies per year was 17,561, the average number of burglaries was 14,101, the average number of stolen vehicles was 12,091, the average number of aggravated assaults was 9,350, the average number of robberies was 5,293, and the average number of homicides was 346.

The unequal distribution in terms of the categories of crime incidents, with 75 percent falling into property-type economic categories (for example, larceny, burglary, and stolen vehicles), suggests that a percentage of the disadvantaged population in the disadvantaged neighborhoods engage in crimes that are motivated by efforts to improve their economic status or economic need by taking property or assets that are owned by other residents. Such incidents usually occur in the same neighborhood or near to where the perpetrator lives. Thus, those residents who live in the same neighborhood or near it are more likely to be more *exposed to* crime because they may live in neighborhoods where these criminal incidents occur.

According to the Federal Bureau of Investigation Uniform Crime Report, incidents of crime are defined as follows:

Aggravated Assault: An unlawful attack by one person upon another wherein the offender uses a weapon or displays it in a threatening manner, or the victim suffers obvious severe or aggravated bodily injury involving apparent broken bones, loss of teeth, possible internal injury, severe laceration, or loss of consciousness.

Burglary/Breaking and Entering: The unlawful entry into a building or other structure with the intent to commit a felony or a theft.

Larceny/Theft Offenses: The unlawful taking, carrying, leading, or riding away of property from the possession or constructive possession of another person.

Robbery: The taking or attempting to take anything of value under confrontational circumstances from the control, custody, or care of another person by force or threat of force or violence and/or by putting the victim in fear of immediate harm.

Stolen Property Offenses: Receiving, buying, selling, possessing, concealing, or transporting any property with the knowledge that it has been unlawfully taken, as by burglary, embezzlement, fraud, larceny, robbery, etc. [This definition includes stolen vehicles.]

Homicide Offenses: The killing of one human being by another. (Federal Bureau of Investigation, 2022)

All of these incidents are related to neighborhood socioeconomic characteristics and the incidents vary accordingly. Thus, crime data on cities including Detroit are not as useful for residents, policy makers, or researchers without the additional information on the characteristics of neighborhoods where these incidents occur. For the purposes of this chapter, a 2015 database was analyzed to assess not only the number of incidents by categories but also *where* the incidents occurred by category and by neighborhood socioeconomic position one year after bankruptcy ended.

Method of analysis

This chapter uses the Darden-Kamel Composite Socioeconomic Index (CSI) method to analyze the data. This is the same method that has been used throughout this book. The method first analyzed the crime incident data by census tract by geocoding the addresses of the crime incidents to the census tract geographic level. O'Brien et al (2022) have argued that census tracts are the most appropriate way to study why crimes are more concentrated in some neighborhoods than in others. Once I determined the number of incidents by census tract, the tracts were then analyzed using the Darden-Kamel CSI, which characterizes each census tract by socioeconomic characteristics using the US Bureau of the Census American Community Survey 2011–15 Five-Year Estimates and the 2016–20 Five-Year Estimates. I used the census reports to *extract* data for nine socioeconomic variables for each census tract. In other words, the Darden-Kamel CSI measures the socioeconomic status of each census tract and assigns a higher score to tracts with high SES, that is, SEP. A high score reflects high-quality socioeconomic characteristics of census tracts (which are surrogates for neighborhoods) and a low score reflects low or poor-quality neighborhood characteristics.

The Darden-Kamel CSI incorporates nine variables (see Chapter 3). Only the names are given here:

1. Percentage below poverty
2. Unemployment rate
3. Median household income
4. Occupational status
5. Educational attainment
6. Median value of dwelling
7. Median household rent
8. Percentage of homeownership
9. Percentage of households with vehicle

For a more detailed discussion of the nine variables, their strengths, and their use in previous research relating to neighborhood characteristics, see Darden et al (2010). The nine variables that I chose are all associated with the quality of life in neighborhoods and have neighborhood effects on residents who live there. The data for the variables were obtained from the US Bureau of the Census (2016) 2011–15 American Community Survey Five-Year Estimates and the US Bureau of the Census (2022) 2016–20 American Community Survey Five-Year Estimates. I have used the Darden-Kamel CSI because it presents an easy-to-understand measure of the extent of inequality between neighborhoods. This ease of understanding makes it very useful for policy makers and federal judges to interpret and determine whether certain socioeconomic conditions impose undue discriminatory hardships on residents in certain neighborhoods.

To standardize the contribution of each census variable included in the CSI, a Z-score was created for each of the nine census tract variables by subtracting the mean from the grand mean for each of the variables used in the study and dividing the resulting figure by the standard deviation of the respective variables for the three counties (Wayne, Oakland, and Macomb) in the Detroit Metropolitan Area as a whole. The Z-scores of all variables were summed together to create a CSI value for each census tract. To ensure that each variable contributed appropriately when calculating this CSI, the Z-scores for two depreciating variables—unemployment rate and percentage of the population below poverty—were multiplied by -1 before they were added to the remaining variables (Darden et al, 2010). The formula for the CSI can be found in Chapter 3 and in Darden et al (2010). Applying the formula to each census tract, the tracts were ranked after computation into the five levels of socioeconomic position (SEP, that is, SES).

Results

The crimes were analyzed for *exposure* by neighborhood characteristics for the years 2015 and 2020. The City of Detroit Open Data Portal database on crimes in the City provided a complete database, and also allowed for the Darden-Kamel CSI to be employed using crime incident data from the City of Detroit Open Portal Data on crime incidents in the city for specific types of crime (aggravated assaults, larceny, burglary, robbery, homicides, and stolen vehicles) for the years 2015 and 2020. The population data were obtained from the US Bureau of the Census for the years 2015 and 2020. The census data were analyzed using the Darden-Kamel CSI to characterize neighborhoods (census tracts) by socioeconomic characteristics. First, the 2015 crime data were analyzed to determine the number of each crime by census tract cluster based on socioeconomic characteristics divided by the population in the cluster multiplied by 100,000. The analysis involved the location of crimes by neighborhoods and whether the crime rate had increased or decreased between 2015 and 2020.

Crimes in the City of Detroit by neighborhood socioeconomic characteristics in 2015

As presented in the literature review of studies on crime in cities, the data on crimes in the City of Detroit were obtained from the City of Detroit Portal Crime Incident Data on crimes in 2015. The analysis of the data revealed that crimes were not evenly distributed, but varied by neighborhood socioeconomic characteristics. The highest crime rates occur in very low socioeconomic characteristic neighborhoods, which are indicated by SEP 1. These neighborhoods, or census tracts, are the location of 60 percent or more of the accounted-for crimes: aggravated assault, larceny, burglary, robbery, homicide, and stolen vehicles. The next highest crime rates occur in low socioeconomic characteristic neighborhoods, which are indicated here as SEP 2. As the socioeconomic characteristics of neighborhoods improve, the crime rate declines. For example, only 4.8 percent of the crimes in 2015 occurred in middle-class neighborhoods (SEP 3). The lowest number of crimes occurred in high socioeconomic characteristic neighborhoods (SEP 4) (1.3 percent) and very high socioeconomic characteristic neighborhoods (SEP 5) (less than 1 percent). In 2015 there were a total of 9,135 aggravated assaults. Out of this total, 8,818 could be analyzed based on neighborhood socioeconomic characteristics and 317 could not be located by census tract coding. Of all assaults, 65.7 percent occurred in SEP 1 neighborhoods and 30.8 percent occurred in SEP 2 neighborhoods. These two types of neighborhoods were also where 97 percent of all homicides occurred in 2015.

Calculating the crime rate by dividing the number of aggravated assaults in the population in the SEP multiplied by 100,000 revealed that the aggravated assault rate in SEP 1 neighborhoods was 1,456.05, while this rate in SEP 5 neighborhoods was 767.60. The highest larceny rate was 2,938.06 in SEP 5 neighborhoods. The highest rate of burglaries was 1,374.38 in SEP 1 neighborhoods. The highest rate of robberies was 654.45 in SEP 4 neighborhoods. Homicide rates were similar to those of aggravated assault; the highest rate was 51.77 in SEP 1 neighborhoods. Finally, the highest rate of stolen vehicles was 2,303.66 and occurred in SEP 4 neighborhoods.

Crimes in the City of Detroit by neighborhood socioeconomic characteristics in 2020 and changes since 2015

The research question here is how did crime rates change between 2015 and 2020? The 2020 City of Detroit crime data and the 2020 Decennial Census were used to assess the population and determine the number of crimes per 100,000 to get the crime rate for six types of crimes mentioned earlier by neighborhood socioeconomic characteristics. Thus, the Darden-Kamel CSI was used to determine the neighborhood socioeconomic characteristics of the tracts. The aggravated assault crime rate was 1,563.48 in SEP 1 neighborhoods—the highest in the city, an increase on the 2015 rate of 1,456.05. The lowest aggravated assault rate was 462.05 in SEP 5 neighborhoods, which marked a decrease from the rate of 767.60 in 2015.

The larceny rate was highest in SEP 5 neighborhoods, where it was 2,536.37, down from 2,938.06 in 2015. This rate was lowest in SEP 2 neighborhoods, where it was 1,457.75, down from 2,153.54 in 2015.

The highest burglary rate was 778.59 in SEP 1 neighborhoods, down from 1,374.38 in 2015. The lowest burglary rate was 383.41 in SEP 5 neighborhoods, a substantial drop compared to the 2015 rate of 1,164.64.

The highest robbery rate was 298.5 in SEP 1 neighborhoods, down from 550.10 in 2015. The lowest robbery rate was 167.9 in SEP 3 neighborhoods, down from 392.48 in 2015.

Of the total serious crimes, residents were most concerned about homicides, which were also not evenly distributed in the city. The highest homicide rate of 59.14 occurred in SEP 1 neighborhoods, up from 51.77 in 2015. The lowest homicide rate was 9.83 in SEP 5 neighborhoods, substantially lower than the 2015 rate of 26.47.

Finally, the highest stolen vehicle rate was 973.26, which occurred in SEP 5 neighborhoods, down from 1,085.23 in 2015.

The answer can be found by comparing the crime rates for 2015 with the crime rates for 2020. Table 8.1 shows the changes in the crime rates of six types of crimes by neighborhood socioeconomic characteristics between 2015 and 2020. The results show whether the crime rate in the City of Detroit increased or decreased five years after bankruptcy. The table provides trends in crimes by type and neighborhood socioeconomic characteristics. The analyses of the trends indicate that the crime rates in Detroit increased in six (20 percent) and decreased in 24 (80 percent) neighborhoods between 2015 and 2020. Thus, overall, it is correct to conclude that *crime rates decreased in most neighborhoods in the City of Detroit between 2015 and 2020.*

Finally, it is important to indicate which neighborhoods are characterized by socioeconomic characteristics. Table 8.1 shows crime rates in the City of Detroit by neighborhood socioeconomic characteristics in 2015. It demonstrates that in 2015, SEP 1 neighborhoods had the highest aggravated assault rate (1,456.05), burglary rate (1,374.38), and homicide rate (51.77). SEP 4 neighborhoods had the highest larceny rate (10,183.25) and stolen vehicle rate (2,303.66). SEP 5 neighborhoods had the lowest stolen vehicle rate (1,085.27).

Table 8.1 shows that in 2020, SEP 1 neighborhoods still had the highest aggravated assault rate (1,563.48), which had increased since 2015. It also shows that SEP 1 neighborhoods had the highest burglary rate (778.59), which had decreased since 2015, and the highest robbery rate (298.54), which had also decreased since 2015. Finally, SEP 1 neighborhoods had the highest homicide rate (59.14), which had increased since 2015. SEP 5 neighborhoods had the lowest aggravated assault rate (462.05), burglary rate (383.4), and homicide rate (9.83).

The two types of crime most residents were concerned about were aggravated assault and homicide. Therefore, I show the pattern of these two types of crimes, not only by SEP but also by neighborhoods. Table 8.2 shows the pattern for occurrences of aggravated assault by neighborhood in 2020. It demonstrates that over 50 percent of aggravated assaults occurred in SEP 1 and SEP 2 neighborhoods. The names of neighborhoods in SEP 1 and 2 are indicated.

They consist of 27 neighborhoods, where over 50 percent of the homicides occurred by name of neighborhood in 2020. They occurred in 26 SEP 1 and SEP 2 neighborhoods across Regent Park to Central Southwest.

Table 8.1: Crime rates in the City of Detroit after bankruptcy (comparing 2015 to 2020 socioeconomic characteristics of neighborhoods)

Crime type	Crime rate in 2015	Crime rate in 2020	Trend 2015–2020
Aggravated assault			
SEP 1	1,456.05	1,563.48	Increase
SEP 2	1,180.98	1,265.32	Increase
SEP 3	659.58	884.58	Increase
SEP 4	863.87	729.61	Decrease
SEP 5	767.60	462.05	Decrease
Larceny			
SEP 1	1,986.55	1,549.64	Decrease
SEP 2	2,153.54	1,457.75	Decrease
SEP 3	2,480.24	1,517.23	Decrease
SEP 4	10,183.25	1,859.16	Decrease
SEP 5	2,938.06	2,536.37	Decrease
Burglary			
SEP 1	1,374.38	778.59	Decrease
SEP 2	1,360.29	699.72	Decrease
SEP 3	929.41	596.25	Decrease
SEP 4	1,151.83	626.93	Decrease
SEP 5	1,164.64	383.41	Decrease
Robbery			
SEP 1	550.10	298.54	Decrease
SEP 2	445.04	237.61	Decrease
SEP 3	392.48	167.96	Decrease
SEP 4	654.45	254.01	Decrease
SEP 5	502.91	226.11	Decrease
Homicide			
SEP 1	51.77	59.14	Increase
SEP 2	34.30	34.26	Decrease
SEP 3	19.08	33.59	Increase

(continued)

Table 8.1: Crime rates in the City of Detroit after bankruptcy (comparing 2015 to 2020 socioeconomic characteristics of neighborhoods) (continued)

Crime type	Crime rate in 2015	Crime rate in 2020	Trend 2015–2020
SEP 4	26.18	32.43	Increase
SEP 5	26.47	9.83	Decrease
Stolen vehicles			
SEP 1	1,091.16	835.53	Decrease
SEP 2	1,185.32	917.65	Decrease
SEP 3	1,207. 41	764.21	Decrease
SEP 4	2,303.66	924.17	Decrease
SEP 5	1,085.23	973.26	Decrease
Population			
SEP 1	397,926	317,881	
SEP 2	230,318	137,198	
SEP 3	36,690	35,723	
SEP 4	3,820	18,503	
SEP 5	3,778	10,172	

Note: Crime rate formula: (Number of Crime Type by SEP/Total Population in Detroit by SEP) *100,000.

Source: Detroit Crime Incident Data (2020); 2020 Decennial Census Data.

Conclusion

This chapter has revealed using the Darden-Kamel CSI that crimes in the City of Detroit are not randomly distributed, but are concentrated in neighborhoods based on social economic characteristics. The highest crime rates occur in two types of neighborhoods: very low socioeconomic characteristic neighborhoods (SEP 1) and low socioeconomic characteristic neighborhoods (SEP 2). There were very few crimes in middle-class neighborhoods, even fewer than occurred in high and very high socioeconomic characteristic neighborhoods (SEP 4 and 5). This chapter has also documented that between 2015 and 2020, however, aggravated assault crimes increased in SEP 1, 2, and 3 types of neighborhoods and decreased in SEP 4 and 5 types of neighborhoods. Larceny decreased in all types of neighborhoods. Burglary also decreased in all types of neighborhoods, and so did robberies. Homicides increased in very low socioeconomic

Table 8.2: Detroit neighborhoods where over 50% of aggravated assaults occurred in 2020 and their neighborhood socioeconomic characteristics (SEP)

Neighborhood		SEP 1	SEP 2	SEP 3	SEP 4	SEP 5
1	Warrendale	X	X			
2	Regent Park	X	X			
3	Outer Drive-Hayes	X				
4	Barton-McFarland	X	X			
5	Brightmoor	X	X			
6	Oakman Blvd Community	X	X			
7	Bethune Community	X				
8	Franklin Park	X	X			
9	Warren Ave Community	X				
10	Cary/St Mary's		X			
11	Claytown	X	X			
12	MorningSide	X	X	X		
13	Fitzgerald-Marygrove	X	X			
14	Moross-Morang	X				
15	Greenfield	X				
16	Mapleridge	X	X			
17	Evergreen Lasher 7/8	X	X			
18	Holcomb Community	X				
19	Yorkshire Woods	X				
20	Bagley		X			
21	Cornerstone Village	X	X			
22	Nolan	X				
23	Central Southwest	X	X			
24	College Park	X	X			
25	Evergreen-Outer Drive		X			
26	O'Hair Park		X	X		
27	Schulze		X	X		
28	Winship		X	X		
29	Dexter-Linwood		X	X		

Source: Data Driven Detroit Crime data: 2020 and 2016–20 ACS.

X indicates which SEP is present in each listed neighborhood.

Table 8.3: Detroit neighborhoods where over 50% of homicides occurred in 2020 and their neighborhood socioeconomic characteristics (SEP)

	Neighborhood	SEP 1	SEP2	SEP 3	SEP 4	SEP 5
1	Regent Park	X	X			
2	MorningSide	X	X	X		
3	Brightmoor	X	X			
4	Fitzgerald-Marygrove	X	X			
5	Outer Drive-Hayes	X				
6	Warrendale	X	X			
7	Claytown	X	X			
8	Holcomb Community	X				
9	Barton-McFarland	X	X			
10	Mapleridge	X	X			
11	Nolan	X				
12	Bethune Community	X				
13	Boynton		X			
14	College Park	X	X			
15	Conner Creek	X				
16	Davison-Schoolcraft	X	X			
17	Franklin Park	X				
18	Greenfield	X				
19	Greenfield-Grand River	X				
20	Hubbell-Lyndon	X				
21	Oakman Blvd Community	X	X			
22	Schoolcraft Southfield	X				
23	Schulze		X	X		
24	West End	X				
25	Bagley		X			
26	Central Southwest	X	X			

Source: Data Driven Detroit Crime data: 2020 and US Census Bureau, *American Community Survey Five-Year Estimates, 2016–20.*

characteristic neighborhoods, decreased in low socioeconomic characteristic neighborhoods, and increased in middle characteristic neighborhoods and high socioeconomic characteristic neighborhoods. However, in very high socioeconomic neighborhoods, homicides decreased. Finally, the number of reported stolen vehicles decreased in every type of neighborhood.

Thus, it is fair to conclude that crime after bankruptcy decreased in the City of Detroit in most neighborhoods. It is very important for residents of Detroit to know that crimes such as aggravated assaults and homicides are not evenly distributed in the City of Detroit. They are concentrated in SEP 1 and SEP 2 neighborhoods. These neighborhoods are very low and low in socioeconomic characteristics. Few occur in SEP 4 and SEP 5 neighborhoods. If these types of crimes are to be addressed, greater attention must be given to the socioeconomic characteristics of neighborhoods.

9

Solving the Problem
of Extreme Race and Class
Inequality: Implementing the
Spatial Mobility Alternative

Introduction

The social and economic characteristics of neighborhoods in Detroit were influenced tremendously by the city's bankruptcy, which made conditions for a large segment of the Detroit population much more difficult. Many residents of Black and Hispanic neighborhoods were exposed to more poverty and higher rates of unemployment. Some residents had more difficulty finding jobs in higher occupations at the management and professional levels (Ihlanfeldt and Sjoquist, 1991). Other residents were not residing in the same neighborhoods as highly educated residents and they experienced wage inequality. Some residents had difficulty becoming homeowners, and those who did own their home often had a lower home value.

When such conditions exist, it is quite common for residents to search for neighborhoods and places that will improve their quality of life, even if this means moving away from the city and the neighborhood where they have lived most of their lives. Urban geographers call this search by residents the *geography of opportunity* (Rosenbaum, 1995; Rosenbaum, Reynolds, and De Luca, 2002; Goering and Feins, 2003; Galster, 2017). The movement away from the city has also been called the spatial *mobility alternative* (Darden and Thomas, 2013: 298–317). In Darden and Thomas' *Detroit: Race Riots, Racial Conflicts, and Efforts to Bridge the Racial Divide* (2013), the argument was made, citing migration theory, that residents often move due to two major factors: (1) push, and (2) pull (Greenwood, 1985; Darden and Thomas, 2013). The push factors impacting residents in Detroit include the already-mentioned factors, plus the low quality of education provided by the Detroit public schools and the lack of affordable quality housing in most neighborhoods. The research questions that this chapter aims to answer are whether the quality of life changed for residents of Detroit after bankruptcy, and what were the social and economic characteristics of municipalities in the suburbs compared to social and economic characteristics of the neighborhoods in Detroit.

In search of the geography of opportunity: evidence of Black and Hispanic suburbanization between 2010 and 2020

The research that has been conducted on Detroit and its suburbs (Darden et al, 1987) has shown that some residents search for greater opportunities, including a reduction in poverty, a reduction in their unemployment rate and greater opportunity for employment, and an increase in their median household income, alongside a higher level of occupation and access to a municipality with a higher level of educational attainment and public school quality (Kain, 1968). In short, many residents have been looking for the *geography of opportunity*. The opportunity is usually greater in municipalities that have a higher socioeconomic status than in municipalities with very low socioeconomic status. Since municipalities provide services that may improve the quality of life for residents, they are like a social and spatial system. We can learn about those municipalities by examining their socioeconomic characteristics and examining the pattern of Black and Hispanic increases in some suburbs rather than others.

Black and Hispanic populations in selected Detroit suburbs

Between 2010 and 2020, most of the suburbs outside of Detroit with a population of 10,000 or more increased in terms of their population. The Black population also increased in most of these suburbs. The largest increase occurred in Eastpointe (23.2 percent), followed by Harper Woods (20.7 percent), Roseville (9.1 percent), Warren (6.8 percent), Wayne (6.6 percent), and Fraser (5.1 percent). Unlike the Black population, the Hispanic population increased in both the City of Detroit and in 40 of the suburbs. The greatest increase occurred in the suburb of Lincoln Park. Hispanics increased to 25.7 percent. Pontiac increased in Hispanic population to 21.8 percent. The third largest increase was in Allen Park, which increased to 12.1 percent.

The focus of this chapter

This chapter will examine a major barrier faced by Black and Hispanic home seekers in terms of their movement into Detroit's suburbs. A comparison will be made using Home Mortgage Disclosure data to measure the mortgage denial rates faced by Blacks and Hispanics compared to that faced by non Hispanic whites (Ladd, 1998). It will also examine the inequality between Blacks, Hispanics, and non Hispanic whites in the following areas of socioeconomic characteristics: percentage in poverty/below the poverty line, median household income, percentage of workers in the highest-ranked occupations (for example, management, business, science, and the arts), the percentage of residents with a bachelor's degree or higher, and the percentage of residents who own their homes (the homeownership rate).

The study areas

The analysis here will be limited to suburban municipalities with a population of 10,000 or higher and where at least 20 mortgage loan applications were made by Black or Hispanic home seekers.

Barriers to achieving geography of opportunity

Among the total population of Detroit, whites were the first residents to leave Detroit in search of a better quality of life. Unlike Blacks and Hispanics, most white Detroit residents received assistance from the federal government to purchase a home in the suburbs (Darden et al, 1987) and did not face barriers in this process. On the other hand, Blacks and Hispanics often experienced barriers to homeownership in the form of mortgage loan denials, which reduced their homeownership rate and their suburbanization percentage. The discussion here will begin with a brief historical look at white suburbanization.

Historically, when the white population in Detroit living in lower socioeconomic characteristic neighborhoods moved to a higher socioeconomic characteristic neighborhood, they usually had financial help and support from the federal government. The federal government disproportionately helped white households with mortgage default insurance that helped them become homeowners in the Detroit suburbs. It did not help most Black households by guaranteeing their mortgages (Darden et al, 1987: 16–17). The effect was that the federal government was enabling white households to become homeowners and accumulate wealth while Black home seekers were denied the same treatment. The Federal Home Loan Programs allowed households—the majority of them white—to build and transfer assets across generations, contributing to glaring racial disparities in homeownership and wealth. Such historical practices that benefit whites more than Blacks and Hispanics still exist today. First, the analyses in this chapter will reveal results of home mortgage denial rates for Blacks, Hispanics and non Hispanic whites (Hanks et al, 2018).

The geographic distribution of loan applications

Contrary to the *preference theory* that each racial group prefers to live only with their own group (Darden, 1987a), these data and analyses demonstrate that the theory is questionable. This is because Blacks applied for mortgage loans in 106 municipalities, while Hispanics applied in 113 municipalities. The municipalities varied in terms of their racial compositions. In the majority of the municipalities, white applicants had a lower mortgage denial rate than Blacks and Hispanics. The mean denial ratio comparing Black applicants and white applicants was 1.5, while it was 1.3 between Hispanic applicants and white applicants. This wide distribution of Blacks and Hispanics who applied for mortgage loans demonstrates that some Blacks and Hispanics prefer to live in municipalities other than the City of Detroit. The 40 municipalities with a population over 10,000 that, including Detroit, are examined in this chapter show that Black applicants and Hispanic applicants applied for mortgage loans in most municipalities in the suburbs that had a higher socioeconomic status than the City of Detroit. The results are based on the actual behavior of Black and Hispanic applicants in their choice of municipalities as opposed to surveys of attitudes about the racial composition of municipalities. This chapter challenges the accuracy of such studies about the preferences of Blacks and Hispanics for suburban locations.

Racial disparities in mortgage loan denial rates in selected suburbs in Detroit

A key barrier to the movement of Blacks and Hispanics to the suburbs of Detroit has been the denial of mortgage loans for home purchases, as they have been denied mortgage loans at a higher rate than non Hispanic white home seekers. The data used are from the *Home Mortgage Disclosure Act* (HMDA), which was passed in 1975. The HMDA required the largest lending institutions to disclose to the public information about where home loans were being made by census tract (Avery et al, 2007), so as to determine whether mortgage lending institutions were adequately serving the needs of all neighborhoods, especially those that were poor, Black, and Hispanic. It was also passed to facilitate the enforcement of the *Federal Fair Housing Act*, which was passed in 1968. The HMDA was amended in 1989; the amendment required that each application include the income, sex, race, and ethnicity of the home seekers applying for credit. The information revealed widespread disparities in the rates of approval of loan applications by race and ethnicity (Goering and Wink, 1996).

This section notes that the widespread racial disparities found in 1996 were still present in Metropolitan Detroit based on the most recent HMDA data and analyses. Using the Home Mortgage Disclosure Act (HMDA) data for 2020, Tables 9.1 and 9.2 present the racial inequality as measured by

Table 9.1: Black, Hispanic, and non Hispanic white mortgage loan denial rates in selected Detroit suburbs and the City of Detroit in 2020

Municipality	Black home seekers (%)	Hispanic home seekers (%)	Non Hispanic white home seekers (%)
Allen Park	10.7	15.9	33.8
Auburn Hills	26.9	16.4	9.6
Birmingham	8.7	11.1	7.2
Dearborn	16.7	24.1	14.6
Eastpointe	17.2	16.7	13.2
Farmington	14.5	9.2	9.2
Farmington Hills	18.8	23.2	13.4
Ferndale	11.1	9.7	6.7
Flat Rock	40.9	32.8	15.1
Fraser	30.8	23.8	9.7
Garden City	20.0	23.9	11.7
Grosse Pointe Park	38.5	16.7	9.7
Grosse Pointe Woods	15.5	12.0	8.4
Hazel Park	25.9	8.7	11.6
Inkster	31.6	31.8	25.9
Lincoln Park	17.3	18.2	12.9
Livonia	14.8	8.1	7.6
Madison Heights	9.1	15.2	8.5
Melvindale	25.0	20.7	16.2
Mount Clemens	37.8	5.1	13.9
Novi	18.9	15.4	7.9
Oak Park	16.9	13.8	7.2
Pontiac	26.1	18.4	14.2
Riverview	24.1	12.5	8.6
Rochester	13.0	4.6	7.4
Rochester Hills	21.1	4.6	7.9
Romulus	23.3	20.0	21.4
Roseville	17.5	2.7	12.8
Royal Oak	12.0	4.6	7.4
South Lyon	34.8	15.8	6.6
Southfield	16.9	9.9	11.1
Southgate	12.2	15.7	12.7

Table 9.1: Black, Hispanic, and non Hispanic white mortgage loan denial rates in selected Detroit suburbs and the City of Detroit in 2020 (continued)

Municipality	Black home seekers (%)	Hispanic home seekers (%)	Non Hispanic white home seekers (%)
St. Clair Shores	13.9	21.1	9.9
Sterling Heights	19.2	13.2	11.7
Taylor	18.5	10.6	15.2
Troy	17.5	12.3	8.4
Warren	17.3	16.9	11.9
Wayne	13.4	20.8	11.8
Westland	14.3	22.1	9.9
Woodhaven	22.5	18.2	8.8
Detroit	*32.3*	*25.1*	*14.1*

Source: Home Mortgage Disclosure Act (HMDA) 2020 Macomb, Oakland and Wayne County Mortgage Loan Data, https://www.consumerfinance.gov/data-research/hmda/.

differences in mortgage loan denial rates between Blacks, Hispanics, and non Hispanic whites in selected suburbs of Detroit.

Using the HMDA 2015 data, the final denial rate percentage was found by identifying the amount of denied applications for each race and ethnicity for each of the five SEPs and the total amount of applications submitted for each race and ethnicity for each of the five SEPs. The amount of denied applications were divided by the total amount of applications for the SEPs: SEP 1, SEP 2, SEP 3, SEP 4, and SEP 5.

In the 40 Detroit suburbs examined, Black home seekers had a higher mortgage loan denial rate than non Hispanic whites in 38 (95 percent) of the suburban municipalities. The only exceptions were Allen Park, where Black home seekers had a denial rate of 10.7 percent compared to 33.8 percent for non Hispanic whites. Southgate was the only other municipality where the denial rate for Black home seekers was lower (12.2 percent) compared to that for non Hispanic whites (12.7 percent). Black home seekers also had a higher loan denial rate than non-Hispanic whites in the City of Detroit (32.3 percent compared to 14.1 respectively).

The mortgage loan denial rates of Hispanics compared with non Hispanic whites were not as unequal in the selected suburbs as those between Blacks and non Hispanic whites. Hispanics had a higher mortgage loan denial rate than non Hispanic whites in 31 (77 percent) of the suburbs. While there were only two Detroit suburbs where Blacks had a lower mortgage loan denial rate than non Hispanic whites, Hispanics had a lower mortgage loan

Table 9.2: Municipality denial rates for Hispanics

Municipality	Denial rate for Hispanics	Denial rate for non Hispanic whites
Allen Park	15.9	33.8
Hazel Park	8.7	11.6
Mount Clemens	5.1	13.9
Farmington	9.2	9.2 (racial equality)
Rochester	4.6	5.6
Roseville	2.7	12.8
Royal Oak	4.6	5.6
Southfield	9.9	11.1
Taylor	10.6	15.2

Sources: Home Mortgage Disclosure Act (HMDA) 2020 Macomb, Oakland and Wayne County Mortgage Loan Data, https://www.consumerfinance.gov/data-research/hmda/.

denial rate than non Hispanic whites in eight (20 percent) suburbs (Table 9.2). The suburbs are listed by percent of denial rates in Table 9.2.

The denial rates between Hispanics and non Hispanic whites in Farmington were both 9.2 percent, which is evidence of racial equality. However, the denial rate in the City of Detroit was 25.1 percent for Hispanics and 14.1 for percent non Hispanic whites. Thus, Hispanics living in Detroit were 1.8 times more likely than non Hispanic whites to be denied a mortgage loan.

Loan denial rates by socioeconomic position and characteristics

Table 9.3 presents mortgage denial rates by socioeconomic characteristics of neighborhoods (SEP, that is, socioeconomic position). The denial rates for each racial group were highest in SEP 1 neighborhoods, which are characterized as having very low socioeconomic characteristics. The denial rate for whites in SEP 1 was 30.3 percent compared to 55.2 percent for Blacks and 56.8 percent for Hispanics. This shows that the characteristics of neighborhoods matter in terms of loan denial rates for all racial and ethnic groups. For example, the denial rates for whites declined from 30.3 percent in SEP 1 neighborhoods to 12.2 percent in SEP 5 neighborhoods (those with very high socioeconomic characteristics).

The denial rate for Blacks declined from 55.2 percent in SEP 1 neighborhoods to 20.4 percent in SEP 5 neighborhoods, while the denial rate for Hispanics declined from 56.8 percent in SEP 1 neighborhoods to 15.7 percent in SEP 5 neighborhoods. The results indicate that the socioeconomic characteristics of neighborhoods matter in relation to loan

Table 9.3: Mortgage loan denial rates by race and socioeconomic position of neighborhoods (SEP) in Metropolitan Detroit

	SEP 1 (%)	SEP 2 (%)	SEP 3 (%)	SEP 4 (%)	SEP 5 (%)
Black, non Hispanic	55.2	36.4	26.9	23.6	20.4
White, non Hispanic	30.3	21.3	17.2	14.4	12.2
Hispanic	56.8	23.4	19.4	16.6	15.7

Sources: Darden, J.T., M. Rahbar, L. Jezierski, M. Li and E. Velie. (2010); United States Bureau of the Census Bureau (2016); American Community Survey, 2011–15; US Bureau of the Census American Community Survey 2016–2020; Home Mortgage Disclosure Act (HMDA) (2015). Macomb, Oakland and Wayne County Mortgage Loan Data, Available from https://www.consumerfinance.gov/data-research/hmda/.

denial rates. The gap between the denial rate for Hispanics and white non Hispanics in SEP 5 neighborhoods (15.7 percent and 12.2 percent respectively) was much smaller than in SEP 1 neighborhoods (Darden et al, 2010; Consumer Financial Protection Bureau, 2017).

Home mortgage loan denial rates by type of loan

Based on the most recent HMDA data, this section examines the Black, Hispanic, and non Hispanic white denial rates by type of loan. It documents that, despite the *Federal Fair Housing Act* of 1968 and the *Federal Home Mortgage Disclosure Act* of 1975, Black and Hispanic applicants are denied mortgage loans at a higher rate than white applicants in most of the selected municipalities with a population of 10,000 or more in Metropolitan Detroit. Finally, the denial rates occurred throughout the Metropolitan Area and in the City of Detroit, and in the inner and outer suburbs. This conclusion is based on the 2017 HMDA data, which shows that for both conventional mortgage loans and Federal Housing Administration (FHA) mortgage loans, Blacks were turned down at a higher rate than non Hispanic white applicants. For conventional loans, they were 2.4 times more likely to be turned down compared to non Hispanic whites and for FHA loans they were 1.5 times more likely than white applicants to be turned down for loans.

A total of 17 percent of Hispanic applicants were denied conventional loans compared to only 12.8 percent of non Hispanic whites (a ratio of 1.3). For FHA loans, 18.8 percent of Hispanics were denied loans compared to 14.6 percent for non Hispanic white applicants (a ratio of 1.3). A total of 16 percent of Hispanic applicants were denied loans. A total of 21 percent of Black applicants were denied home purchase loans, compared to only

10 percent of non Hispanic white applicants (a ratio of 2.1); for Hispanic applicants, the denial rate was 11.9 percent (a ratio of 1.2). The largest ratios between each of the racial ethnic groups and white applicants were for home improvement loans rather than home purchase or refinance loans.

Racial inequality between Blacks and whites in Detroit's selected suburbs and in the City of Detroit

This section examines five of the nine variables discussed throughout the book: percentage in poverty/below the poverty line, median household income, educational attainment, occupational status, and homeownership. The objective is to determine the extent to which these characteristics exist among the Black and white population in each of the selected suburbs and in the City of Detroit.

Racial inequality in the poverty rate between Black and white households

Although many whites left the City of Detroit following each census, research suggests that one of the major reasons many moved to the suburbs was to live in a neighborhood with improved socioeconomic characteristics, especially the opportunity to buy a home and to escape poverty. Some poor residents have lived in the suburbs since their existence. However, many Detroit suburbs were areas where the population was overwhelmingly white. Since the *Fair Housing Act* of 1968, more and more Blacks have moved to the suburbs of Detroit. Some of the Blacks who moved there were motivated by the same desires as the white population who moved there.

Racial inequality in the poverty rate between Black and non Hispanic white households

The discussion here begins with the poverty rate. The results reveal that out of the 40 Detroit suburbs examined, the Black poverty rate was higher than the non Hispanic white poverty rate in 31 (77 percent) of the selected suburbs. The Black poverty rate was also higher in the City of Detroit, where it was 34.7 percent for Blacks and 33.4 percent for non Hispanic whites. The Black poverty rate was lower in all of the Detroit suburbs than in the City of Detroit, with the exceptions of Hazel Park (42 percent) and Flat Rock (37.5 percent). The poverty rate for non Hispanic whites was 17.7 percent in Hazel Park and 11.1 percent in Flat Rock. There were nine suburbs (22 percent) where the Black poverty rate was lower than the rate for non Hispanic whites. These are listed in Table 9.4.

Table 9.4: Municipalities where the percentage of Black poverty rate was lower than the rate for non Hispanic white poverty rate

Municipality	Black poverty rate (%)	Non Hispanic white poverty rate (%)
Grosse Pointe Park	1.7	6.0
Grosse Pointe Woods	2.0	4.2
Inkster	32.6	35.8
Madison Heights	8.5	14.2
Melvindale	13.6	21.6
Novi City	3.0	4.0
Rochester Hills	2.6	5.4
Southfield	10.2	12.2
Southgate	5.3	10.0

Source: calculated by the author from data obtained from US Bureau of the Census (2022).

The poverty rate for Blacks and non Hispanic whites in Oak Park was equal (13.9 percent) (see Table 9.5).

Racial inequality in terms of median household income

Of the 40 selected Detroit suburbs, Blacks had a lower median household income than non Hispanic white households in every Detroit suburb except Melvindale ($50,879 compared to $42,216), Rochester ($91,528 compared to $88,678), Romulus ($50,901 compared to $50,526), and Southfield ($55,884 compared to $55,208). The census data did not provide median household income data for Blacks living in Ferndale.

Since most studies compare the racial groups living in the suburbs with the racial groups living in the city, it is important to note that the Black median household income in the selected Detroit suburbs was higher than the Black median household income for residents who remained in the City of Detroit ($30,062), with the exception of Hazel Park ($21,613) and Mount Clemens ($28,509) (see Table 9.6).

Racial inequality in the occupational structure

Within the occupational structure, the Office of Management and Budget has listed occupations based on their rank from highest to lowest. At the top of the hierarchy are management, business, science, and arts occupations. These occupations include not only business but also computer and science occupations, community service, media, healthcare practitioners, and

Table 9.5: The poverty rate for Blacks, non Hispanic whites, and Hispanics in the City of Detroit and selected suburbs in 2020

Municipality	Black poverty rate (%)	Non Hispanic white poverty rate (%)	Hispanic poverty rate (%)
Allen Park	11.8	8.8	1.4
Auburn Hills	16.3	11.2	18.9
Birmingham	16.8	4.6	0.0
Dearborn	28.9	28.4	13.1
Eastpointe	18.7	11.3	11.9
Farmington	10.7	8.0	1.5
Ferndale	27.7	7.7	12.4
Flat Rock	37.5	11.1	28.9
Fraser	26.7	10.3	0.0
Garden City	13.4	10.0	4.2
Grosse Pointe Park	1.7	6.0	11.4
Grosse Pointe Woods	2.0	4.2	9.2
Harper Woods	21.4	10.9	0.0
Hazel Park	42.0	17.7	8.7
Inkster	32.6	35.8	54.8
Lincoln Park	28.5	18.4	21.4
Livonia	12.7	4.8	6.0
Madison Heights	8.5	14.2	1.9
Melvindale	13.6	21.6	22.5
Mount Clemens	27.9	16.0	35.0
Novi City	3.0	4.0	4.3
Oak Park	13.9	13.9	19.6
Pontiac	30.9	29.8	29.5
Riverview	28.6	7.3	4.7
Rochester	7.9	6.7	4.5
Rochester Hills	2.6	5.4	2.5
Romulus	20.0	15.5	14.5
Roseville	22.2	13.0	23.0
Royal Oak	20.0	5.6	6.5
South Lyon	18.9	5.9	0.0
Southfield	10.2	12.0	23.3
Southgate	5.3	10.0	17.6

Table 9.5: The poverty rate for Blacks, non Hispanic whites, and Hispanics in the City of Detroit and selected suburbs in 2020 (continued)

Municipality	Black poverty rate (%)	Non Hispanic white poverty rate (%)	Hispanic poverty rate (%)
St. Clair Shores	15.6	7.2	3.8
Sterling Heights	12.2	11.2	12.0
Taylor	31.8	12.3	7.3
Troy	7.7	4.8	7.7
Warren	23.9	14.7	18.9
Wayne	30.6	19.7	1.1
Westland	18.4	12.9	22.5
Woodhaven	17.3	4.6	9.5
Detroit	*34.7*	*33.4*	*34.3*

Source: calculated by the author from data obtained from US Bureau of the Census (2022).

Table 9.6: Non Hispanic white, Black, and Hispanic median household income in Detroit and selected suburbs in 2020

Municipality	Non Hispanic white	Black	Hispanic
Allen Park	$69,800	$49,483	$64,468
Auburn Hills	$62,788	$49,820	$72,303
Birmingham	$124,088	$97,813	$127,946
Dearborn	$52,691	$48,750	$65,987
Eastpointe	$50,324	$48,316	$56,250
Farmington	$81,200	$45,238	$48,930
Farmington Hills	$81,733	$67,729	$84,672
Ferndale	$75,016	X	$49,583
Flat Rock	$60,972	$36,518	$55,903
Fraser	$58,737	$45,096	$64,883
Garden City	$57,079	$32,321	$50,559
Grosse Pointe Park	$117,256	$80,972	X
Grosse Pointe Woods	$106,058	$84,612	$106,719
Hazel Park	$40,978	$21,613	$56,136
Inkster	$35,104	$31,713	$23,967

(continued)

Table 9.6: Non Hispanic white, Black, and Hispanic median household income in Detroit and selected suburbs in 2020 (continued)

Municipality	Non Hispanic white	Black	Hispanic
Lincoln Park	$46,355	$30,344	$46,563
Livonia	$79,975	$55,114	$88,882
Madison Heights	$57,573	$45,102	$45,221
Melvindale	$42,216	$50,879	$31,270
Mount Clemens	$50,352	$28,503	$46,875
Novi	$93,762	$77,838	$90,000
Oak Park	$56,610	$49,360	$29,956
Pontiac	$35,599	$32,004	$35,082
Riverview	$57,928	$34,258	$64,238
Rochester	$88,678	$91,528	$83,056
Rochester Hills	$90,291	$80,556	$95,714
Romulus	$50,526	$50,901	$107,708
Roseville	$50,265	$36,940	$58,594
Royal Oak	$82,979	$35,938	$93,901
South Lyon	$71,908	X	$155,036
Southfield	$55,218	$55,884	$39,860
Southgate	$57,586	$38,508	$72,330
St. Clair Shores	$61,031	$53,636	$68,162
Sterling Heights	$63,939	$60,000	$66,639
Taylor	$53,620	$35,568	$51,607
Troy	$95,415	$74,464	$85,270
Warren	$51,519	$39,670	$46,280
Wayne	$50,700	$38,806	$44,806
Westland	$51,843	$43,125	$55,781
Woodhaven	$64,586	$50,368	$58,152
Detroit	$38,145	$30,062	$32,754

Note: X = data not listed.

Source: calculated by the author from data obtained from the US Bureau of the Census (2022).

technical occupations. Second in rank are service occupations; third are sales and office occupations; fourth are natural resources, construction, and maintenance occupations. Ranked fifth (or last) in the hierarchy are production, transportation, and material-moving occupations. The racial inequality in the occupational structure between Blacks and whites is measured in Detroit and selected suburbs by determining the percentage of Black and white households that held the highest occupational status.

I have also measured the racial inequality in more detail for the City of Detroit. I measured the five major occupations and the difference in the percentage of Blacks and whites occupying these five occupations in order to determine whether the distribution over these was even. I used the index of dissimilarity to determine the extent of evenness. The results of Blacks and whites in occupations in the selected Detroit suburbs highlight that Black residents are underrepresented in management, business, science, and arts occupations. The data show that white residents in management, business, service, and arts occupations had a higher percentage than Blacks in 33 of the 40 suburban municipalities, or 82 percent. White residents also had a higher percentage in these occupations than Blacks in the City of Detroit. However, there were some municipalities where there was a higher percentage of Blacks in these occupation than whites.

Black inequality in the occupational structure

In 33 of the 40 Detroit suburbs examined (82 percent), there were fewer Blacks than non Hispanic whites in the highest occupations. There were only nine municipalities where a higher Black percentage of the employed population occupied these occupations than the percentage of non Hispanic whites. The nine municipalities were Allen Park (50.4 percentage for Blacks compared to 34.7 for non Hispanic whites); Birmingham (68.2 compared to 67.1); Eastpointe (36.1 compared to 21.5); Inkster (19.1 compared to 18.7); Rochester Hills (58.9 compared to 53.2); Romulus (18.9 compared to 17.9); Southgate (39.4 compared to 28.8); St Clair Shores (32.1 compared to 25.5); Woodhaven (37.3 compared to 34.9).

Of all occupations held by Blacks in the City of Detroit, 21.8 percent were in very high-rated occupations compared to 35.7 percent of all non Hispanic whites in Detroit. In 29 (72 percent) of the suburbs, there was a higher percentage of Blacks in this high occupational status than for those who remained in the City of Detroit. Blacks were also underrepresented in natural resources, construction, and maintenance occupations in Detroit—of all occupations held by Blacks, 5.2 percent fell into this category, compared to 6.7 percent of all occupations held by whites. Blacks were overrepresented in service occupations at 30.5 percent compared to 21 percent of all whites, a difference of 9.5 percentage points. Also, 25.7 percent of all Blacks were in sales and office occupations, compared to 23.4 percent of all whites. Blacks were also overrepresented in production, transportation, and material-moving occupations, where they held 16.9 percent. Whites comprise 13.3 percent of these occupations. If the Detroit occupational structure reflected racial equality, the distribution of Blacks and whites in these occupations would

Table 9.7: The percentage of Blacks, non Hispanic whites, and Hispanics in the highest occupational category (management, business, science, and arts occupations) in 2020

Municipality	Blacks	Whites	Hispanics
Allen Park	50.4	34.7	63.0
Auburn Hills	40.3	41.8	15.4
Birmingham	68.2	67.1	58.8
Dearborn	33.1	39.3	40.3
Eastpointe	36.1	21.5	18.4
Farmington	36.2	51.8	36.8
Farmington Hills	46.6	51.8	36.8
Ferndale	24.2	46.4	45.3
Flat Rock	6.1	35.4	33.3
Fraser	15.8	33.3	17.7
Garden City	19.9	24.2	16.1
Grosse Pointe Park	38.1	64.0	70.5
Grosse Pointe Woods	53.3	54.4	56.8
Hazel Park	14.9	22.8	18.0
Inkster	19.1	18.7	29.8
Lincoln Park	14.9	20.2	18.3
Livonia	29.8	42.1	47.5
Madison Heights	25.6	26.2	16.7
Melvindale	17.8	23.0	25.1
Mount Clemens	28.4	33.1	37.9
Novi City	42.6	52.1	36.0
Oak Park	31.5	41.8	50.3
Pontiac	18.5	21.3	11.2
Riverview	0.0	33.5	11.9
Rochester	46.5	53.7	64.4
Rochester Hills	58.9	53.2	50.0
Romulus	18.9	17.9	3.7
Roseville	18.7	21.9	14.4
Royal Oak	46.1	53.4	56.9
South Lyon	13.9	47.0	35.0
Southfield	38.2	49.3	35.1
Southgate	39.4	28.8	15.2
St. Clair Shores	32.1	25.5	24.6

Table 9.7: The percentage of Blacks, non Hispanic whites, and Hispanics in the highest occupational category (management, business, science, and arts occupations) in 2020 (continued)

Municipality	Blacks	Whites	Hispanics
Sterling Heights	30.1	34.8	30.1
Taylor	20.1	20.6	20.9
Troy	40.6	55.2	55.6
Warren	21.8	26.4	17.3
Wayne	20.1	21.9	28.0
Westland	18.4	27.0	24.5
Woodhaven	37.3	34.9	42.6
Detroit	**21.8**	**35.7**	**10.6**

Source: calculated by the author from data obtained from the United States Bureau of the Census (2022).

be equal to an index of dissimilarity of zero. The index of dissimilarity of the Black and white occupational distribution was 15.4. The higher the index, the higher the extent of racial inequality.

In sum, most Blacks who moved to the Detroit suburbs did improve their occupational status.

Black inequality in the educational attainment in selected suburbs of Detroit and the City of Detroit

How educated a population in a municipality is influences the strength of the municipality, including residential neighborhoods. I used the highest level of educational attainment to determine whether the percentage of Blacks and whites who had obtained a bachelor's degree or higher was equal. The analyses revealed that for the 40 Detroit suburbs, there was a higher percentage of white bachelor's degree holders than Black bachelor's degree holders in 33 (82 percent) of the suburbs. There was also a higher percentage of white bachelor's degree holders in the City of Detroit.

However, in the suburbs, the percentage of Blacks with a bachelor's degree or higher was greater than the percentage of non Hispanic whites: Allen Park (30.2 percent of Blacks and 28.3 percent of non Hispanic whites); Flat Rock (37.1 percent of Blacks and 17.4 percent of non Hispanic whites); and Livonia (40.6 percent of Blacks and 37.8 percent of non Hispanic whites). In Melvindale, Blacks with bachelor's degrees or higher were 12.1 percent compared to 10.8 percent for non Hispanic whites. In Romulus, 21.4 percent of Blacks had a bachelor's degree or

Table 9.8: Black and white occupational inequality in the City of Detroit in 2020

Percentage of		Percentage of		**Absolute difference**
Black residents in management, business, science, and arts occupations	21.7%	white residents in management, business, science, and arts occupations	35.6%	−13.9
Percentage of Black residents in service occupations	30.5%	Percentage of white residents in service occupations	21.0%	+ 9.5
Percentage of Black residents in sales and office occupations	25.7%	Percentage of white residents in sales and office occupations	23.4%	+ 2.3
Percentage of Black residents in natural resources, construction, and maintenance occupations	5.2%	Percentage of white residents in natural resources, construction, and maintenance occupations	6.7%	−1.5
Percentage of Black residents in production, transportation, and material-moving occupations	16.9%	Percentage of white residents in production, transportation, and material-moving occupations	13.3%	+3.6
TOTAL	**100**		**100**	**30.8**
INDEX OF DISSIMILARITY = 15.4				

Source: calculated by the author from data obtained from United States Bureau of the Census (2022).

higher, compared to 16.8 percent for non-Hispanic whites. In Roseville, 14.3 percent of Blacks had a bachelor's degree or higher, compared to 13.3 percent for non Hispanic whites. In St. Clair Shores, 26.4 percent of Blacks had a bachelor's degree or higher, compared to 26.1 percent of non Hispanic whites. In Taylor, 22.8 percent of Blacks had a bachelor's degree or higher, compared to 11.6 percent of non Hispanic whites. In Wayne, 14.9 percent of Blacks had a bachelor's degree or higher, compared to 14.7 percent of non Hispanic whites. Finally, in Woodhaven, 32.7 percent of Blacks had a bachelor's degree or higher compared to 22.7 percent of non Hispanic whites. Among the Blacks who lived in the suburbs compared to Blacks who remained in the City of Detroit, their educational attainment as defined by bachelor's degree holders was higher in 31, or 77 percent, of the suburbs than the percentage of bachelor's degree holders for Blacks in Detroit (see Tables 9.9a and 9.9b).

Table 9.9a: Black bachelor's degree holders, compared to white bachelor's degree holders

Municipality	Blacks with bachelor's degree (%)	Whites with bachelor's degree (%)
Allen Park	30.2	28.3
Flat Rock	37.1	17.4
Livonia	40.6	37.8
Melvindale	12.1	10.8
Romulus	21.4	16.8
Roseville	14.3	13.3
St. Clair Shores	26.4	26.1
Taylor	22.8	11.6
Wayne	14.9	14.7
Woodhaven	32.7	22.7

Source: calculated by the author from data obtained from the US Bureau of the Census (2022).

Black inequality in homeownership

The Black homeownership rate was lower than the non Hispanic white homeownership rate in all of the 40 suburbs examined. The Black homeownership rate was also lower than the non Hispanic white homeownership rate in the City of Detroit. Unlike the other socioeconomic variables, the racial inequality between Blacks and non Hispanic whites was complete.

Homeownership among the five variables examined is the most important because it is most directly related to the wealth disparity between Blacks and whites. This is the only variable examined that had s100 percent racial inequality in the suburbs and in the City of Detroit. There was not a single municipality where the Black homeownership rate was higher than the rate for non Hispanic whites or even equal to the rate for non Hispanic whites. The largest gap between Black and non Hispanic white homeownership rates was in South Lyon, where no Blacks who lived there owned a home, compared to 79.4 percent of non Hispanic whites who owned their own homes. The smallest gap in homeownership rates between Blacks and non Hispanic whites was in Inkster, a predominantly Black suburb, and in Detroit, a predominantly Black city. In Inkster, the Black homeownership rate was 39.9 percent, compared to 50.2 percent for whites. In the City of Detroit the Black homeownership rate was 45.8 percent compared to 53.3 percent for non Hispanic whites (see Table 9.10).

Table 9.9b: Bachelor's degree holders for Blacks, Hispanics, and non Hispanic whites in Detroit and selected Detroit suburbs

Municipality	Bachelor's degree or higher level of educational attainment Black households (%)	Bachelor's degree or higher level of educational attainment white households (%)	Bachelor's degree or higher level of educational attainment Hispanic households (%)
Allen Park	30.2	28.3	10.7
Auburn Hills	26.2	37.3	32.0
Birmingham	55.9	77.9	68.0
Dearborn	24.6	65.9	34.1
Eastpointe	16.1	17.4	12.7
Farmington	26.0	53.2	64.2
Farmington Hills	32.7	53.2	54.8
Ferndale	34.8	52.5	44.0
Flat Rock	37.1	17.4	0.0
Fraser	12.2	24.4	37.0
Garden City	7.1	13.5	11.3
Grosse Pointe Park	45.3	69.4	73.0
Grosse Pointe Woods	20.3	65.6	61.0
Harper Woods	20.4	33.5	55.7
Hazel Park	14.1	16.2	19.3
Inkster	9.8	8.8	21.5
Lincoln Park	11.4	11.7	7.9
Livonia	40.6	37.8	31.3
Madison Heights	24.3	24.9	21.4
Melvindale	12.1	10.8	2.4
Mount Clemens	8.8	17.5	6.8
Novi City	30.6	54.4	65.8
Oak Park	25.3	43.0	15.4
Pontiac	10.5	18.1	7.1
Riverview	11.2	22.9	4.5
Rochester	36.9	60.6	53.1
Rochester Hills	51.7	54.2	67.8
Romulus	21.4	16.8	4.3
Roseville	14.3	13.3	13.6
Royal Oak	33.8	59.6	63.0

Table 9.9b: Bachelor's degree holders for Blacks, Hispanics, and non Hispanic whites in Detroit and selected Detroit suburbs (continued)

Municipality	Bachelor's degree or higher level of educational attainment Black households (%)	Bachelor's degree or higher level of educational attainment white households (%)	Bachelor's degree or higher level of educational attainment Hispanic households (%)
South Lyon	28.6	46.3	71.6
Southfield	35.3	43.7	40.3
Southgate	12.3	19.8	16.2
St. Clair Shores	26.4	26.1	24.6
Sterling Heights	23.9	27.3	23.5
Taylor	22.8	11.6	12.4
Troy	49.7	55.8	60.1
Warren	16.5	17.9	13.3
Wayne	14.9	14.7	13.7
Westland	19.2	20.4	11.6
Woodhaven	32.7	22.7	17.3
Detroit	**12.9**	**36.2**	**8.0**

Source: calculated by the author from data obtained from United States Bureau of the Census (2022).

Furthermore, it is important to reveal that in every Detroit suburb examined, the majority of whites owned their homes. The majority of non Hispanic whites living in Detroit also owned their homes. On the other hand, the majority of Blacks (85 percent) living in 35 of the 40 Detroit suburbs examined did not own their homes (see Table 9.10). Nor did the majority of Hispanics own their homes.

The seven Detroit suburbs where the majority of Blacks living there did own their own homes were: Allen Park (56.6 percent); Eastpointe (52 percent); Flat Rock (62.8 percent); Grosse Pointe Woods (72.5 percent); Livonia 52.6 percent); Oak Park (50.8 percent); and Romulus (55.9 percent). In sum, based on the census data and analyses, it is clear that from the socioeconomic variables examined (percentage in poverty/below the poverty line, median household income, occupational status, educational attainment, and homeownership) racial discrimination is still a factor in explaining the racial inequality in Detroit's selected suburbs and in the City of Detroit after bankruptcy. Racial inequality remains a fact of life.

The next section will examine inequality between Hispanics and non Hispanic whites.

Table 9.10: Black, non Hispanic white, and Hispanic homeownership rates in Detroit and selected Detroit suburbs in 2020

Municipality	Black (%)	Non Hispanic white (%)	Hispanic (%)
Allen Park	56.6	85.6	93.2
Auburn Hills	28.1	56.8	49.5
Birmingham	15.7	76.2	41.6
Dearborn	21.8	69.3	59.6
Eastpointe	52.0	78.7	55.3
Farmington	26.0	75.8	52.4
Farmington Hills	43.0	74.7	36.7
Ferndale	27.3	71.4	52.8
Flat Rock	62.8	76.5	32.8
Fraser	12.3	75.4	93.0
Garden City	32.3	82.3	88.2
Grosse Pointe Park	41.5	77.5	56.1
Grosse Pointe Woods	72.5	91.6	59.5
Hazel Park	29.9	52.9	64.3
Inkster	39.9	50.2	24.2
Lincoln Park	21.0	74.6	72.5
Livonia	52.6	87.9	91.6
Madison Heights	12.4	66.8	40.0
Melvindale	25.6	59.7	48.3
Mount Clemens	37.8	60.7	42.9
Novi City	31.2	73.1	45.8
Oak Park	50.8	61.9	63.9
Pontiac	36.8	50.9	56.8
Riverview	7.7	64.4	46.6
Rochester	46.7	66.5	49.0
Rochester Hills	40.4	80.0	63.6
Romulus	55.9	76.6	76.1
Roseville	19.0	73.4	42.8
Royal Oak	12.6	70.0	49.3
South Lyon	0.0	79.4	100
St. Clair Shores	44.6	83.3	65.8
Sterling Heights	36.5	76.0	74.0
Taylor	16.3	76.3	74.6
Troy	23.7	80.7	56.6

Table 9.10: Black, non Hispanic white, and Hispanic homeownership rates in Detroit and selected Detroit suburbs in 2020 (continued)

Municipality	Black (%)	Non Hispanic white (%)	Hispanic (%)
Warren	31.5	78.7	70.0
Wayne	26.7	68.3	61.1
Westland	30.1	68.7	40.3
Woodhaven	23.6	75.4	74.6
Detroit	**45.8**	**53.3**	**53.2**

Source: calculated by the author from data obtained from United States Bureau of the Census (2022).

Table 9.11: Detroit suburbs where the Hispanic poverty rate was lower than the non Hispanic white poverty rate

Municipality	Hispanic poverty rate (%)	Non Hispanic poverty rate (%)
Allen Park	1.4	8.3
Birmingham	0.0	4.6
Farmington	1.5	8.0
Fraser	0.0	10.3
Garden City	4.2	10.0
Hazel Park	8.7	17.7
Madison Heights	1.9	14.2
Riverview	4.7	7.3
Rochester Hills	2.5	5.4
Romulus	14.5	15.5
South Lyon	0.0	5.9
St. Clair Shores	3.8	7.2
Taylor	7.3	12.3
Wayne	1.1	19.7

Source: calculated by the author from data obtained from United States Bureau of the Census (2022).

Hispanic inequality in the poverty rate

The percentage of Hispanics in poverty was higher than non Hispanic white households in 22 (55 percent) of the 40 suburbs examined. Hispanics also had a higher poverty rate in the City of Detroit than non Hispanic white households. However, there were a few suburbs where the Hispanic poverty rate was lower than that for non Hispanic white households. Such suburbs and the poverty rates are shown in Table 9.12.

In examining the racial inequality between Hispanics and non Hispanic whites based on the poverty rate, it is clear that Hispanics in the suburbs of Detroit were better off economically than Hispanics who remained in the City of Detroit. Of the 40 suburbs where Hispanics resided, only two—Inkster (54.8 percent) and Mount Clemens (35 percent)—had a poverty rate higher than that for Hispanics in the City of Detroit (34.3 percent). Hispanics in Metropolitan Detroit took advantage of the geography of economic opportunity, and improved their economic status and condition by residing in the suburbs, just as non Hispanic whites had done earlier. The next socioeconomic indicator to assess inequality between Hispanics and non Hispanic whites is median household income. Hispanics had a lower median household income than non Hispanic whites in 21 (50 percent) of the 40 Detroit suburbs examined (see Table 9.12). However, in 20 (50 percent) of the suburbs, Hispanics had a higher median household income than non Hispanic whites.

Table 9.12: Suburbs where the Hispanic median household income was higher than the median household income of white households

Municipality	Hispanic income	Non Hispanic white income
Auburn Hills	$72,303	$62,788
Birmingham	$127,946	$124,088
Dearborn	$65,987	$52,691
Eastpointe	$56,250	$50,324
Farmington Hills	$84,672	$81,733
Fraser	$64,883	$58,737
Grosse Pointe Woods	$106,719	$106,058
Hazel Park	$56,136	$40,970
Lincoln Park	$46,563	$46,355
Livonia	$88,882	$79,975
Riverview	$64,238	$57,928
Rochester Hills	$95,714	$90,291
Romulus	$107,708	$50,526
Roseville	$58,594	$50,265
Royal Oak	$93,901	$82,979
South Lyon	$155,036	$71,908
Southgate	$72,330	$57,586
St. Clair Shores	$68,162	$61,031
Sterling Heights	$66,639	$63,939
Westland	$55,781	$51,843

Source: calculated by the author from data obtained from United States Bureau of the Census (2022).

The next indicator was measured by the differences in the percentage of Hispanics holding the highest occupations (management, business, science, and arts occupations). I also examined the percentage of Hispanics and non Hispanic whites in the City of Detroit who are distributed in the other four categories of occupations. I used the index of dissimilarity to determine how unevenly the two groups are distributed over these occupations. Table 9.7 shows that Hispanics and non Hispanic whites were more unevenly distributed over the occupations in the City of Detroit than Blacks were. The index of dissimilarity between the two groups was 30.

In terms of the distribution of Hispanics in the highest occupational category compared to non Hispanic whites in the 40 Detroit suburbs examined, the results revealed that Hispanics had a lower percentage of their population in management, business, science, and arts occupations than non Hispanic whites in 27 (67 percent) of the suburbs. Hispanics also had a lower percentage of their population in these occupations in the City of Detroit. In fact, Hispanics had the lowest representation in these occupations in Romulus (3.7 percent) (see Table 9.7). However, in the following municipalities, Hispanics had a higher percentage of their population than whites in these occupations.

Table 9.13: Management, business, science, and arts occupations where Hispanics had a higher percentage than non Hispanic whites in the suburbs

Municipality	Hispanics (%)	Non Hispanic whites (%)
Allen Park	63.0	34.7
Dearborn	40.3	39.3
Grosse Pointe Woods	56.8	54.4
Inkster	29.8	18.7
Livonia	47.5	42.1
Melvindale	25.1	23.0
Mount Clemens	37.9	33.1
Oak Park	50.3	41.8
Rochester	64.4	53.7
Royal Oak	56.9	53.4
Taylor	20.9	20.6
Troy	55.6	55.2
Wayne	28.0	21.9
Woodhaven	42.6	34.9

Source: calculated by the author from data obtained from United States Bureau of the Census (2022).

Table 9.14: Suburbs where Hispanics had a higher percentage of bachelor's degree holders than non Hispanic whites

Municipality	Hispanics (%)	Non Hispanic whites (%)
Farmington	64.2	3.2
Farmington Hills	54.8	53.2
Fraser	37.0	24.4
Grosse Pointe Park	73.0	69.4
Harper Woods	55.7	33.5
Hazel Park	19.3	16.2
Inkster	21.5	8.8
Novi City	65.8	54.4
Rochester Hills	67.8	54.2
Roseville	13.6	13.3
Royal Oak	63.0	59.6
South Lyon	71.6	46.3
Taylor	12.4	11.6
Troy	60.1	55.8

Source: calculated by the author from data obtained from United States Bureau of the Census (2022).

Like the other indicators, there were 14 (35 percent) of the suburbs where a higher percentage of Hispanics had a bachelor's degree or higher than non Hispanic white households. These are shown in Table 9.14.

Finally, the racial inequality between the percentage of Hispanics and non Hispanic white households that owned their own homes was examined in selected suburbs of Detroit. Non Hispanic whites had a higher homeownership rate than Hispanics in 32 (80 percent) of the 40 suburbs examined. However, Hispanics in the City of Detroit had an equal percentage of homeownership compared to non Hispanic whites (53 percent). The Detroit suburbs were where Hispanics had a higher percentage of homeownership than non Hispanic whites (see Table 9.15).

Hispanics had a higher homeownership rate than those who stayed in the City of Detroit. In general, Hispanics in the suburbs of Detroit were more likely to be homeowners than those who remained in the city, although the majority of Hispanics in Detroit (53 percent) owned their own home. This is equal to the percentage of non Hispanic whites who own their homes. In terms of homeownership, this is racial equality. However, Blacks have not reached racial equality in Detroit in terms of their homeownership rate (only 45.8 percent). Thus, after bankruptcy there was not a single Detroit

Table 9.15: Suburbs where Hispanics had a higher homeownership rate than non Hispanic whites

Municipality	Hispanic households (%)	Non Hispanic white households (%)
Allen Park	93.2	85.6
Fraser	93.0	75.4
Garden City	88.2	82.3
Hazel Park	64.3	52.9
Livonia	91.6	87.9
Oak Park	63.9	61.9
Pontiac	56.8	50.9
South Lyon	100	79.7
Southgate	74.6	71.1

Source: calculated by the author from data obtained from United States Bureau of the Census (2022).

suburb where Blacks had a higher homeownership rate than non Hispanic whites. Blacks also do not have a homeownership rate higher than non Hispanic whites in the City of Detroit.

Conclusion

The United States Bureau of the Census in 2020 shows an increase in the Black and Hispanic population that moved to the suburbs of Detroit between 2010 and 2020. However, data from the *Home Mortgage Disclosure Act* database revealed that barriers remain for Black and Hispanic home seekers. Both groups continue to experience a higher percentage of mortgage loan denials than their non Hispanic white counterparts. Racial differences in mortgage loan denial rates were apparent in different loan types, such as conventional loans and FHA loans. In both types, Blacks were turned down at a higher rate than non Hispanic white home seekers, and so were Hispanics. In fact, the ratio of loan denials between Blacks and non Hispanic whites was 2.4, which means that Black home seekers were more than twice as likely as non Hispanic white home seekers to be denied a mortgage loan (Immergluck, Earl, and Powell, 2019). For Hispanics, the denial rate was also higher. They were denied conventional loans and FHA loans at 1.3 times the rate for non Hispanic whites.

The analysis in this chapter has shown that Blacks and Hispanics were also denied mortgage loans at a higher rate as a result of the socioeconomic characteristics of neighborhoods in which they lived. The denial rate was highest for very low socioeconomic characteristic neighborhoods and lowest for those with very high socioeconomic characteristics. This chapter has also measured racial inequality in the suburbs of Detroit. The following socioeconomic variables were analyzed: percentage in poverty/ below the poverty line, median household income, educational attainment, occupational status, and homeownership. Racial inequality was evident in the 40 suburbs with a population of 10,000 or more and where at least 20 applications were made for mortgage loans by Black and Hispanic home seekers. The racial inequality was greater between Blacks and non Hispanic whites than between Hispanics and non Hispanic whites in all of the suburbs. Compared to Blacks, there were more suburbs where Hispanics had a lower poverty rate, a higher median household income, and a higher percentage of workers employed in management, business, science, and arts occupations than non Hispanic whites.

The data show that the inequality gap between Blacks and non Hispanic whites was much greater than the inequality gap between Hispanics and non Hispanic whites. The major inequality difference was in the homeownership rate. Although Hispanics had homeownership rates that were higher than or equal to those of non Hispanic whites in some suburbs, the Black homeownership rate was lower than the non Hispanic white rate in every suburb. Racial discrimination, as revealed by mortgage loan denials, seems to be more of a barrier to racial equality than the other socioeconomic variables since mortgage denials reduce the Black homeownership rate. Homeownership is the most important socioeconomic variable among those examined in selected Detroit suburbs and in the City of Detroit. It is clear from the findings given in this chapter that the City of Detroit after bankruptcy did not achieve the objective of racial inclusiveness and racial equality.

10

Conclusions: The Status
of the Residents of Detroit
after Bankruptcy

The aim of the book has been to provide a detailed analysis of patterns of development in Detroit after bankruptcy and determine whether or not these developments have been equitable and inclusive. Over the course of the last nine chapters I have measured: (1) changes in trends toward an inclusive city; (2) whether more racial equality occurred after bankruptcy; and (3) whether the data and analyses answered the question of whether Detroit met its overall objective of becoming a more racially inclusive city after bankruptcy.

I started the book by focusing on the antecedents to bankruptcy. On July 18, 2013, Black lawyer Kevyn Orr was appointed Emergency Manager by Republican Governor of Michigan Rick Snyder. Orr's task was to conduct research on the predominantly Black city and recommend a legal decision to declare the City of Detroit bankrupt. According to *Bloomberg News* (2013), Emergency Manager Kevyn Orr rushed the $18 billion bankruptcy petition into federal court on July 18 just minutes before a state judge could stop him. The decision by the Emergency Manager made the City of Detroit the largest city in the US to experience bankruptcy.

Chapter 1 examined the historical, economic, social, demographic, racial, and non cooperative relationship between the State of Michigan and the City of Detroit that led to the bankruptcy decision. There is evidence to suggest that the seeds for Detroit's bankruptcy were planted over time by the actions of investors, who reduced their investments in the City of Detroit and increased investment in the suburbs over a period of 60 years (Darden et al, 1987). These actions resulted in increased unemployment in the city, the outmigration of the white middle class, a decline in property values, an increase in housing abandonment, and a reduction in tax revenue for city services (Gillette, 2014). Instead of financial assistance from the State, Detroit, like other cities in Michigan, was faced with a reduction in revenue sharing (Lavelle, 2014; Sapotichne et al, 2015). Such disinvestment by the private sector and a reduction in revenue sharing by the State made the financial problems of the city very difficult to solve (McFarland and Pagano, 2014).

Instead of providing the financial support needed, the Governor used a new, stronger Republican-passed Emergency Manager Law in 2011 to remove the democratically elected African American Mayor and the City Council from power (Pew Charitable Trusts, 2013). The Governor then appointed an Emergency Manager to govern Detroit. The Emergency Manager served on behalf of the Governor, who made the final political decision to declare bankruptcy.

Chapter 2 examined Detroit's struggle to survive financially during the bankruptcy period—a struggle that it lost. On July 18, 2013, Detroit filed for the largest municipal bankruptcy in US history. The city emerged nearly 17 months later with a Plan of Adjustment. This chapter examined: (1) the legal origin of the city's bankruptcy; (2) the summary of oral opinion and reasons why the decision was made for bankruptcy by Judge Steven Rhodes; (3) the characteristics of the decision makers; and (4) the characteristics of the creditors and of winners and losers resulting from the Grand Bargain. The legal origin of the bankruptcy can be traced back to 1937, when Congress enacted new municipal bankruptcy provisions by adding Chapter IX to the 1934 *Bankruptcy Act*.

The Plan of Adjustment that the City of Detroit filed with the US Bankruptcy Court for the Eastern District of Michigan on February 21, 2014 represented a critical step toward the city's rehabilitation and recovery from a decades-long downward spiral. The Plan provided for the adjustment of up to as much as $18 billion in secured and unsecured debt, and offered the greatest possible recoveries for the city's creditors while simultaneously allowing for meaningful and necessary investment in the city.

Emergency Manager Orr concluded that despite aggressive cost-cutting measures already implemented by the city and good faith negotiations, no reasonable alternatives for restructuring the city's operations and obligations existed other than Chapter IX. Without Chapter IX relief, there was no clear path to rectifying the city's financial emergency, and its deteriorating financial cycle would not only continue but would also accelerate. Thus, Orr recommended that the city be authorized to proceed under Chapter IX bankruptcy. The case was then turned over to Judge Steven Rhodes, a white male who was the United States Bankruptcy Judge for the Eastern District of Michigan. He made the final decision on Detroit's bankruptcy and supported a plan that: (1) dissolved more than $7 billion of the city's $18 billion of debt; (2) enhanced the city's credit rating; and (3) included a ten-year, $1.7 billion investment in the city's services (Gulick, 2015). The third decision maker was US District Chief Judge Gerald Rosen, who was a white male appointed judge of the United States District Court for the Eastern District of Michigan in 1990 by then Republican President George W. Bush. Rosen negotiated the $816 million Grand Bargain, which produced funds to help with city pensions and protect the Detroit Institute of Arts from having to sell many of its prized possessions.

Chapter 3 and the remaining chapters examined whether the city has become more inclusive in terms of race and class after bankruptcy—in other words, whether there was more racial equality between Blacks and whites, and between Hispanics and non Hispanic whites. Chapter 3 was based on an analysis of the class, or social structure, and spatial structure of the Detroit Metropolitan Area. It also examined the racial residential segregation by socioeconomic neighborhood characteristics. For the purposes of this book, the study area consisted of Wayne, Oakland, and Macomb Counties. Such analysis allowed for the measurement of the extent of racial residential segregation combined with inequality in neighborhood socioeconomic characteristics related to the racial composition of neighborhoods. To analyze these three counties for the purposes of determining the extent of inequality, I used census tracts as spatial units as they are surrogates for neighborhoods. Inequality by both class and race in Metropolitan Detroit can best be understood if examined using data on the characteristics of neighborhoods—that is, census tracts.

The neighborhoods were analyzed using census data from the American Community Survey Five-Year Estimates. Most of the analyses were based on data from the 2011–15 and 2016–20 Five-Year Estimates databases. I used the Darden-Kamel Composite Socioeconomic Index (CSI) to analyze Metropolitan Detroit by neighborhoods in order to determine the extent of class inequality (Darden et al, 2010). I used the index of dissimilarity to determine the extent of racial residential segregation and socioeconomic neighborhood inequality by race (Darden et al, 2010). The Darden-Kamel CSI incorporates nine variables:

- Unemployment rate
- Median household income
- Occupational status
- Educational attainment
- Median value of dwelling
- Median rent of dwelling
- Percentage of homeownership
- Percentage of households with vehicle available
- Percentage of poverty/below the poverty line

The social and spatial structure of Metropolitan Detroit, based on US Census data from 2011–15 and 2016–20, shows that the neighborhoods are extremely unequal, creating five distinctly different Detroits. One Detroit is where very low socioeconomic characteristic neighborhoods (SEP 1) are located, occupied by people who live a different life than people living in other neighborhoods. There are also neighborhoods that are low in socioeconomic characteristics (SEP 2) and these neighborhoods are distinctly different from other neighborhoods, but they are not as low in socioeconomic characteristics as SEP 1 neighborhoods. There is also a middle-class Detroit (SEP 3), which has residents that are higher in socioeconomic characteristics than those in Detroit (SEP 1 and SEP 2). At a higher level than those in SEP 3 are those neighborhoods where the population resides in a high socioeconomic status (SEP 4). Finally, there are very high socioeconomic characteristic neighborhoods (SEP 5), where the most well-off Detroiters reside.

The analysis of the data shows that the inequality gap between neighborhoods increased between 2011–15 and 2016–20. This inequality has impacted Black and Hispanic residents more than white residents. This is because Black and Hispanic residents disproportionately reside in neighborhoods with very low and low socioeconomic characteristics. Most whites, on the other hand, reside in neighborhoods with high and very high socioeconomic characteristics. Therefore, the quality of life for residents in Metropolitan Detroit differs by race and ethnicity, based on the neighborhood characteristics where the racial and ethnic groups tend to live.

The analysis of the distribution of the racial groups revealed that Black residents live in neighborhoods that are separate and unequal to whites, indicating an index of dissimilarity of 56.3 in the 2011–15 period. The index of dissimilarity declined only slightly to 51 according to the 2016–20 census data. Hispanics were not as separate and unequal as Black residents; in 2011–15, the index of dissimilarity for Hispanics was 34.3, which fell to 32 in 2016–20.

In Chapter 4, I answered the question of whether gentrification had occurred in Detroit and if so which neighborhoods had experienced it. I had to first define gentrification and then measure it. Gentrification is a concept that has not been easy to define. It has also been difficult to measure it (Vigdor et al, 2002; Freeman, 2005; Lees et al, 2010; Brown-Saracino, 2013). The concept was first introduced by sociologist Ruth Glass in 1964 to describe "working class quarters [that] have been *invaded* by the middle class" (Glass, 1964: xvii). Glass (1964) first defined gentrification as a *process* of change in the social structure of deprived working-class neighborhoods characterized by the arrival of middle- and upper-class citizens and the subsequent requalification of the housing stock, and the displacement of incumbent residents. I noticed her use of the same words used by E.W Burgess (1925) to describe movement of the low-income population into middle-class neighborhoods in the City of Chicago.

The objectives of Chapter 4 were as follows: (1) to determine whether gentrification occurred in Detroit as defined by the Darden-Kamel CSI;

(2) to determine the location of the neighborhoods where gentrification occurred using geographic information system (GIS) techniques to map the location; (3) to determine whether gentrification resulted in an increase in the white population; (4) to determine whether the white population and the Black population are less residentially segregated in the gentrified census tracts than they were before the tracts became gentrified; and (5) to determine whether the City of Detroit's public–private model for economic development leading to gentrification has provided useful assistance to neighborhood residents in their efforts to negotiate with developers in their neighborhoods through the process of community benefits agreements.

The analysis in this chapter found that: (1) gentrification occurred in 12 neighborhoods (census tracts) in Detroit between 2011–15 and 2016–20; (2) gentrification resulted in an increase in the white population; (3) the white population and the Black population were more residentially segregated in the gentrified census tracts than they were before the tracts became gentrified; and (4) the Detroit Model was able to provide useful assistance to predominantly Black and poor neighborhoods. The assistance involved efforts to negotiate with wealthy white developers who were selected to redevelop projects in their neighborhoods. The negotiation was called the process of community benefits agreements. These agreements led developers to agree to include 20 percent of their units for low- and moderate-income renters, thereby reducing the outmigration of some low- and moderate-income residents from the gentrified neighborhoods. Future evaluations of the influence of community benefits agreements will be necessary in order to determine whether it is only wealthy white developers who benefit from gentrification or if poor Black neighborhood residents also benefit.

In Chapter 5, I described that, after emerging from bankruptcy on December 11, 2014, city officials were desperate for investments in rehabilitated apartments and condos to provide economic development in the neighborhoods as well as businesses downtown in order to increase the tax base. The bankruptcy left Detroit with numerous deteriorating and abandoned buildings, vacant lots, and very cheap land—an investor's dream (Davey and Walsh, 2014a). Meanwhile, the residents who had remained in Detroit through the bankruptcy period had a 40 percent poverty rate and an unemployment rate twice that of the State average (US Bureau of the Census, 2016). When the Republican Governor Rick Snyder announced that governance was returning to the elected city officials on December 14, 2014, Detroit's Mayor and City Council were given the challenge of rebuilding the city by attracting investments in housing (rehabilitated and new apartments and condos) while ensuring that long-term existing residents would not experience rents so high that they could not afford to remain in their neighborhoods.

Two years after bankruptcy, according to the city's building permit data, several building permits had been issued to developers requesting permission to build apartments and condos in certain neighborhoods, provided Detroit extend to them the highest tax advantages and subsidies to invest. At this time, Detroit was governed by a white mayor and a nine-member City Council (seven Blacks, one Hispanic, and one white). In 2016, Detroit's population was 683,443, with Blacks comprising 80 percent, non Hispanic whites 10 percent, Hispanics 8 percent, and Asians 1.4 percent (US Bureau of the Census, 2016).

In this stressful time for Detroit, developers—who were overwhelmingly white and male—saw an opportunity to make significant profits and get the highest tax advantages and subsidies by agreeing to take part in the economic redevelopment of this predominantly Black city. They started to pressure city officials to award them with high tax advantages and subsidies without affordable housing agreements in exchange. At the same time, city residents pressured City Council members not to agree to such terms unless guaranteed numbers of affordable housing units formed part of the deals. There was already a lot of very cheap land, and a large number of deteriorating and abandoned buildings and vacant lots before the bankruptcy. However, following bankruptcy, the city bottomed out and was desperate to build. Still, pressure from neighborhood groups forced city officials not to bargain, at any cost, with developers, but to also satisfy the needs of the low-income, predominantly Black residents in the city with a certain percentage of affordable housing.

Midtown was another area that experienced redevelopment in Detroit following bankruptcy. The challenges of advancing redevelopment in neighborhoods instead of downtown and midtown, and the development of more affordable housing, led the Detroit City Council to pass an inclusionary housing ordinance that required developers to provide a stipulated percentage of their developments for low- and moderate-income residents. The ordinance mandated that developers who received city-owned property at less than the true market value and/or public funding set aside 20 percent of their units for residents earning no more than 80 percent of the Detroit Metropolitan Area's median income. Investors were reluctant to invest in the redevelopment of neighborhoods without strong incentives such as tax forgiveness and other advantages from the city, the State, or the federal government. Examples of neighborhoods that were redeveloped and in which affordable housing units were built were summarized in this chapter.

Chapter 5 also discussed the importance of the Land Bank Authority to redevelopment in neighborhoods. The Detroit Land Bank Authority is the city's largest landowner and controls 30,000 residential structures, representing 25 percent of all parcels in the city. It sells the properties at auction on the traditional real estate market in Detroit. As of May 15, 2019, it owned 91,669 properties, divided into four categories: (1) owned vacant land; (2) owned vacant lots for sale; (3) owned structures; and (4) owned structures for sale.

Finally, this chapter examined whether poor residents in Detroit were benefiting economically from the Opportunity Zone legislation passed by Congress in 2017, and whether the investors that received so much in incentives from the governments agreed to include a proportionate percentage of Black developers from Detroit. The evidence revealed that after bankruptcy, the city has not achieved the goal of being an "inclusive city" as measured by whether Blacks and the poor in Detroit are receiving an equal share of the economic benefits of redevelopment downtown and in residential neighborhoods. The results of studies on the Opportunity Zone legislation showed that it was the affluent white developers who received most of the benefits from the legislation and not the poor Black and Hispanic residents living in the City of Detroit.

Before and during bankruptcy, Black and Hispanic business owners were extremely underrepresented compared to their populations in the City of Detroit. In Chapter 6, I examined Black and Hispanic-owned businesses. The objective of this chapter was to assess the extent of underrepresentation of Blacks in the area of business ownership in Detroit. This chapter focused on Black businesses with paid employees instead of focusing on sole-proprietor Black businesses. These are usually large firms and they have an impact on employment because they have jobs they offer to the population in the City of Detroit. After Detroit bankruptcy ended, some key questions that this chapter answered were: (1) what is the extent of Black businesses with paid employees?; (2) what was the number of employees working in the Black-owned businesses?; (3) were there additional Black businesses with paid employees founded or created after bankruptcy?; (4) what was the extent to which Black businesses with paid employees were located in the City of Detroit compared to the Detroit suburbs?; (5) what were the types of businesses with paid employees that Black owners operated?; and (6) where were the municipalities located where Black and Hispanic businesses received Paycheck Protection Program loans to maintain their businesses during the COVID-19 pandemic before and during bankruptcy? The data were obtained from *Crain's Detroit Business* database, the *Survey of Business Owners*, and the United States Small Business Administration Paycheck Protection Program Report.

The kinds of businesses owned by Blacks differed from the kinds of white-owned businesses. Black-owned businesses were very underrepresented in construction, real estate, rental and leasing, retail trade, and professional, scientific, and technical services. On the other hand, compared to white-owned firms, Black-owned businesses were overrepresented in healthcare and social assistance, excluding public administration. The extreme underrepresentation of Blacks in the construction sector has not changed. Based on the 2014 Survey of Business Ownership, there were only 123 Black-owned firms with paid employees in construction compared to

6,918 white-owned firms in Metropolitan Detroit. Instead, the two kinds of businesses that continued to dominate Black business ownership with paid employees were healthcare and social service, as they did earlier before bankruptcy.

Based on recent data, Blacks are disproportionately more likely to own smaller businesses and pay more for access to capital, due in part to systemic racial discrimination. According to *Crain's Detroit Business*, there were 32 large Black-owned businesses with paid employees in the Detroit Metropolitan Area (that is, Wayne, Oakland, and Macomb Counties) in January 2021. The revenue ranged from $12 million for Jenkins Construction to $2,876.3 for the Piston Group. Only 16, or 50 percent, of the Black-owned businesses with paid employees were located in the City of Detroit in January 2021. Six, or 19 percent, of the businesses were located in suburban Southfield, including the largest Black-owned business with paid employees (the Piston Group). The one Black-owned business with paid employees that was established in 2017, after bankruptcy ended in 2014, was ACE Petroleum.

Black-owned businesses are still extremely underrepresented in Detroit after bankruptcy. Only one new Black-owned business was founded after the city's bankruptcy ended in 2014. Only 32 large Black-owned businesses existed in Wayne, Oakland, and Macomb Counties, with half of the businesses located in the City of Detroit. Most of the businesses were associated with and dependent on the auto industry to a certain extent. Where information was provided, Black-owned businesses with paid employees had a total of 8,674 employees in January 2021.

Hispanics are disproportionately more likely to own smaller businesses and pay more for access to capital than non Hispanic white-owned businesses, due in part to systemic racial discrimination (US Bureau of the Census, 2015). Like Black business owners, new businesses owned by Hispanics are more likely to be discouraged from applying for loans and are more likely to have their applications denied by banks compared to non Hispanic white business owners. According to *Crain's Detroit Business*, there were eight large Hispanic-owned businesses with paid employees in the Detroit Metropolitan Area in January 2021. Data were provided on the revenue of five of those businesses in 2020. The revenue of these companies ranged from $37.2 million for Aztec Manufacturing Corporation to $319.2 million for Elder Automotive Group.

Seven of the nine businesses provided data on the number of employees as of January 2021, which ranged from 33 at Three Star to 364 at the Ideal Group. For the location of the Hispanic-owned businesses, the data were provided for all eight. Only two of the Hispanic-owned businesses were located in the City of Detroit. The majority of the Hispanic-owned businesses were located in the following suburbs of Detroit: Troy, Warren, Romulus, Dearborn, and Wayne.

Most of the PPP loans were given to white-owned businesses after the PPP was first implemented in 2020 to aid businesses impacted by the COVID-19 pandemic as part of the *CARES Act*, which passed in March of 2020. The municipalities receiving the largest number of business loans were Detroit, which received nine, and Troy, which received seven. Of the 45 businesses that received the PPP loans, only one is Hispanic-owned: Ideal Contracting Company. It is engaged in commercial and institutional building construction and is located in Detroit. It received $10 million and maintained 417 jobs. One company is Black and is located in Detroit: Detroit Manufacturing Systems. It received $8,185,662 and maintained 500 jobs. It is engaged in motor vehicle seating and interior trim manufacturing. Thus, neither Black-owned businesses nor Hispanic-owned businesses reduced the disparity in business ownership and became more representative after bankruptcy. The chapter on the underrepresentation of Black- and Hispanic-owned businesses in Detroit revealed that the major problem was a lack of capital and access to it.

During the research undertaken for the book, there appeared to be some evidence in 2021 and 2022 that some foundations and some affluent developers and organizations started to begin providing capital and other loans to Black-owned businesses in order to economically develop neighborhoods in Detroit. In 2021 Dan and Jennifer Gilbert developed their plans for investment in Detroit neighborhoods. They targeted what Dan Gilbert called the scourge of property tax debt and foreclosures in Detroit. The billionaire mortgage mogul announced that $15 million would be given to pay the back-due property taxes of an estimated 20,000 low-income Detroit city residents.

Chapter 7 examined the racial inequality between student academic achievement and proposed a neighborhood solution for the problem. Since the City of Detroit came out of bankruptcy, a major question for many Black parents living in the city where their children *must* attend schools was whether their children—who attend racially segregated schools—receive an equal education to white students living in Wayne County (outside of the city), Macomb County, and Oakland County. The objective of this chapter was to answer that question using the most appropriate data and methods. Much of these data were obtained from the Educational Opportunity Project at Stanford University. The researcher there used public school test scores in grades 3–8 from 2008–09 to 2017–18 in order to create the first comprehensive database on educational opportunity in the US. For this chapter the database used from the Stanford Project focused on overall average district test scores for Black, white, and Hispanic students. Student scores were compared to the national average test scores.

The evidence was strong that racial segregation of Black students at the elementary and at higher-grade levels, especially in Wayne County, is denying Black students an equal education to that of white students. Thus, postbankruptcy Detroit has not achieved a level of racial equity, equal opportunity, or inclusion in the field of education. The race of students is still the dominant factor that matters in relation to educational quality in Wayne County, where the City of Detroit is located. The State of Michigan has failed to provide Black students with an equal education after the *Brown v. Board of Education* decision in 1954.

Michigan has instead provided Detroit students more charter schools. The solution is not to produce more charter schools, the quality of which is not significantly different from that of noncharter schools. The solution, based on the data, must be related to changing the State law that prohibits Black, Hispanic, and white students from attending schools outside of their school district and neighborhood. Most school districts and neighborhoods are racially segregated and differ in terms of quality by racial composition (Michigan Department of Education, 2021). Furthermore, for any student attending a low-achieving school, the State of Michigan should pay the transportation costs for that student to attend a high-achieving school that may exist in another neighborhood. These conclusions are consistent with the findings of the Stanford University Educational Project, which found that average student test scores are influenced by home environments, early childhood experiences, community resources, and schools. The trend or change in average student test scores from one year to the next indicates whether educational opportunities are improving in Detroit.

Where the trend is positive, students' opportunities to learn are improving; the opposite is also true. The trend in Detroit is negative. In terms of learning rates, students learn 1.7 percent less each grade than the US average. Opportunities may improve over time because of changes in school quality or changes in family resources, home environments, early childhood experiences, and/or community resources.

Chapter 8 examined the unequal exposure to crime in the City of Detroit across neighborhoods. In this chapter it was argued that *place* matters in understanding why crimes occur in some neighborhoods more than others. Many years ago, urban researchers at the University of Chicago examined the correlation between characteristics of neighborhoods and delinquency (Shaw, 1929). This chapter examined crime incidents as the unequal *exposure* of certain neighborhoods to crimes based on neighborhood socioeconomic characteristics. Following the theoretical concept of *neighborhood effects* advanced by Wilson (1987), crimes are directly related to neighborhood characteristics where residents in concentrated poverty reside.

This chapter revealed, using the Darden-Kamel CSI to characterize neighborhoods by socioeconomic characteristics, that crimes in the City of Detroit are not randomly distributed, but are concentrated in neighborhoods based on social and economic characteristics. The highest crime rates occur in two types of neighborhoods: low and very low socioeconomic characteristic neighborhoods. There are fewer crimes in neighborhoods with middle, high, and very high socioeconomic characteristics. This chapter also documented that between 2015 and 2020, aggravated assault crimes increased in low and very low socioeconomic characteristic neighborhoods. Aggravated assaults decreased in high and very high socioeconomic characteristic neighborhoods. Larceny decreased in all types of neighborhoods. Burglaries also decreased in all types of neighborhoods and so did robberies. Homicides increased in very low, middle, and high socioeconomic characteristic neighborhoods. Homicides decreased in low and very high socioeconomic characteristic neighborhoods. Finally, incidents of stolen vehicles decreased in every type of neighborhood. Thus, it is fair to conclude that crime after bankruptcy decreased in the City of Detroit in most neighborhoods. Characteristics of neighborhoods indicated that such crimes as aggravated assaults and homicides are concentrated in low and very low socioeconomic characteristic neighborhoods.

If crimes are to be reduced in the City of Detroit, the Mayor and the City Council must pass and implement policies that provide greater priority and address the needs of the very low and low socioeconomic characteristic neighborhoods. For more on the correlation between crime and neighborhood characteristics, see the recent book written by criminologist John Hipp (2022), *How Physical and Social Distance Drive the Spatial Location of Crime*. Neighborhoods and their characteristics help us understand why crime occurs in some neighborhoods more often than in others. The book reinforces many of the findings of Chapter 8.

In Chapter 9, I examined the problem of extreme race and class inequality, and whether some Blacks and Hispanics tried to reduce the inequality by changing their place of residence from Detroit to the suburbs. The social and economic characteristics of neighborhoods in Detroit were influenced tremendously by the bankruptcy, which made conditions for a large segment of the Detroit population much more difficult. Some residents of Black and Hispanic neighborhoods were exposed to more poverty; some residents had more difficulty finding jobs in management, business, science, and arts occupations. Other residents did not reside in the same neighborhoods as highly educated residents—that is, residents with bachelor's degrees or higher. Some Black and Hispanic residents had difficulty becoming homeowners due to differential mortgage-lending denial rates from lending institutions. When such conditions exist, it is quite common for residents to search for neighborhoods and places that will improve their quality of life, even if it means moving away from the city and neighborhood where they had lived for most of their lives (Chetty, Hendren, Jones, and Porter, 2020). Urban geographers refer to this search by residents as the *geography of opportunity* (de Souza Briggs et al, 1999).

The US Bureau of the Census in 2020 shows an increase in the Black and Hispanic population that moved to the suburbs of Detroit between 2010 and

2020. However, data from the *Home Mortgage Disclosure Act* database revealed that barriers remain to Black and Hispanic home seekers. Both groups continue to experience a higher percentage of mortgage loan denials than their non Hispanic white counterparts. The racial difference in mortgage loan denial rates were found in different loan types. For both conventional loans and Federal Housing Administration (FHA) loans, Blacks were turned down at a higher rate than non Hispanic white home seekers; the same was true for Hispanics.

In fact, the ratio of loan denial between Blacks and non Hispanic whites was 2.4, which means that Black home seekers were more than twice as likely as non Hispanic white home seekers to be denied a mortgage loan. For Hispanics, the denial rate was also higher than for non Hispanic whites. The analysis showed that Blacks and Hispanics were also denied mortgage loans at a higher rate based on the socioeconomic characteristics of the neighborhoods in which they lived. The denial rate was higher in the very low socioeconomic characteristic neighborhoods and lower in the very high socioeconomic characteristic neighborhoods.

This chapter also measured the racial inequality in the suburbs of Detroit. The following socioeconomic variables were analyzed: percentage in poverty/below the poverty line; median household income; educational attainment; occupational status; and homeownership. Racial inequality was evident in the 40 suburbs with a population of 10,000 or more and where at least 20 applications were made for mortgage loans by Black and Hispanic home seekers. The racial inequality was greater between Blacks and non Hispanic whites than between Hispanics and non Hispanic whites in all of the suburbs. Compared to Blacks, there were more suburbs where Hispanics had a lower poverty rate, a higher median household income, and a higher percentage of workers employed in management, business, arts, and science occupations than non Hispanic whites.

The major socioeconomic variable was in the homeownership rate. Although some Hispanics had higher homeownership rates or equal rates compared to non Hispanic whites in some suburbs, the Black homeownership rate was lower than the rate for non Hispanic whites in every suburb. Racial discrimination, as revealed by the differences by race in the home mortgage loan denial rates, matters most because it reduces the homeownership rate for Blacks especially and also Hispanics to a lesser degree. Homeownership is the most important socioeconomic variable among those examined in the selected suburbs and in the City of Detroit. In the City of Detroit after bankruptcy, the denial rate for Blacks was 32.3 percent compared to 25.1 percent for Hispanics and only 14.1 percent for non Hispanic whites. The Black homeownership rate in the City of Detroit after bankruptcy is 45.8 percent compared to the white homeownership rate of 53.3 percent and the Hispanic homeownership rate of 53.2 percent. The real disadvantaged group is Blacks in terms of homeownership.

Action is needed to address the problem. The Mayor and the City Council in Detroit should address this problem of differential treatment in mortgage loan denials negatively impacting the Black homeownership rate by: (1) requesting that all banks operating in the City of Detroit provide specific data annually, by race, on the number of applications made by Blacks, Hispanics, and non Hispanic whites, and the number of denials by race, the racial composition of the census tracts (neighborhoods), and why the denials occurred; (2) using this information to make decisions about where they will deposit the city's funds. Are the funds deposited in banks or other financial institutions that do not deny mortgage loans to Blacks and Hispanics at a higher rate than loans to whites; and (3) distributing the data from the annual report to residents, neighborhood organizations, and nonprofit organizations concerned with civil rights so that they too can use the information to make deposits.

Nationwide, the data show that Black households remained less likely to own their own homes compared to white households, even after controlling for factors such as education, income, age, geographic region, state, and marital status (Ruggles et al, 2020; Federal Reserve Bank of St. Louis, 2021; US Bureau of the Census, 2022). The data demonstrate that *race matters.* According to Ruggles et al (2020), college-educated Black households in the US are less likely to own their own homes than white households whose occupants never finished high school. According to the most recent report by the Joint Center for Housing Studies at Harvard University, the proportion of the population owning their own homes in early 2022 was 45.3 percent for Black households and 74 percent for white households, amounting to a gap in the homeownership rate of 28.7 percentage points. The Hispanic homeownership rate was 49.1 percent, amounting to a gap in the homeownership rate of 24.9 percentage points compared to white households.

According to the same report, the particularly large disparity between Black and white homeownership rates reflects the nation's long history of racial discrimination in housing markets, including covenants barring Black households from purchasing homes in many communities and mortgage-lending practices limiting their access to financing. But today's homeownership gaps, according to the report, also reflect discriminatory treatment in the broader economy that has constrained the earning power of Blacks and has kept their household income low. But the report also notes the fact that even for Blacks with middle and high levels of income, the homeownership gap remains. Race still matters in explaining the lower Black homeownership rate compared to that for whites.

Let me return to the City of Detroit, which had the Black homeownership rate of 45.8 percent and a non Hispanic white homeownership rate of 53.3 percent—a gap of 7.5 percentage points. The homeownership rate is related to the mortgage-lending denial rates. In the City of Detroit, the Black mortgage-lending denial rate was 32.3 percent compared to 14.1 percent for non Hispanic whites—a gap of 18.2 percentage points. Detroit is an overwhelmingly Black city with a majority-Black City Council. The question for residents to ask is as follows: what more aggressive actions can the City Council take in order to address these racial inequities?

Data limitations

The Black and Hispanic population undercount and the overcount of the white population

This book relies heavily on US Census data. As a result, there are two limitations that should be noted. One is that the US Bureau of the Census data have undercounted the Black and Hispanic population in the 2020 Census and in the 2016–20 American Community Survey census data (Benson, 2022). At the same time, the Bureau has overcounted the white and Asian populations. Census Bureau Director Robert Santos, who was confirmed after the 2020 Census was completed, noted that there are "limitations" presented by the overcount and the undercount (Barrett, 2022).

The Black population was undercounted at a rate of 3.3 percent, up from 2.1 percent in 2010. The findings suggested that the 2020 Census missed Hispanics and Latinos at three times the rate as in 2010 (an undercount rate of roughly 5 percent, as opposed to 1.5 percent in 2010).

The COVID-19 pandemic presented a significant hurdle to this census process, impacting the Census Bureau's ability to achieve the most accurate count. The undercount has been a long-term problem for Detroit. Detroit Mayor Mike Duggan cited race as a primary factor and said an audit of 2020 census data by Michigan researchers suggests an intentional effort to undercount the majority-Black city's population (Associated Press, 2022). Researchers from the University of Michigan and Wayne State University estimated an 8 percent undercount in a selection of neighborhoods across the city. The report by the independent researchers laid out compelling evidence of a likely undercount in Detroit in the 2020 Census. Mayor Duggan said the independent analysis by the researchers proves that the 2020 data is inaccurate, which has massive implications on city finances and federal aid (Cooney et al, 2021). He said the undercount was not a mistake, blaming former President Donald Trump for ending the 2020 count early and accusing the US Census Bureau of purposefully prioritizing other areas over Detroit. I recommend that the Census Bureau correct this undercount in the 2020 Census.

The Census Bureau identifying Middle Eastern population as white

The US Bureau of the Census has continued to identify the Middle Eastern population as white. It must adhere to the 1997 Office of Management and Budget standards on race and ethnicity, which guide it in terms of classifying written responses to the race question. Therefore, in terms of identity, "White" is defined as a person having origins in any of the original peoples of Europe, the Middle East, or North Africa (US Bureau of the Census, 2021). According to the US Bureau of the Census, the racial categories included in the census questionnaire generally reflect a social definition of race recognized in this country and not an attempt to define race biologically, anthropologically, or genetically. In addition, it is recognized that the categories of race include racial and national origin, or sociocultural groups. People may choose to report more than one race to indicate their racial mixture, such as "American Indian" and "White." People who identify their origin as Hispanic, Latino, or Spanish may be of any race. The Office of Management and Budget require the US Bureau of the Census to include five minimum categories: White, Black or African American, American Indian or Alaska Native, Asian, and Native Hawaiian or Other Pacific Islander. No separate category exists for Middle Easterners.

The US is different from other predominantly white countries in defining Middle Easterners. The Canadian census, for example, does not define Middle Easterners as white; instead, they are considered "visible minorities" and are defined as people with ancestry, origins, or citizenship from the Middle East, which includes Western Asia and North Africa. Included in the group from West Asia are Lebanese, Iranians, Arabs, Palestinians, Israelis, Afghans, Syrians, Turks, and Iraqis. Other Middle Easterners from West Central Asia and North Africa include Kurds, Jordanians, Assyrians, Moroccans, Egyptians, Algerians, Tunisians, and Sudanese (Statistics Canada, 2021).

Classifying the largest population of Dearborn, Michigan as "White" presents a need for caution for researchers. The US Bureau of the Census stated that the white population in Dearborn in 2020 was 95,037, but the city has the largest Arab American population in the US. It is 42 percent Arab (40,000 residents). Yet in Dearborn, the largest ethnic groups from the Middle Eastern countries are Lebanese, Syrians, Palestinians, Iraqis, and Yemenis. I recommend that the US Census Bureau correct this error of counting Middle Easterners as white in the next census. The results will enable the Middle Eastern population to measure the extent of inequality between the Middle Easterners and the white population. Notwithstanding these limitations on the census data, other data enabled me to provide answers to the questions of whether Detroit after bankruptcy became more racially inclusive and more equal by neighborhood socioeconomic characteristics. The results showed that in some areas progress was made but in most areas neighborhood socioeconomic characteristics remain separate and unequal by race and class.

References

Abbey-Lambertz, K. (2013) "Michigan Emergency Manager Law in effect in 6 cities after Detroit appointment (MAP)," *HuffPost* [online] March 15, Available from: https://www.huffpost.com/entry/michigan-emergency-manager-law-cities_n_2876777?ec_carp=8238058477429527525

Afana, D. (2016) "Dan Gilbert's $100M Brush Park project construction begins next week," *MLive* [online] November 29, Available from: https://www.mlive.com/news/detroit/2016/11/city_modern.html

Alonso, W. (1964) *Location and Land Use*, Cambridge, MA: Harvard University Press.

Anderson, M.W. (2011) "Democratic dissolution: radical experimentation in state takeovers of local governments," *Fordham Urban Law Journal*, 39(3): 577–624.

Andresen, M.A. and Shen, J.L. (2019) "Journey to crime: how far does the criminal travel? Final Report," Institute for Canadian Urban Research Studies, Simon Fraser University. Burnaby BC. Available from: https://martinxandresen.files.wordpress.com/2022/01/ocr-go_jtc_report_andresen_shen.pdf

Associated Press (2022) "Detroit is largest city to challenge 2020 census numbers," *KTAR News* [online] April 6, Available from: https://ktar.com/story/4989063/detroit-is-largest-city-to-challenge-2020-census-numbers/

Avery, R., Brevoort K. and Canner, G. (2007) "Opportunities and issues in using HMDA data," *Journal of Real Estate Research*, 29(4): 351–80.

Baldas, T. (2017) "Gerald Rosen, the judge who helped save Detroit, retires," *Detroit Free Press* [online] January 21, Available from: https://www.freep.com/story/news/local/detroit-reborn/2017/01/21/gerald-rosen-judge-detroit-retirement/96850154/

Baradaran, M. (2017) *The Color of Money: Black Banks and the Racial Wealth Gap*, Cambridge, MA: Harvard University Press.

Barrett, K. (2022) "Census Bureau releases estimates of undercount and overcount in 2020 Census," *United States Census Bureau* [online] March 10, Available from: https://www.census.gov/newsroom/press-releases/2022/2020-census-estimates-of-undercount-and-overcount.html

Barth, J. and Kelly, K. (2019) "Missed Opportunity Zone investments: minority-owned banks," *Crain's Detroit Business* [online] October 22, Available from: https://www.crainsdetroit.com/other-voices/missed-opportunity-zone-investments-minority-owned-banks

Bates, T. (1993) "Black businesses and legacy of racism," *Focus*, 21(6): 5–6.

Bates, T. (1997) "Unequal access: financial institution lending to Black- and white-owned small business start-ups," *Journal of Urban Affairs*, 19(4): 487–95.

Bates, T. (1997) *Race, Self-Employment and Upward Mobility: An Elusive American Dream*, Washington, DC: Johns Hopkins University Press.

Bates, T. and Robb, A. (2015a) "Has the Community Reinvestment Act increased loan availability among small businesses operating in minority neighborhoods?" *Urban Studies*, 52(9): 1702–21.

Bates, T. and Robb, A. (2015b) "Impacts of owner race and geographic context on access to small-business financing," *Economic Development Quarterly*, 30(2): 159–70.

Baxamusa, M.H. (2008) "Empowering communities through deliberation: the model of community benefits agreements," *Journal of Planning Education and Research*, 27(3): 261–76.

Beck, B. (2020) "Policing gentrification: stops and low-level arrests during demographic change and real estate reinvestment," *City and Community*, 19(1): 245–72.

Been, V. (2017) "What more do we need to know about how to prevent and mitigate displacement of low- and moderate-income households from gentrifying neighborhoods," *A Shared Future: Fostering Communities of Inclusion in an Era of Inequality*. Cambridge, MA: Joint Center for Housing Studies. Available from: https://www.jchs.harvard.edu/sites/default/files/media/imp/a_shared_future_what_more_do_we_need_to_know_0.pdf

Benson, S. (2022) "Census undercounted Black people, Hispanics and Native Americans in 2020," *Politico* [online] March 10, Available from: https://www.politico.com/news/2022/03/10/2020-census-undercount-black-people-hispanics-native-americans-00016138

Berman, D.R. (1995) "Takeovers of local governments: an overview and evaluation of state policies," *Publius: The Journal of Federalism*, 25(3): 55–70.

Berman, D.R. (2003) *Local Government and the States: Autonomy, Politics, and Policy*, New York: M.E. Sharpe.

Bernasco, W. (2010) "A sentimental journey to crime: effects of residential history on crime location choice," *Criminology*, 48(2): 389–416.

Blakely, T.A. and Woodward, A.J. (2000) "Ecological effects in multi-level studies," *Journal of Epidemiology & Community Health*, 54(5): 367–74.

Bloomberg News (2013) "Orr's fast filing could be key to Chapter 9 fight, analysts say," *Crain's Detroit Business* [online] July 23, Available from: https://www.crainsdetroit.com/article/20130723/NEWS01/130729965/orrs-fast-filing-could-be-key-to-chapter-9-fight-analysts-say

Bostic, R.W. and Martin, R.W. (2003) "Black home-owners as a gentrifying force? Neighbourhood dynamics in the context of minority home-ownership," *Urban Studies*, 40(12): 2427–49. Available from: http://www.jstor.org/stable/43100507

Bradley v. Milliken (1971) Civil Action 35257 Eastern Division Michigan.

Brown v. Board of Education (1954) 347 US 483.

Brown, D. (2021) *The Whiteness of Wealth*, New York: Crown.

Brown-Saracino, J. (2013) *The Gentrification Debates: A Reader*, New York: Routledge.

Burgess, E.W. (1916) "Juvenile delinquency in a small city," *Journal of the American Institute of Criminal Law and Criminology*, 6(5): 724–8.

Burgess, E.W. (1925) "The growth of the city," in R.E. Park, E.W. Burgess and R.D. McKenzie (eds) *The City*, Chicago: University of Chicago Press, pp 85–97.

Carrns, A. (2019) "'Opportunity Zones' offer tax breaks and, maybe, help for communities," *New York Times* [online] February 15, Available from: https://www.nytimes.com/2019/02/15/business/opportunity-zone-tax-break-controversy.html?searchResultPosition=1

Castagnola, M. (2015) "Gentrification without displacement," Doctoral dissertation, Massachusetts Institute of Technology.

Cavalluzzo, K.S., Cavalluzzo, K.L. and Wolken, J.D. (2002) "Competition, small-business financing, and discrimination: evidence from a new survey," *Journal of Business*, 75(4): 641–79.

Chetty, R., Hendren, N., Jones, M.R. and Porter, S.R. (2020) "Race and economic opportunity in the United States: an intergenerational perspective," *Quarterly Journal of Economics*, 135(2): 711–83.

Chopin, J., Caneppele, S. and Beauregard, E. (2020) "An analysis of mobility patterns in sexual homicide," *Homicide Studies*, 24(2): 178–202.

Citizens Research Council (2000) *CRC Memorandum 1054, Michigan's Unrestricted Revenue Sharing Program: Retrospect and Prospects*, http://crcmich.org/PUBLICAT/2000s/2000/memo1054.pdf

City of Detroit (2014a) "Overview of Detroit's Plan of Adjustment," Available from: https://detroitmi.gov/Portals/0/docs/EM/Announcements/Summary_PlanOfAdjustment.pdf

City of Detroit (2014b) "Summary of oral opinion on the record in the City of Detroit's bankruptcy judge Steven Rhodes, conclusion of oral opinion," November 7.

City of Detroit (2015) 2015–2019 Housing and Urban Development Consolidated Plan and 2015–2016 Annual Action Plan. Housing and Revitalization Department, Available from: https://detroitmi.gov/sites/detroitmi.localhost/files/2018-06/2015-2019ConsolidatedPlan-Detroit8.19.16-Standard.pdf

City of Detroit (2020) "FY 2024 Neighborhood Revitalization Strategy Areas," Available from: https://detroitmi.gov/sites/detroitmi.localhost/files/2020-10/City%20of%20Detroit%20%20FY%202020-2024%20NRSA%20Application%20Draft%2010-19-20-%20NW%20Edits.pdf

City of Detroit (2022) "The Mayor's Office presents vision for Gratiot/7 Mile neighborhoods as part of Strategic Neighborhood Fund," Available from: https://detroitmi.gov/news/city-detroit-presents-vision-gratiot7-mile neighborhoods-part-strategic-neighborhood-fund

City of Detroit Open Data DET (2015) *Crimes by Year, 2015*, Available from: https://data.detroitmi.gov/

City of Detroit Open Data Portal (2020) *Crimes by Year, 2020*, Available from: https://data.detroitmi.gov/

City of Detroit Open Data Portal (2021) *DLBA Owned Properties*, Available from: https://data.detroitmi.gov/datasets/detroitmi::dlba-owned-properties/about

City of Detroit Open Data Portal (2022) *Crime Incident Data, 2020*, Available from: https://data.detroitmi.gov/

Clark, E. (2005) "The order and simplicity of gentrification: a political challenge," in R. Atkinson and G. Bridge (eds) *Gentrification in a Global Context: The New Urban Colonialism*, New York: Routledge, pp 261–9.

Consumer Financial Protection Bureau (2015) *Home Mortgage Disclosure Act, Macomb, Oakland and Wayne County Mortgage Loan Data*, Available from: https://www.consumerfinance.gov/data-research/hmda/

Consumer Financial Protection Bureau (2017) *Home Mortgage Disclosure Act, Macomb, Oakland and Wayne County Mortgage Loan Data*, Available from: https://www.consumerfinance.gov/data-research/hmda/

Consumer Financial Protection Bureau (2020) *Home Mortgage Disclosure Act, Macomb, Oakland and Wayne County Mortgage Loan Data*, Available from: https://www.consumerfinance.gov/data-research/hmda/

Cooney, P., Farley, R., Juabed, S., Metzger, K., Morenoff, J., Neidert, L. and Rodriguez-Washington, R. (2021) "Analysis of the Census 2020 Count in Detroit," *Poverty Solutions, University of Michigan*, Available from: http://sites.fordschool.umich.edu/poverty2021/files/2021/12/PovertySolutions-Census-Undercount-in-Detroit-PolicyBrief-December2021.pdf

Corporation for a Skilled Workforce (2016) Detroit data update—July 2016, Hartland, MI, Available from https://skilledwork.org/publications/detroit-data-update-july-2016/

Costello, J. (2019) "US Opportunity Zone legislation is moving capital," *Real Capital Analytics Insights* [online] June 4, Available from: www.rcanalytics.com/opportunity-

Crain's Detroit Business (2020) *2020 Book of Lists*, Available from: https://www.crainsdetroit.com/businessdata/sf1/2020-book-of-lists

Crain's Detroit Business (2021) *Crain's Data Center*, Available from: https://www.crainsdetroit.com/data-lists

Darden, J.T. (1987a) "Choosing neighbors and neighborhoods: the role of race in housing preference," in G. Tobin (ed) *Divided Neighborhoods: Changing Patterns of Racial Segregation*, London: Sage Publications, pp 15–42.

Darden, J.T. (1987b) "Socioeconomic status and racial residential segregation: Blacks and Hispanics in Chicago," *International Journal of Comparative Sociology*, 28: 1–13.

Darden, J.T. (2007) "Black business development in Michigan, 1987–2002," in J. Darden, C. Stokes and R. Thomas (eds) *The State of Black Michigan, 1967–2007*, East Lansing: Michigan State University Press, pp 69–79.

Darden, J.T. and Kamel, S.M. (2000) "Black residential segregation in the city and suburbs of Detroit: does socioeconomic status matter?" *Journal of Urban Affairs*, 22(1): 1–13.

Darden, J.T. and Thomas, R.W. (2013) *Detroit: Race Riots, Racial Conflicts, and Efforts to Bridge the Racial Divide*, East Lansing: MSU Press.

Darden, J.T. and Rubalcava, L. (2018) "The measurement of neighborhood socioeconomic characteristics and Hispanic and non-Hispanic white residential segregation in Metropolitan Detroit," *Hispanic Journal of Behavioral Sciences*, 40(3): 312–29.

Darden, J.T., Hill, R., Thomas, J. and Thomas, R. (1987) *Detroit: Race and Uneven Development*, Philadelphia: Temple University Press.

Darden, J.T., Rahbar, M., Jezierski, L., Li, M. and Velie, E. (2010) "The measurement of neighborhood socioeconomic characteristics and Black and white residential segregation in Metropolitan Detroit: implications for the study of social disparities in health," *Annals of the Association of American Geographers*, 100(1): 137–58.

Data Driven Detroit (2020) *Crime Data, 2016–2020*, Available from: https://datadrivendetroit.org

Davey, M. (2013) "Bankruptcy lawyer is named to manage an ailing Detroit," *New York Times* [online] March 14, Available from: https://www.nytimes.com/2013/03/15/us/gov-rick-snyder-kevyn-orr-emergency-manager-detroit.html

Davey, M. and Walsh, M.W. (2014a) "Billions in debt, Detroit tumbles into bankruptcy," *New York Times* [online] July 18, Available from: https://www.nytimes.com/2013/07/19/us/detroit-files-for-bankruptcy.html

Davey, M. and Walsh, M.W. (2014b) "Plan to exit bankruptcy is approved for Detroit," *New York Times* [online] November 24, Available from: https://www.nytimes.com/2014/11/08/us/detroit-bankruptcy-plan-ruling.html

Dawsey, C.P. (2014) "Emergency manager or emperor? Why Michigan's law stirs contempt," *Bridge Magazine* [online] July 10, Available from: https://www.bridgemi.com/michigan-government/emergency-manager-or-emperor-why-michigans-law-stirs-contempt

De Souza Briggs, X., Darden, J.T. and Aidala, A. (1999) "In the wake of desegregation: early impacts of scattered-site public housing on neighborhoods in Yonkers, New York," *Journal of the American Planning Association*, 65(1): 27–49.

Detroit NAACP (2013) *Emergency Manager complaint*, https:www.detroitnaacp.org

Dixon, J. (2019) "Bedrock got nearly free land, millions in incentives—based on Dan Gilbert promises," *Detroit Free Press* [online] December 15, Available from: https://www.freep.com/in-depth/news/investigations/2019/09/06/dan-gilbert-bedrock-projects/2207973001/

Downtown Detroit Partnership (2023) Measuring Development and Investment, Available from: https://downtowndetroit.org/downtown-dashboard/

Duggan, M. and Jemison, A. (2014) "City of Detroit Neighborhood Revitalization Strategy Areas Plan," Available from: https://detroitmi.gov/sites/detroitmi.localhost/files/2018-06/City%20of%20Detroit%20NRSA%20Application%202015%2001%2005_1.pdf

Dunn, T. and Holtz-Eakin, D. (2000) "Financial capital, human capital, and the transition to self-employed: evidence from intergenerational links," *Journal of Labor Economics*, 18(2): 282–305.

Dutko, P., Ploeg, M. and Farrigan, T. (2012) "Characteristics and Influential Factors of Food Deserts, ERR-140," United States Department of Agriculture, Economic Research Service. Available from: https://www.ers.usda.gov/publications/pub-details/?pubid=45017

Educational Opportunity Project at Stanford University (n.d.) "Methods," Available from: https://edopportunity.org/methods/

Eisenberg, A., Mehdipanah, R. and Dewar, M. (2019) "'It's like they make it difficult for you on purpose': barriers to property tax relief and foreclosure prevention in Detroit, Michigan," *Housing Studies*, 35(6): 1–27.

Ellen, I.G. (2017) "Can gentrification be inclusive?" *President and Fellows of Harvard College*.

Ernsthausen, J. and Elliott, J. (2019) "How a tax break to help the poor went to NBA owner Dan Gilbert," *ProPublica* [online] October 25, Available from: https://www.propublica.org/article/how-a-tax-break-to-help-the-poor-went-to-nba-owner-dan-gilbert

ESRI ArcGIS (n.d.) *Light Gray Canvas*, Available from: https://www.arcgis.com/home/item.html?id=979c6cc89af9449cbeb5342a439c6a76

Fairlie, R.W. (1999) "The absence of the African American-owned business: an analysis of the dynamics of self-employment," *Journal of Labor Economics*, 17(1): 80–108.

Fairlie, R.W. and Meyer, B.D. (2000) "Trends in self-employment among white and Black men during the twentieth century," *Journal of Human Resources*, 35(4): 643–69.

Fairlie, R.W. and Robb, A. (2007a) "Families, human capital and small businesses: evidence from the Characteristics of Business Owners Survey," *IRL Review*, 60(2): 225–45.

Fairlie, R.W. and Robb, A. (2007b) "Why are Black-owned businesses less successful than white-owned businesses? The role of families, inheritances, and business human capital," *Journal of Labor Economics*, 25(2): 289–323.

Fairlie, R.W., Robb, A. and Robinson, D.T. (2022) "Black and white: access to capital among minority-owned start-ups," *Management Science*, 68(4): 2377–400.

Farley, R. (2015) "The bankruptcy of Detroit: what role did race play?" *City and Community*, 14(2): 118–37.

Farley, R., Danziger, S. and Holzer, H.J. (2000) *Detroit Divided*, New York: Russell Sage Foundation.

Federal Bureau of Investigation Crime Data Explorer (2022) "Uniform Crime Reporting Program," Available from: https://cde.ucr.cjis.gov/LATEST/webapp/#/pages/home

Federal Financial Institutions Examination Council (2021) *HMDA 2021 Loan Application Register Data*, Available from: https://ffiec.cfpb.gov/data-publication/modified-lar

Ferretti, C. (2018) "Detroit bankruptcy 'threw everything into chaos for retirees,'" *Detroit News* [online] July 18, Available from: https://www.detroitnews.com/story/news/local/detroit-city/2018/07/18/detroit-bankruptcy-retirees-reaction/783828002/

First Independence Bank (2022) "About us," Available from: https://www.firstindependence.com/about/presidents-message/

Fisher, P.S. and Peters, A.H. (1998) "Industrial incentives: competition among American states and cities," *Employment Research Newsletter*, 5(2): 1.

Florida, R. (2002) *The Rise of the Creative Class*, New York: Basic Books.

Frank, A. (2018) "$31 million Midtown Detroit development gets brownfield tax break," *Crain's Detroit Business* [online] June 18, Available from: https://www.crainsdetroit.com/real-estate/31-million-midtown-detroit-development-gets-brownfield-tax-break

Frank, A. (2019) "Duggan unveils $250 million bond plan to rid Detroit of blight in 5 years," *Crain's Detroit* [online] September 16, Available from: https://www.crainsdetroit.com/government/duggan-unveils-250-million-bond-plan-rid-detroit-blight-5-years

Frank, A. (2021) "Detroit revamps its blight efforts, tries to turn around program beset by controversy," *Crain's Detroit Business* [online] November 1, Available from: https://www.crainsdetroit.com/government/detroit-revamps-blight-efforts-tries-turn-around-program-beset-controversy

Frank, A. and Livengood, C. (2021) "Election 2021: What do Detroit business and civic leaders want to see next?" *Crain's Detroit Business* [online] October 31, Available from: https://www.crainsdetroit.com/elections/election-2021-what-do-detroit-business-and-civic-leaders-want-see-next

Frankenberg, E., Siegel-Hawley, G. and Wang, J. (2010) "Choice without equity: charter school segregation and the need for civil rights standards," *Civil Rights Project/Proyecto Derechos Civiles*, Available from: https://www.civ ilrightsproject.ucla.edu/research/k-12-education/integration-and-divers ity/choice-without-equity-2009-report

Freeman, L. (2005) "Displacement or succession? Residential mobility in gentrifying neighborhoods," *Urban Affairs Review* 40(4): 463–91.

Freeman, L. (2006) *There Goes the Hood: Views of Gentrification from the Ground Up*, Philadelphia: Temple University Press.

Freeman, L. and Cai, T. (2015) "White entry into black neighborhoods: advent of a new era?" *The Annals of the American Academy of Political and Social Science*, 660: 302–18. Available from: http://www.jstor.org/stable/ 24541839

Fusfeld, D.R. (1981) "The economy of the urban ghetto," in J.T. Darden (ed) *In the Ghetto: Readings with Interpretations*, Washington, DC: Kennikat Press, pp 131–55.

Gallagher, J. (2018a) "Detroit Land Bank many wins including 10,000 side-lot sales," *Detroit Free Press* [online] September 23, Available from: https:// www.freep.com/story/money/business/john-gallagher/2018/09/23/detr oit-land-bank/1358663002/

Gallagher, J. (2018b) "Dan Gilbert about to break ground on Detroit's next big thing," *Detroit Free Press* [online] December 13, Available from: https:// www.freep.com/story/money/business/john-gallagher/2018/12/13/gilb ert-downtown-project-detroit/2287508002/

Galster, G. (2017) "The geography of opportunity 20 years later," *Housing Policy Debate*, 27(6): 941–3.

Ghaffari, L., Klein, J.L. and Angulo Baudin, W. (2018) "Toward a socially acceptable gentrification: a review of strategies and practices against displacement," *Geography Compass*, 12(2): e12355.

Gibbons, J., Barton, M. and Brault, E. (2018) "Evaluating gentrification's relation to neighborhood and city health," *PLoS ONE*, 13(11): e0207432.

Gillette, C.P. (2014) "Dictatorships for democracy: takeovers of financially failed cities," *Columbia Law Review*, 114: 1373.

Glass, R. (1964) *London: Aspects of Change*, London: MacGibbon & Kee.

Goering, J.M. and Feins, J.D. (eds) (2003) *Choosing a Better Life? Evaluating the Moving to Opportunity Social Experiment*, Washington, DC: Urban Institute Press.

Goering, J.M. and Wienk, R.E. (eds) (1996) *Mortgage Lending, Racial Discrimination, and Federal Policy*, Washington, DC: Urban Institute Press.

Gould, E., Lacoe, J. and Sharygin, C.A. (2013) "Do foreclosures cause crime?" *Journal of Urban Economics*, 74: 59–70.

Graif, C., Gladfelter, A.S. and Matthews, S.A. (2014) "Urban poverty and neighborhood effects on crime: incorporating spatial and network perspectives," *Social Compass*, 8(9): 1140–55.

Greenwood, M.J. (1985) "Human migration: theory, models, and empirical studies," *Journal of Regional Science*, 25(4): 521–44.

Grengs, J. (2010) "Job accessibility and the modal mismatch in Detroit," *Journal of Transport Geography*, 18(1): 42–54.

Gross, A. (2019) "Help for Wayne County people facing foreclosure," *Detroit Free Press* [online] January 26, Available from: https://www.freep.com/story/news/local/michigan/detroit/2019/01/26/wayne-county-hearings-tax-foreclosure/2682434002/

Gulick, J. (2015) "Steven Rhodes: engineer of Detroit's bankruptcy," *Detroit News* [online] November 5, Available from: https://www.detroitnews.com/story/news/michigan/michiganians-of-year/2015/11/05/michiganians-year-bankruptcy-court-judge-steven-rhodes/75262870/

Hackworth, J. (2019) *Manufacturing Decline: How Racism and the Conservative Movement Crush the American Rust Belt*, New York: Columbia University Press.

Hanks, A., Solomon, D. and Weller, C.E. (2018) "Systematic inequality: how America's structural racism helped create the Black–white wealth gap," *Center for American Progress* [online] February 21, Available from: https://www.americanprogress.org/issues/race/reports/2018/02/21/447051/systematic-inequality

Harris, C.D. and Ullman, E.L. (1945) "The nature of cities," *Annals of the American Academy of Political and Social Science*, 242(1): 7–17.

Harvard Joint Center for Housing Studies (2022) *The State of the Nation's Housing 2022*, Available from: https://www.jchs.harvard.edu/sites/default/files/reports/files/Harvard_JCHS_State_Nations_Housing_2022.pdf

Hipp, J.R. (2010) "A dynamic view of neighborhoods: the reciprocal relationship between crime and neighborhood structural characteristics," *Social Problems*, 52(2): 205–30.

Hipp, J.R. (2022) *The Spatial Scale Of Crime: How Physical and Social Distance Drive the Spatial Location of Crime*, New York: Taylor & Francis.

Hipp, J.R. and Kim, Y.A. (2017) "Measuring crime concentration across cities of varying sizes: complications based on the spatial and temporal scale employed," *Journal of Quantitative Criminology*, 33(3): 595–632.

Hoffman, L. (2018) "Capital Access: Detroit, Hamtramck, Highland Park. The Eckblad Group and New Economy Initiative," Available from: https://neweconomyinitiative.org/wp-content/uploads/2019/01/Capital-Access-final.pdf

Holcomb, H.B. and Beauregard, R.A. (1981) "Revitalizing cities: resource publications in geography," *Association of American Geographers*, Available from: https://eric.ed.gov/?id=ED235085

Honadle, B.W., Cigler, B. and Costa, J.M. (2004) *Fiscal Health for Local Governments*, Amsterdam: Elsevier.

Hout, M. and Rosen, H.S. (2000) "Self-employment, family background, and race," *Journal of Human Resources*, 35(4): 670–92.

Hoyt, H. (1939) *The Structure and Growth of Residential neighborhoods in American Cities*, Washington, DC: Federal Housing Administration.

Hsieh, C.C. and Pugh, M.D. (1993) "Poverty, income inequality, and violent crime: a meta-analysis of recent aggregate data studies," *Criminal Justice Review*, 18(2): 182–202.

Hutson, M.A. (2018) We Live Here Too: Incorporating Residents' Voices in Mitigating the Negative Impacts of Gentrification, Cambridge, MA: Harvard University Joint Center for Housing Studies.

Hwang, J. and Ding, L. (2020) "Unequal displacement: gentrification, racial stratification, and residential destinations in Philadelphia," *American Journal of Sociology*, 126(2): 354–406.

Hwang, J. and Lin, J. (2016) "What have we learned about the causes of recent gentrification?" *Cityscape*, 18(3): 9–26.

Hynes, R.M. and Walt, S.D. (2015) "Fair and unfair discrimination in municipal bankruptcy," *Campbell Law Review*, 37: 25.

Ihlanfeldt, K.R. and Sjoquist, D.L. (1991) "The role of space in determining the occupations of black and white workers," *Regional Science and Urban Economics*, 21(2): 295–315.

Immergluck, D. (2002) "Redlining redux: Black neighborhoods, Black-owned firms, and the regulatory cold shoulder," *Urban Affairs Review*, 38(1): 22–41.

Immergluck, D, Earl, S. and Powell, A. (2019) "Black homebuying after the crisis: appreciation patterns in fifteen large metropolitan areas," *City and Community*, 18(3): 983–1002.

Jibrell, A. (2019) "Affordable housing project in Detroit's Oakman Boulevard neighborhood completed," *Crain's Detroit Business* [online] July 17, Available from: https://www.crainsdetroit.com/real-estate/affordable-housing-proj ect-detroits-oakman-boulevard-neighborhood-completed

Johnson, S.D. (2010) "A brief history of the analysis of crime concentration," *European Journal of Applied Mathematics*, 21(4–5): 349–70.

Johnson, S.D. and Summers, L. (2015) "Testing ecological theories of offender spatial decision making using a discrete choice model," *Crime & Delinquency*, 61(3): 454–80.

Kain, J.F. (1968) "Housing segregation, negro employment, and metropolitan decentralization," *Quarterly Journal of Economics*, 82(2): 175–97.

Kang, L. (2020) *Dismantled: The Breakup of an Urban School System: Detroit, 1980–2016*, New York: Columbia University Press.

Kawachi, I., Kennedy, B.P. and Wilkinson, R.G. (1999) "Crime: social disorganization and relative deprivation," *Social Science & Medicine*, 48(6): 719–31.

Kennedy, M. and Leonard, P. (2001) "Gentrification: practice and politics," *Washington, DC: Local Initiatives Support Corporation Center for Homeownership and Knowledge Sharing Initiative.*

Kim, M.J., Lee, K.M., Brown, J.D. and Earle, J.S. (2021) "Black entrepreneurs, job creation, and financial constraints," *IZA Discussion Paper 14403*, Bonn, Germany: IZA Institute of Labor Economics.

Kim, S., LaGrange, R.L. and Willis, C.L. (2013) "Place and crime: integrating sociology of place and environmental criminology," *Urban Affairs Review*, 49(1): 141–55.

Kirkland, E. (2008) "What's race got to do with it? Looking for the racial dimensions of gentrification," *Western Journal of Black Studies*, 32(2): 18–30.

Krivo, L.J., Byron, R.A., Calder, C.A., Peterson, R.D., Browning, C.R., Kwan, M.P. and Lee, J.Y. (2015) "Patterns of local segregation: do they matter for neighborhood crime?" *Social Science Research*, 54: 303–18.

Ladd, H.F. (1998) "Evidence on discrimination in mortgage lending," *Journal of Economic Perspectives*, 12(2): 41–62.

Laniyonu, A. (2018) "Coffee shops and street stops: policing practices in gentrifying neighborhoods," *Urban Affairs Review*, 54(5): 898–930.

Lavelle, M. (2014) "Understanding trends in State revenue sharing with local governments in Michigan," *Chicago Fed Letter, No. 329*, Available from: https://www.chicagofed.org/publications/publication-listing?page=8&filter_topic=FD18F3C19602452C8168D3178E9FB3C7

Lawrence III, C.R. (1977) "Segregation misunderstood: the Milliken decision revisited," *University of San Francisco Law Review*, 12(1): 15-56.

Lederer, A., Oros, S., Bone, S., Christensen, G. and Williams, J. (2020) *Lending Discrimination within the Paycheck Protection Program*, Available from: https://ncrc.org/lending-discrimination-within-the-paycheck-protection-program/

Lee, A. (2015) "City of Detroit employees get unique mortgage opportunity," *Daily Detroit* [online] June 8, Available from: http://www.dailydetroit.com/2015/06/08/city-of-detroit-employees-get-unique-mortgage-opportunity/

Lee, H. and Bostic, R.W. (2020) "Bank adaptation to neighborhood change: mortgage lending and the Community Reinvestment Act," *Journal of Urban Economics*, 116: 103211.

Lee, Y., Eck, J.E. and Martinez, N.N. (2017) "How concentrated is crime at places? A systematic review from 1970 to 2015," *Crime Science*, 6(1): 1–16.

Lees, L. and Ley, D. (2008) "Introduction to special issue on gentrification and public policy," *Urban Studies*, 45(12): 2379–84.

Lees, L., Slater, T. and Wyly, E.K. (2010) *The Gentrification Reader (Vol. 1)*, Abingdon: Routledge.

Levy, D.K., Comey, J. and Padilla, S. (2007) "In the face of gentrification: case studies of local efforts to mitigate displacement," *Journal of Affordable Housing and Community Development Law*, 16(3): 238–316.

Lewis, O. (2021) "Michigan advocates for vaccine equity, but it's unclear whether it's delivering," *Bridge Detroit* [online] February 11, Available from: https://www.bridgedetroit.com/michigan-advocates-for-vaccine-equity-but-its-unclear-whether-its-delivering/

Looney, A. (2018) "Will Opportunity Zones help distressed residents or be a tax cut for gentrification?" *Brookings Institution* [online] February 26, Available from: https://www.brookings.edu/blog/up-front/2018/02/26/will-opportunity-zones-help-distressed-residents-or-be-a-tax-cut-for-gentrification/

Marklew, T. (2018) "A brief history of Corktown, Detroit's historic Irish neighborhood," https://theculturetrip.com/north-america/usa/michigan/articles/a-brief-history-of-corktown-detroits-historic-irish-neighborhood/

Martin, I.W. and Beck, K. (2018) "Gentrification, property tax limitation, and displacement," *Urban Affairs Review*, 54(1): 33–73.

Martin L. (2007) "Fighting for control: political displacement in Atlanta's gentrifying neighborhoods," *Urban Affairs Review*, 42(5): 603–28.

Massey, D.S. and Denton, N.A. (1993) *American Apartheid: Segregation and the Making of the Underclass*, Cambridge, MA: Harvard University Press.

McCaffrey, M. (2022) *Introduction to Swaps Investopedia*. Available from: https//www.investopedia.com/arleder/optioninvestor/07/swaps-asp

McCollum, B. (2021) "Hitsville transformed: first look at Motown Museum's new plaza as expansion fund hits $32M," *Detroit Free Press* [online] October 10, Available from: https://www.freep.com/story/entertainment/music/brian-mccollum/2021/10/10/motown-museum-expansion-plaza-renderings/6023468001/

McFarland, C. and Pagano, M.A. (2014) "City Fiscal Conditions 2014. National League of Cities," *Center for City Solutions and Applied Research*. Available from: https://www.nlc.org/wp-content/uploads/2016/12/CSAR_City_Fiscal_Conditions_20140_0.pdf

McKinney, J. (2020) "Black-owned fuel supplier wins $27 million contract with City of Detroit," *Black Enterprise* [online] January 8, Available from: https://www.blackenterprise.com/black-owned-fuel-supplier-wins-27-million-contract-detroit/

Mich. Const. [1963] art. 7, sec. 217.

Mich. Leg. Emergency Manager Law Public Act 72 [2011] State of Michigan.

Mich. Leg. Local Financial Stability and Choice Act 435 [2012] State of Michigan.

Mich. Leg. Local Government and School District Fiscal Accountability Act 4 [2011] State of Michigan.

Mich. Leg. Michigan's Manual [2009] State of Michigan.

Mich. Leg. Public Act 101 [1988] State of Michigan.

Michigan Department of Education (2005) *Design and Validity of the MEAP Test*.

Michigan Department of Education (2014) *Michigan Educational Assessment Program (MEAP)*, Available from: https://www.mischooldata.org/DistrictSchoolProfiles/Assessments.

Michigan Department of Education (2021) "Racial Census Report by School Districts for 2020–2021," Available from: https://www.michigan.gov/-/media/Project/Websites/mde/Year/2021/06/17/RacialCensus0506.pdf?rev=c55620b6f1d6441ea0c883f3c98e2d1f

Michigan Department of Treasury (2012) *Executive Budget Appendix on Tax Credits, Deductions, and Exemptions: Fiscal Years 2013 and 2014*, Available from: https://www.michigan.gov/treasury/-/media/Project/Websites/treasury/Budget/ExecutiveBudgetAppendixOnTaxCreditsDeductionsAndExempts_FY_2013and2014.pdf?rev=6781c638c7bc4c90a2e43359ab776c07&hash=153F018813BC3038B8F3D8F9857A698B

Michigan Department of Treasury (n.d.) *Fiscal Indicator Scoring*, Available from: https://www.michigan.gov/documents/treasury/Fiscal Indicator Scoring_223016_7.pdf

Michigan Department of Treasury (n.d.) "Frequently asked questions regarding Public Act 72 of 1990, Local Government Fiscal Responsibility Act, and the appointment of emergency financial managers," Available from: http://www.michigan.gov/documents/treasury/FiscalEmerg_271926_7.pdf

Michigan Legislature (2016) "Emergency Manager," Available from: www.michigan.gov/documents/snyder/EMF_Fact_Sheet2_347889_7.pdf

Milliken v. Bradley [1974] 418 US 717.

Monroe, S.D. and Shaw, S.C. (2011) "Retail gentrification and race: the case of Alberta Street in Portland, Oregon," *Urban Affairs Review*, 47(3): 413–32.

Moore, K.S. (2009) "Gentrification in Black face? The return of the Black middle class to urban neighborhoods," *Urban Geography*, 30(2): 118–42.

Nadworny, E. and Turner, C. (2019) "This Supreme Court case made school district lines a tool for segregation," *National Public Radio* [online] July 25, Available from: https://www.npr.org/2019/07/25/739493839/this-supreme-court-case-made-school-district-lines-a-tool-for-segregation

Nagl, K. (2022) "Vinnie Johnson, founder and owner, Piston Group," *Crain's Detroit Business* [online] January 10, Available from: https://www.crainsdetroit.com/awards/vinnie-johnson-2021-newsmaker

New York Times (2019) "Opportunity Zone—for billionaires," *New York Times* [online] November 16, Available from: https://www.nytimes.com/2019/11/16/opinion/trump-tax-opportunity-zones.html

Niche.com (2022) *Detroit Public Schools Community School District*, Available from: https://www.niche.com/k12/d/detroit-public-schools-community-school-district-mi/#students

Nieuwenhuis, J., Kleinepier, T. and van Ham, M. (2021) "The role of exposure to neighborhood and school poverty in understanding educational attainment," *Journal of Youth and Adolescence*, 50(5): 872–92.

Nobles, M.R., Ward, J.T. and Tillyer, R. (2016) "The impact of neighborhood context on spatiotemporal patterns of burglary," *Journal of Research in Crime and Delinquency*, 53(5): 711–40.

Nordquist, R. (2019) "The principle of least effort: definition and examples of Zipf's law," *ThoughtCo.* [online] July 3, Available from: https://www.thoughtco.com/principle-of-least-effort-zipfs-law-1691104

O'Brien, D.T, Ciomek, A. and Tucker, R. (2022) "How and why is crime more concentrated in some neighborhoods than others? A new dimension to community crime," *Journal of Quantitative Criminology*, 38(2): 295–321.

Ocbazghi, E. (2019) "Detroit's gentrification is its compromise for economic recovery," *Business Insider* [online] July 30, Available from: https://www.businessinsider.com/what-detroit-has-compromised-for-its-economic-recovery-2019-7

Olsen, S. (2018) "Black and white homeownership rate gap has widened since 1900," *Zillow* [online] April 10, Available from: https://www.zillow.com/research/homeownership-gap-widens-19384/

Ong, P.M. (1981) "Factors influencing the size of the black business community," *Review of Black Political Economy*, 11(3): 313–19.

Orfield, G. and Lee, C. (2005) "Why segregation matters: poverty and educational inequality," *Civil Rights Project at Harvard University*, Cambridge, MA: Harvard University, Available from: https://www.civilrightsproject.ucla.edu/research/k-12-education/integration-and-diversity/why-segregation-matters-poverty-and-educational-inequality/orfield-why-segregation-matters-2005.pdf

Orozco, M., Tareque, I., Oyer, P. and Porras, J. (2020) "State of Latino entrepreneurship," *Stanford Latino Entrepreneurship Initiative*, Stanford, CA: Stanford University, Available from: https://uploads-ssl.webflow.com/5f2883288707a1d898871825/61b0e5228b3e4f1cf0f90b44_report-2020-state-of-latino-entrepreneurship.pdf

Orr, K. (2013a) *City of Detroit: Proposal for Creditors*, Available from: http://www.detroitmi.gov/Portals/0/docs/EM/Reports/City%20of%20Detroit%20Proposal%20for%20Creditors1.pdf

Orr, K. (2013b) *Re: Recommendations Pursuant to Section 18 (1) of PA 436*, Available from: https://michigan.gov/documents/Snyder/Detroit_EM_Kevyn_Orr_Chapter_9_Recommendation_427831_7.pdf

Perry, A.M. and Romer, C. (2020) "To expand the economy, invest in Black businesses," *Brookings* [online] December 31, Available from: https://www.brookings.edu/essay/to-expand-the-economy-invest-in-black-businesses/

Peterson, R.D. and Krivo, L.J. (2010) *Divergent Social Worlds: Neighborhood Crime and the Racial–Spatial Divide*, New York: Russell Sage Foundation.

Pew Charitable Trusts (2013) "The State of States Report," *PEW* [online] January 23, Available from: https://www.pewtrusts.org/en/research-and-analysis/reports/2013/01/23/state-of-the-states-2013

Pinho, K. (2013) "Detroit prepares for EM; Snyder mulls pick," *Crain's Detroit Business* [online] February 24, Available from: https://www.crainsdetroit.com/article/20130224/NEWS/302249956/detroit-prepares-for-em-snyder-has-short-list-of-candidates

Pinho, K. (2019) "Major development/redevelopment requests for proposals Detroit has issued under Mayor Mike Duggan," *Crain's Detroit Business* [online] January 13, Available from: https://www.crainsdetroit.com/real-estate/major-developmentredevelopment-requests-proposals-detroit-has-issued-under-mayor-mike

Pinho, K. (2021) "Why Target finally made its move in Detroit," *Crain's Detroit Business* [online] October 31, Available from: https://prod.crainsdetroit.com/retail/why-target-finally-made-its-move-detroit

Public School Review (2022) *Michigan School Districts*, Available from: https://www.publicschoolreview.com/michigan/school-districts

Reardon, S.F., Fahle, E.M., Ho, A.D., Shear, B.R., Kalogrides, D., Saliba, J. and Kane, T.J. (2022) Stanford Education Data Archive (Version SEDA 2022), Available from: http://purl.stanford.edu/db586ns4974

Reardon, S.F., Weathers, E.S., Fahle, E.M., Jang, H. and Kalogrides, D. (2022) "Is separate still unequal? New evidence on school segregation and racial academic achievement gaps," *Stanford Center for Education Policy Analysis, CEPA Working Paper No. 19.06*, Available from: https://cepa.stanford.edu/wp19-06

Reynolds, P. and White, S.B. (1997) *The Entrepreneurial Process: Economic Growth, Man, Women, and Minorities*, Westport, CT: Quorum Books.

Robb, A. (2002) "Entrepreneurship: a path for economic advancement for women and minorities?" *Journal of Developmental Entrepreneurship*, 7(4): 383–97.

Robb, A.M. and Fairlie, R.W. (2007) "Access to financial capital among US businesses: the case of African American firms," *Annals of the American Academy of Political and Social Science*, 613(1): 47–72.

Rosenbaum, J.E. (1995) "Changing the geography of opportunity by expanding residential choice: lessons from the Gautreaux program," *Housing Policy Debate*, 6(1): 231–69.

Rosenbaum, J.E., Reynolds, L. and DeLuca, S. (2002) "How do places matter? The geography of opportunity, self-efficacy, and a look inside the black box of residential mobility," *Housing Studies*, 17(1): 71–82.

Roth, S., Bondy, M. and Sager, L. (2019) "Crime is in the air: the contemporaneous relationship between air pollution and crime," *Journal of the Association of Environmental and Resource Economists*, 7(3): 555–85.

Rouse, C.E. and Barrow, L. (2006) "US elementary and secondary schools: equalizing opportunity or replicating the status quo?" *The Future of Children*, 16(2): 99–123.

Ruggles, S., Flood, S., Ronald, R., Grover, J., Meyer, E., Pacas, J. and Sobek, M. (2020) "IPUMS USA: Version 10.0 [dataset]," Minneapolis, MN: IPUMS, Available from: https://www.ipums.org/projects/ipums-usa/d010.v10.0

Sands, G. and Skidmore, M. (2014) "Making ends meet: options for property tax reform in Detroit," *Journal of Urban Affairs*, 36(4): 682–700.

Sands, G. and Skidmore, M. (2015) *Detroit and the Property Tax: Strategies to Improve Equity and Enhance Revenue*. Lincoln Institute of Land Policy, Available from: https://www.lincolninst.edu/sites/default/files/pubfiles/detroit-and-the-property-tax-full_0.pdf

Sapotichne, J., Rosebrook, E., Scorsone, E.A., Kaminski, D., Doidge, M. and Taylor, T. (2015) "Beyond state takeovers: reconsidering the role of state government in local financial distress, with important lessons for Michigan and its embattled cities," *MSU Extension White Paper*, East Lansing, MI: Michigan State University.

Schnake-Mahl, A.S., Jahn, J.L., Subramanian, S.V., Waters, M.C. and Arcaya, M. (2020) "Gentrification, neighborhood change, and population health: a systematic review," *Journal of Urban Health*, 97(1): 1–25.

Shaw, C.R. (1929a) "Delinquency and the social situation," *Religious Education*, 24(5): 409–17.

Shaw, C.R. (1929b) *Delinquency Areas: A Study of the Geographic Distribution of School Truants, Juvenile Delinquents and Adult Offenders in Chicago*, Chicago: University of Chicago Press.

Shaw, C.R. and McKay, H.D. (1942) *Juvenile Delinquency and Urban Areas*, Chicago: University of Chicago Press.

Shaw, K. (2008) "Gentrification: what it is, why it is, and what can be done about it," *Geography Compass*, 2(5): 1697–728.

Shlay, A.B. (2006) "Low-income homeownership: American dream or delusion?" *Urban Studies*, 43(3): 511–31.

Siegel, L.J. and McCormek, C. (2006) *Criminology in Canada: Theories, Patterns, and Typologies*, Toronto: Thomson Nelson.

Smith, N. (1979) "Toward a theory of gentrification: a back to the city movement by capital, not people," *Journal of the American Planning Association*, 45(4): 538–48.

Smith, N. (1996) *The New Urban Frontier: Gentrification and the Revanchist City*, New York: Routledge.

Solomon, D., Maxwell, C. and Castro, A. (2019) "Systemic inequality: displacement, exclusion, and segregation," *Center for American Progress*, 7, Available from: https://www.americanprogress.org/article/syste mic-inequality-displacement-exclusion-segregation/

Spiotto, J.E., Acker, A.E. and Appleby, L.E. (2012) "Municipalities in distress: how states and investors deal with local government financial emergencies," Charlotte, NC: Chapman and Cutler LLP.

Statistics Canada (2021) "Census Profile, 2021 Census of Population," *Statistics Canada*, Available from: https://www12.statcan.gc.ca/census-rece nsement/index-eng.cfm?MM=1

Stoll, M.A., Raphael, S. and Holzer, H.J. (2004) "Black job applicants and the hiring officer's race," *ILR Review*, 57(2): 267–87.

Sugrue, T.J. (1996) *The Origins of the Urban Crisis: Race Inequality in Postwar Detroit*, Princeton: Princeton University Press.

Tankersley, J. (2019) "Treasury completes rules for Opportunity Zone tax break," *New York Times* [online] December 20, Available from: https://www.nytimes.com/2019/12/20/business/tax-breaks-opportunity-zones.html?searchResultPosition=1

Tanner, K. and Dixon, J. (2018) "How does Detroit Land Bank Authority know how many homes are occupied?" *Detroit Free Press* [online] July 19, Available from: https://www.freep.com/story/news/local/2018/07/19/how-does-detroits-land-bank-count-squatters/783733002/

Tanner, K. and Dixon, J. (2019) "How does Detroit Land Bank know how many homes are occupied?" *Detroit Free Press* [online] July 19, Available from: https://www.freep.com/story/news/local/2018/07/19/how-does-detroits-land-bank-count-squatters/783733002/

Task Force on Local Government Services and Fiscal Stability (2006) *Final Report to the Governor*, Available from: https://www.michigan.gov/docume nts/FINAL Task Force Report_5 _23_164361_7.pdf

The Editorial Board (2019) "Opportunity Zone—for billionaires," *New York Times* [online] November 16, Available from: https://www.nytimes.com/2019/11/16/opinion/trump-tax-opportunity-zones.html

The Educational Opportunity Project at Stanford University (n.d.) "Methods," Available from: https://edopportunity.org/methods/

Theodos, B., Hangen, E., Gonzalez, J. and Meixell, B. (2020) "An early assessment of Opportunity Zones for equitable development projects: nine observations on the use of the incentive to date," *Urban Institute* [online] June 5, Available from: https://policycommons.net/artifacts/813355/an-early-assessment-of-opportunity-zones-for-equitable-development-projects/1686899/

Townsley, M. and Sidebottom, A. (2010) "All offenders are equal, but some are more equal than others: variation in journeys to crime between offenders," *Criminology*, 48(3): 897–917.

US Const. [1983] amend XIV *Sec 42.*

United States Bankruptcy Court Easter District of Michigan (2014) *Summary of Oral Opinion on the Record: In re City of Detroit Bankruptcy Following the Conclusion of the Oral Opinion, November 7, 2014,* Available from: http://www.mieb.uscourts.gov/sites/default/files/notices/Press_Summary-Judge_Rhodes_Detroit_Confirmation_Oral_Opinion_FINAL.pdf

United States Bureau of the Census (2014) *American Community Survey 2009–2013, Five-Year Estimates,* Available from: https://www.census.govdata

United States Bureau of the Census (2015) *American Community Survey 2010–2014, Five-Year Estimates,* https://www.census.gov/programs-surveys/acs/technical-documentation/table-and-geography-changes/2014/5-year.html

United States Bureau of the Census (2015) *2012 Survey of Business Owners.*

United States Bureau of the Census (2016) *American Community Survey 2011–2015 Five-Year Estimates,* Available from: https://www.census.gov/programs-surveys/acs/technical-documentation/table-and-geography-changes/2015/5-year.html

United States Bureau of the Census (2016) *Survey of Business Owners (SBO)— Survey Results: 2012,* Available from: https://www.census.gov/library/publications/2012/econ/2012-sbo.html

United States Bureau of the Census (2018) *Annual Business Survey.*

United States Bureau of the Census (2018) *Survey of Income and Program Participation (SIPP) Data,* Available from: https://www.census.gov/programs-surveys/sipp/data/datasets/2018-data/2018.html

United States Bureau of the Census (2019) *2018 Annual Business Survey,* Available from: https://www.census.gov/en.html

United States Bureau of the Census (2020) *2019 Annual Business Survey,* Available from: https://www.census.gov/en.html

United States Bureau of the Census (2021) "About the topic of race," https://www.census.gov/topics/population/race/about.html

United States Bureau of the Census (2021) "Homeownership rate by race and ethnicity: non-Hispanic white alone in the United States [NHWAHORUSQ156N]," *Federal Reserve Bank of St. Louis* [online] May 7, Available from: https://fred.stlouisfed.org/series/NHWAHORUSQ156N

United States Bureau of the Census (2022) *American Community Survey 2016–2020 Five-Year Estimates,* Available from: https://www.census.gov/programs-surveys/acs/technical-documentation/table-and-geography-changes/2020/5-year.html

United States Federal Reserve (2019) *Federal Reserve's Survey of Consumer Finances,* Available from: https://www.federalreserve.gov/econres/scfindex.htm

United States Small Business Administration (2021) *Paycheck Protection Program Report: Approvals through 05/31/2021*, Available from: https://www.sba.gov/document/report-paycheck-protection-program-weekly-reports-2021

Vandeviver, C. and Bernasco, W. (2017) "The geography of crime and crime control," *Applied Geography*, 86: 220–5.

Vigdor J.L., Massey, D.S. and Rivlin, A.M. (2002) "Does gentrification harm the poor?" *Brookings-Wharton Papers on Urban Affairs*, pp 133–82, Brookings Institution Press, Available from: https://muse.jhu.edu/pub/11/article/35609/pdf?casa_token=9YjHSOmoGd4AAAAA:4eSQau29Nv7giDoMsaWrU5OFzNZg2jnyNAFETdJ8ClzjsZEojcNDzNAeFVZ4Ewd-qTyJbv2tww

Vojnovic, I. and Darden, J.T. (2013) "Class/racial conflict, intolerance, and distortions in urban form: lessons for sustainability from the Detroit region," *Ecological Economics*, 96: 88–98.

Wainer, A. and Zabel, J. (2020) "Homeownership and wealth accumulation for low-income households," *Journal of Housing Economics*, 47: 101624.

Walsh, D. (2018) "Ford: Corktown plan aims to 'curate' mobility's future," *Crain's Detroit Business* [online] September 12, Available from: https://www.crainsdetroit.com/detroit-homecoming/ford-corktown-plan-aims-curate-mobilitys-future

Weisburd, D. (2015) "The law of crime concentration and the criminology of place," *Criminology*, 53(2): 133–57.

Wilcox, P. and Eck, J.E. (2011) "Criminology of the unpopular: implications for policy aimed at payday lending facilities," *Criminology and Public Policy*, 10(2): 473–82.

Williams, C. (2013) "Bankruptcy expert named Detroit Emergency Manager," *Associated Press* [online] March 14, Available from: https://detroit.cbslocal.com/2013/03/14/bankruptcy-expert-named-detroit-emergency-manager/

Wilson, W.J. (1987) *The Truly Disadvantaged: The Inner City, the Underclass, and Public Policy*, Chicago: University of Chicago Press.

Wright, T. (2015) "The art of bankruptcy and what role the DIA played in the case," *NPR Detroit* [online] November 15, Available from: https://wdet.org/2015/11/15/the-art-of-bankruptcy-and-what-role-the-dia-played-in-the-case/

Wyly, E.K. and Hammel, D.J. (1999) "Islands of decay in seas of renewal: housing policy and the resurgence of gentrification," *Housing Policy Debate*, 10(4): 711–71.

Xopolis LLC. African-American Entrepreneurs: Contributions and Challenges Small Business Research Summary, No. 459. Washington, DC: U Small Business Administration Office of Advocacy, Available from: https://cdn.advocacy.sba.gov/wp-content/uploads/2022/05/24110 442/Research-Summary_-African-American-Entrepreneurs-508c.pdf

Zipf, G.K. (1949) *Human Behavior and the Principle of Least Effort: An Introduction to Human Ecology*, Boston: Addison-Wesley Press.

Index

References to figures appear in *italic* type; those in **bold** type refer to tables. Since Detroit is the major subject of this title, entries have been kept to a minimum under this heading and readers are advised to seek more specific references.